Imagining

A PHENOMENOLOGICAL STUDY

Studies in Phenomenology and Existential Philosophy

Imagining

A PHENOMENOLOGICAL STUDY

EDWARD S. CASEY

INDIANA UNIVERSITY PRESS

Bloomington and London

Published in Canada by Fitzhenry & Whiteside, Don Mills, Ontario

Manufactured in the United States of America

Library of Congress Cataloging in Publication Data

Casey, Edward S   1939–
    Imagining: a phenomenological study.
    (Studies in phenomenology and existential philosophy)

    Includes index.
    1. Imagination.   2. Phenomenology.   I. Title.

BF411.C37 1976   153.3   76-12370
ISBN 0-253-32912-4   1 2 3 4 5 81 80 79 78 77 76

For Brenda, Eric, and Erin
—The Better Imaginers

CONTENTS

Preface

*Imagination, not slavery to fact, is the
source of whatever is good in human life.*
—Bertrand Russell

Keine Phantasie ist am Ende.
—Edmund Husserl

The ultimate aim of this book is to demonstrate that imagination is an autonomous mental act: independent in status and free in its action. Such a thesis can gain full cogency only if it is based on an accurate anatomy of imaginative experience itself: we must know *what* imagining is before we can establish *that* it is autonomous in its operations. Accordingly, a major portion of the book will be devoted to a careful and rigorous description of imagination's fundamental features. In pursuing a phenomenology of imagining, I shall impose certain restrictions on the overall scope of the project. No attempt will be made to show how imaginative autonomy is exhibited in such diverse domains as mythico-poetic thinking and political action—to name only two of the many areas of human endeavor in which imagining plays a shaping role. Nor will any express inquiry be made into the more extraordinary forms of imaginative experience—e.g., those that occur under the influence of drugs or in other extreme states of mind or body—or into the disciplined development of imaginative powers (as in the preparatory stages of certain meditative and mystical experiences). The investigation will instead take the form of a descriptive account of imagination in its ordinary, even banal, modes of activity. If the autonomy of imagining can be confirmed in such commonplace cases, it will be all the more convincingly demonstrable in more unusual instances.

Closely linked with my primary objective of establishing imagination's autonomy on a sound descriptive basis is a secondary aim of rectifying the tendency on the part of many Western philosophers to belittle imagination—or, still worse, to neglect it altogether. Preoccu-

pied by logocentric concerns, philosophers have been consistently
skeptical of imagining and its products. Their skepticism stems largely
from a conception of philosophical thinking as image-free. As Francis
Galton observed at the beginning of this century:

> A habit of suppressing mental imagery must therefore characterize men
> who deal with abstract ideas; and as the power of dealing easily and
> firmly with these ideas is the surest criterion of a high order of intellect,
> we should expect that the visualizing faculty would be starved by disuse
> among philosophers, and this is precisely what I found on inquiry to be
> the case.[1]

But the important question for our purposes concerns not so much
what philosophers actually do in their reflective activities as what they
think they are doing or should be doing. Most Western philosophers
would agree with Plato's stern judgment: "a theoretical inquiry no
more employs images than does a factual investigation."[2] Ever since
Plato, philosophers have condemned recourse to imagery as an inferior
form of mental activity—as at best a crutch for, and at worst a debase-
ment of, pure reflection. Philosophical thinking, proclaims Heidegger,
is "charmless and image-poor."[3] It remains moot, however, whether
there is or can be such a thing as strictly imageless thinking, a thinking
that dispenses with images altogether to become "thought thinking itself," in Aristotle's provocative and revealing phrase.[4]

Whether or not such image-free thought exists, there can be little
doubt as to what the predominant philosophical attitudes toward imagining have been. They range from distrust to disgust, from malevo-
lence to *méconnaissance*. The fact is that the claims of imagination
have been rebuffed or ignored at almost every critical juncture. Far
from being the "Queen of the faculties" revered by Poe and Baudelaire,
imagining has been regarded, with rare exceptions, as the impoverished
chimneysweep of mind, performing tasks (if it is given any tasks at all)
that are considered beneath the dignity of other psychical powers.

In view of this tradition of condemnation and neglect, the central
purpose of the following inquiry will be to vindicate the efforts of those
advocates of imagination—from Avicenna to Ficino, from Vico to San-
tayana—who have sought for imagining a more judicious treatment
than it has usually received. We need not agree with Anatole France

1. *Inquiries into Human Faculty* (London: Dent, 1907), p. 76.
2. *Phaedo*, 100.
3. Martin Heidegger, *Vorträge und Aufsätze* (Pfullingen: Neske, 1954), p. 229:
"Das Wort des Denkens ist bildarm und ohne Reiz."
4. *Metaphysics*, XII, 1072b 20.

that "to know is nothing at all; to imagine is everything."[5] But we do need to acknowledge the amplitude and intrinsic power of imagining and to recognize it as an autonomous act that is comprehensible and significant in its own right.

5. *The Crime of Sylvestre Bonnard*, trans. L. Hearn (New York: Harper, 1890), pt. II, ch. 2.

Acknowledgments

A book, like a person, is finally the expression of many people. Among philosophers it was above all William Earle who first encouraged and guided my interest in imagination; I am deeply grateful to him for his genial and generous help over the years. David Carr and Don Ihde read an early manuscript version and offered crucial criticisms. At a later point Robert Jaeger and Merold Westphal provided specific suggestions for improvements. Special thanks must go to Rulon Wells and Calvin Schrag, who discerned shortcomings and indicated means of amelioration. Mikel Dufrenne has been a continuing source of insight and support. A guiding spirit throughout has been John Niemeyer Findlay, in whose borrowed office I first received the inspiration for this book.

I am thankful to Yale University and to its Department of Philosophy for having awarded me a Morse Fellowship for 1972–73. During this year of rumination and writing I was extremely fortunate in being able to test out my conception of imagining in presentations at the Phenomenology Workshop at Washington University (where Herbert Spiegelberg was a true *spiritus rector*), the British Society for Phenomenology at Oxford University, and the C.G. Jung Institute in Zurich.

I have profited greatly over the past few years from discussions with psychologists and psychoanalysts on the subject of imagination. Stanley A. Leavy and Roy Schafer brought their rich clinical experience and analytical acumen to bear on my early and often naive efforts. Jerome Singer disclosed new facets of the subject by introducing me to his work on daydreaming and fantasy and by pointing to research in guided imagery techniques. James Hillman's seminal 1972 Terry Lectures (now published as *Re-Visioning Psychology*) taught me that imagining has many more dimensions than I had dreamed of; subsequent conversations with Hillman have convinced me of the existence of archetypal aspects of imagination, aspects which are not stressed in my phenomenological approach.

I wish to thank Lila Freedman and Susan Fernandez for their excellent editorial assistance; they aided enormously in converting the incoherent into the communicable. The typing and retyping of the manuscript was done gallantly and well by Nan Manochi and especially by Barbara Bahti.

Those to whom this book is dedicated have contributed most of all. Brenda Casey has given graciously and preciously of her time, patience, and literary skills in ways too numerous to mention. The cherubic cheerfulness of Eric and Erin Casey has sustained me in my more saturnine moments. I am immeasurably indebted to all three for their forbearance: too often they have had to imagine me in their midst.

List of Terms

P. F. Strawson has warned that "the uses, and applications, of the terms 'image', 'imagine', 'imagination', and so forth, make up a very diverse and scattered family. Even this image of a family seems too definite. It would be a matter of more than difficulty to identify and list the family's members, let alone their relationships of parenthood and cousinhood."[1] The glossary of somewhat specialized terms given below is offered in the interest of clarification. But, in keeping with Strawson's cautionary statement, this list of terms does not pretend to constitute a distinct family or to achieve exact definitions. Rather, it merely gives a preliminary indication of particular usages (some of ordinary acceptance, some slightly idiosyncratic) that will be used in the text of this book.

act phase: imagining *qua* act or enactment.

object phase: the totality of *what* we imagine in a specific act of imagining.

imagination: the complete phenomenon, composed in each case of an act phase and an object phase. As such, the term is synonymous with the coordinate terms "imaginative experience" and (emphasizing its intentional character) "imaginative act-*cum*-presentation" or "act-presentation." The expressions "the imagination" and "an imagination," which are unnecessarily reifying, have been eliminated wherever possible. It should be noted that the generic term "imagination" as used in this essay is not interchangeable with *creative* imagination. Creative imagination—or more exactly, the creative *use* of imagination—is an application or extension of imagination proper.

imagining: Taken in a broad sense (e.g., as found in the title of this book), this word will be synonymous with "imagination" in the full meaning just discussed; in a narrower sense and in accordance with an intentional analysis, it will denote the act phase of imagination.

imaginative: the primary adjectival form of "imagination." Only rarely, however, will this term bear the honorific connotation it enjoys in everyday parlance.

imaginal: an alternative adjectival form of "imagination," to be found principally in such semitechnical terms as "imaginal margin," "imaginal space," and "imaginal time."

1. "Imagination and Perception" in *Experience and Theory*, L. Foster and J. W. Swanson, eds. (Amherst: University of Massachusetts Press, 1970), p. 31.

imaginational: an adjectival expression that will be mostly avoided because of its awkwardness.

imaginary: As an adjective, this term will be used only infrequently because of its dishonorific connotation of 'merely fictitious'; as a noun ("the imaginary"), it will designate the totality of a given range of imagined objects or, at the limit, the sum of all imagined objects.

imaginative presentation: Strictly speaking, this refers to two of the three main components of the object phase of imagination: the specific imagined content and the surrounding imaginal margin. More loosely, it refers to the object phase of imagination in its entirety; in this sense it is equivalent to the term "intentional correlate of imagining," i.e., the *whole* of what is imagined on a given occasion. (In this respect it corresponds to colloquial usage of the term "image," as in the locution "I had an image of Susan.")

image: The noun form of this word will be used almost exclusively to denote the manner in which the imaginative presentation (in the narrower sense) is given; in this capacity it is the third main component of the object phase. The ordinary usage of the noun form in the misleading locution "mental image" has been avoided so far as possible. The verb form, "to image," will be employed to designate one (and only one) of the major forms that the act of imagining can assume.

imaginatum: a Latinate form used occasionally as a substitute for "specific imagined content."[2]

2. The original Latin verb from which the English verb "to imagine" derives is *imaginari*, which is akin to *imitari*, "to copy." Similarly, *imago*, the root of "image" and "imagination," means an imitation, copy, or likeness. Thus a mimetic function is implicitly ascribed to the group of English words founded on the *imag-* stem; and the British empiricist thesis that (mental) images are copies of sensations receives linguistic sanction. Since the empiricist thesis is highly problematic, however, it is unfortunate that a different series of terms, based on the polysemous Greek word *phantasia*, is not available for use. But *phantasia*, which includes any kind of mental seeing or "impression in the soul" (Zeno), has given rise to the much narrower English words "fantasy" and "phantasy."

INTRODUCTION

The Problematic Place of Imagination

> This World is all one continued Vision of
> Fancy or Imagination.
> —WILLIAM BLAKE

I

"IMAGINATION" IS A WORD which has come to promise more than it can possibly deliver. Since the Romantic movement (and even more distantly, the Renaissance), the term has acquired such honorific connotations that the experience it ostensibly names is unable to live up to all that is expected of it. In this orgy of overestimation, rhetoric has overruled dispassionate description. "Imagination created the world," exulted Baudelaire midway through the nineteenth century.[1] Closer to the present, those who concern themselves with imagination in practice or in theory continue to be inordinate in their praise. Wallace Stevens, himself deeply indebted to the Romantic tradition in poetry, proclaims that "imagination is the only genius";[2] and, on a less poetic plane, we witness a seemingly unending stream of popular and semipopular publications which adulate imagining while purporting to fathom its mystery.

There are signs, however, that another assessment has been gathering force in the twentieth century—one which attempts to avoid panc-

1. Charles Baudelaire, "La Reine des Facultés" in *Curiosités esthétiques* [et] *L'Art romantique*, ed. H. Lemaitre (Paris: Garnier, 1962), p. 321.
2. Wallace Stevens, *The Necessary Angel* (New York: Vintage, 1965), p. 139. On Stevens as a late Romantic poet, see Harold Bloom, "Notes toward a Supreme Fiction: A Commentary" in *Wallace Stevens*, ed. Marie Boroff (Englewood Cliffs: Prentice-Hall, 1963), pp. 76-95. Bloom claims that the poem on which he comments so tellingly in this article brings "to a climax the whole movement of poetry in the Romantic tradition" (p. 77).

gyric in order to illuminate the experience of imagining itself. This new assessment is provided by phenomenology. Edmund Husserl, lecturing in Göttingen in the first years of this century, paid scrupulous attention to the detailed infrastructure of *Phantasie*. In so doing, he refused to regard imagining as a "productive" act in the manner of Kant and Schiller, Fichte and Schelling. Instead, his patient phenomenological probings uncovered an activity that can "presentify" (*vergegenwärtigen*, to make intuitively present to mind), yet cannot achieve the amplitude and plenitude that characterize sensory perception.[3] Eugen Fink, Husserl's trusted assistant, tried to specify the peculiar "image world" (*Bildwelt*) to which imagining as intuitive presentification furnishes access. But Fink's prizewinning essay of 1927, "Vergegenwärtigung und Bild," like Husserl's own seminal research, remains only the torso of a project that was never completed.[4] It took the persevering labors of Jean-Paul Sartre, during more than a decade of intensive work on the subject, to present a phenomenological account of imagination that could claim certainty, if not completeness. Yet *L'Imaginaire*, published in 1940 (though stemming from the *diplôme* thesis of 1927, "L'Image"), undermines itself in the end by falling back into several of the same pre-phenomenological misconceptions that Sartre himself had exposed so devastatingly in his earlier essay, *L'Imagination*.[5]

Sartre's formidable but flawed efforts represent not merely a culmination of Husserl's and Fink's pioneering attempts to provide a phenomenology of imagination. They also bring to a head an increasing though still somewhat subdued skepticism on the part of twentieth-century philosophers toward exaggerated claims for imagination's efficacy. When Sartre curtly denies that there is any world of imagination (imagining exhibits at best an "anti-world"), he is not only challenging Fink's contentions but at the same time articulating a general philosophical doubt as to the extensiveness of imaginative powers. Are these powers capable of engendering a coherent and cohesive experiential domain? Are they creative or productive in any significant sense? To

3. For a brief account of Husserl's lectures of 1904–1905, see Rudolf Boehm's Introduction to *Zur Phänomenologie des Inneren Zeitbewusstseins* (The Hague: Nijhoff, 1966). These lectures are presently being prepared for publication in a new volume of *Husserliana* (The Hague: Nijhoff, 1950–).

4. Fink's essay is in his *Studien zur Phänomenologie* (The Hague: Nijhoff, 1966), pp. 1-78. As it stands, this essay represents Part I of a longer work which has never appeared in its complete form. Fink's treatment of the *Bildwelt*, perhaps his most original contribution, is confined to the last five pages of the essay cited.

5. For a fuller account of the misconceptions in question and the manner in which Sartre manages to fall into them himself, see my essay "Sartre on Imagination" (forthcoming in *The Philosophy of Jean-Paul Sartre*, ed. P. A. Schilpp [La Salle, Ill.: Open Court]).

such questions Sartre's answer is resolutely negative: imagination suffers from an incurable "essential poverty," a "nothingness of being."[6] The actual experience of imagining, when soberly assayed by Sartre's highly reflective phenomenological method, reveals itself to be devoid of the riches that Romantics had imputed to it. Beneath their inflated rhetoric Sartre discerns a nihilating mental act which is quite impoverished and threadbare in comparison with the psychical activity rhapsodized by the poets and philosophers of Romanticism.

Yet matters are considerably more complicated than either Sartre or the Romantics admit. Imagining itself is *neither* superproductively world-generating *nor* utterly devoid of intrinsic resources. If we should not claim too much for imaginative activity, we also should not claim too little. The task of a renewed phenomenology of imagination is to claim for imagining only what a detailed description allows us to claim, no more and no less.

The starting-point for any such description lies in an initial recognition of the phenomenon's inherent ambiguity, its tendency to invite opposite evaluations. No one has acknowledged this ambiguity more tellingly than Samuel Beckett, who writes in a recent prose piece:

No trace anywhere of life, you say, pah, no difficulty there, imagination not dead yet, yes, dead, good, *imagination dead imagine*.[7]

In these enigmatic and yet emblematic words we can see reflected *in nuce* all the ambivalence and unease which the experience of imagining stirs up in the mind of anyone who approaches it in an open and unblinkered fashion. *Imagination* as a fixed faculty is indeed dead, eviscerated in the "objective" accounts of many modern thinkers. But *imagining* is very much alive, its potency as an act manifesting itself in daily feats of fancy as well as in the productions of poets. What this means is that although imagination is no longer the only genius—regarded as a reified psychical process, it may even be distinctly moribund —the ongoing activity of imagining survives splendidly. It continues to flourish, whether in art (as Beckett's own novels and plays attest) or in more mundane contexts. Artists or not, we are irrepressible imaginers in everyday life, where we indulge in imaginative activity persistently and not merely as an occasional *divertissement*. Despite its airy indeterminateness, imagining arises constantly in the midst of concrete actions

6. Jean-Paul Sartre, *L'Imaginaire* (Paris: Gallimard, 1940), pp. 20-21, 25, 28, 73, 171. (English trans. by B. Frechtman, *Psychology of Imagination* [New York: Washington Square Press, 1966], pp. 11-12, 16, 19, 67, 170.)

7. *Imagination Dead Imagine* (London: Calder & Boyars, 1965), p. 7. My italics.

and events. Indeed, it is often the case that the more pressing the project, the greater our temptation to indulge in imagining as sheer evasion.

Yet the act of imagining is not always and not only an escape, an irresponsible flight into the unreal. It can accompany and even precipitate intensely involving experiences, as in the cathartic effects of free associating in psychoanalysis.[8] In certain situations, it is even more difficult *not* to imagine than to imagine in the first place. Like the aggressive and sexual fantasies which we so often have (and just as often deny having), imagining occurs more frequently and more influentially than we care to admit to ourselves or to others. Imagining is the *influenza* of mind—part of its pathology. But it is also an auspicious influence. Even when it is most remote or most remiss, and in spite of its basic independence from other mental acts, imagining remains inseparable from the life of mind as a whole, essential to its welfare, indeed to its identity and very existence.

II

But to attest to the familiarity and frequency of an activity such as imagining is one thing; to provide a coherent account of this same activity is something else again. Imagining is easy enough to enact or experience, but it is extremely difficult to capture in midair for purposes of scrutiny and examination. In Kant's classical formulation, imagination is "a blind but indispensable function of the soul, without which we should have no knowledge whatsoever, but of which we are scarcely ever conscious."[9] If this is so—if imagining indeed lies beneath the level of explicit awareness—then we are driven to ask: Must we murder to dissect? Will imagination as analyzed be the *same* imagination as that which we experience so effortlessly in everyday life and with such relish in art?

The skeptical tenor of these questions is heightened when we realize that imagining poses particular problems for philosophical analysis. More than most mental acts, it defies attempts at explanation—and

8. It is significant that when Freud first discusses the technique of free association in *The Interpretation of Dreams,* he quotes with approval a letter of Schiller in which imagination is favorably contrasted with reason on the basis of its open and noncritical attitude. It is due to precisely such a suspension of critical judgment as is effected in imagination that free association becomes possible. Yet Freud stops short of explicitly claiming that free association is itself a form of imagining. Cf. Sigmund Freud, *The Standard Edition of the Complete Psychological Works* (London: Hogarth Press, 1971), V, 102-103. Hereafter referred to as *Standard Edition.*

9. Immanuel Kant, *Critique of Pure Reason,* trans. Norman Kemp Smith (New York: Humanities Press, 1950), A78, p. 112.

even, as we shall have abundant occasion to witness, efforts at elementary description. Here we must say of imagination what Stevens said of poetry: it "resist[s] the intelligence almost successfully."[10] True, there have been a number of perspicuous philosophical accounts, both explanatory and descriptive, of imagination. But it is a signal fact that most of these accounts prove to be unsatisfactory, since they fail to establish what is distinctive about imagining in comparison with other mental acts. Moreover, the very multiplicity of such accounts suggests that there are as many kinds of imagination as there are explanations or descriptions of it. Viewed from the perspective of British empiricism, imagination is little more than warmed-over sensation: "decaying sense" in Hobbes's pithy phrase.[11] As seen through the lens of the Romantic sensibility, however, imagination becomes the sole source of creativity. In Coleridge's well-known words:

> The primary IMAGINATION I hold to be the living power and prime Agent of all human Perception, and as a repetition in the finite mind of the eternal act of creation in the infinite I AM.[12]

A number of positions lying between these two extreme views could be cited as well, e.g., those theories which define imagination as a form of play. What is important at this point, however, is not to summarize all the various accounts that have been given, but simply to acknowledge their sheer diversity. This diversity serves to challenge, and perhaps even to mock, efforts at a unified account—not excepting the present one. It also leads us to pose a second pair of skeptical questions. How can we reach even a minimal agreement as to what imaginative experience consists in? What can we say for certain about the imagining that everyone does?

III

Two characteristics of everyday imagining are perhaps immediately apparent to all: it is easily accessible to the imaginer and it is almost always successfully executed. Let us briefly consider both of these char-

10. The full statement is: "The poem must resist the intelligence almost successfully." It is from Stevens' poem "Man Carrying Thing" in *The Collected Poems of Wallace Stevens* (New York: Knopf, 1954), p. 350.

11. Thomas Hobbes, *Leviathan*, ed. C. B. Macpherson (London: Pelican, 1968), p. 88.

12. Samuel Taylor Coleridge, *Biographia Literaria*, ed. George Watson (London: Dent, 1965), p. 167.

acteristics, which serve in a preliminary way to distinguish imagining from other mental acts.

First of all, imagining is remarkably easy to enter into. It is nearly always available to us as an alternative to whatever else we may be doing at a given time, whether it be perceiving, remembering, reflecting, or whatever. The ease with which we are able to slip into what was once called an "imaginate" state at practically any moment testifies to the ready accessibility of imagining in the ordinary course of events. For the most part, we can imagine *whenever* we wish to, that is, except for those infrequent occasions when the demands or distractions of a particular situation make imagining difficult to initiate or to sustain.

Second, we can also imagine *whatever* and *however* we wish to. At any rate, we can do so within very broad limits, limits which only rarely impede us from summoning up precisely the imaginative scene or situation that is desired. Though in a certain strict sense we cannot be said to fail in our projects of imagining, neither can we be said to succeed— at least not in any strong sense. To be more exact, we should say that the success with which we habitually imagine has a built-in, self-incurred character. It is a success that often takes place without any concerted effort, and it sometimes seems to occur even in spite of ourselves. Apart from negligible exceptions, we cannot *not* imagine what and how we want to. Or to put it paradoxically: it is more difficult to fail than to succeed in imagining. When we are told, in the familiar example, "not to imagine a black bear," we tend to succeed in imagining such a bear despite the express directive not to do so. And the outcome is similar in many cases in which imagining occurs spontaneously and without any conscious effort at all: then we are still less tempted to speak of failure.

This kind of self-guaranteed success is rare, perhaps even unique, among mental acts. Most other acts exhibit a basic capacity for failure —a "fallibility" in the literal sense of the term. It is, for instance, all too possible to fail to perceive clearly or to predict correctly on a given occasion. In perceiving and predicting there is often a distinct discrepancy between intention and realization, with the result that the latter seems only contingently connected with the former. For this reason we frequently put a great deal of effort into a given realization, and attempt to ensure that future realizations can be counted upon. Nevertheless, many perceptual or predictive intentions remain empty or unfulfilled. Such emptiness of intention may eventually be overcome—as when we scrutinize more closely a complex three-dimensional object that we have so far perceived only in part. But the state of unfulfillment may also be unremediable: my intention of the square root of -2 will never find a satisfactory fulfillment in intuitive terms. In most imagining, by contrast, no sooner do I intend a certain object or state of affairs than it appears before me, and in just the form I intended. When I conjure up an image of Pegasus, for example, I may not apprehend exactly the same Pegasus as the next person, but I do experience the precise Pegasus *I* wanted: tinted a certain shade of white, with wings outspread in a certain specific manner, flying through a certain kind of sky, etc. In such a trite but typical act of imagining, little can count as failure and almost everything signifies success. However modest this success may be, it does not occur so consistently and with so few qualifications in other kinds of mental activity.

In view of the perspicuousness of these two distinguishing features of imaginative activity—ease of access and predominantly successful execution—the nature of leading theories elucidating this activity is all the more perplexing. These theories are not only diverse; they are also confused, inconsistent, and even self-contradictory. It is as if the very availability and self-ensured success of imaginative experience hindered rather than helped its comprehension in theoretical terms. Indeed, a theoretical account of imagination may run a greater risk of being a travesty of the phenomenon than a theory of an inherently less evanescent experience such as perception. Not only is there a tendency not to take something so ephemeral as imagining seriously, but its very ephemerality renders it resistant to conceptual specification of a precise sort. Although we normally apprehend an imagined object with remarkable facility, we do so only for an instant, since it tends to elude us in the very next instant: "one glimpse and vanished," says Beckett.[13] An imagined object does not remain present to us in an abiding manner, as do many perceptual objects; to keep it before our mental gaze, we must constantly *re*-imagine it, and even then it is difficult to say whether we are continuing to imagine exactly the *same* object again and again.

In the case of imagination, then, we are dealing with an extraordinarily elusive phenomenon, one that easily slips off the tenterhooks of both observation and theory. In fact, we do not, strictly speaking, *observe* what we imagine at all, for we are not in a position to subject imagined objects and events to the kind of scrutinizing that may be directed toward what we perceive. At the limit, imagining (particularly in the specific form of visualizing) may *seem* to resemble observing, but it can never count as *bona fide* observation: by imagining, we ascertain nothing that we did not know beforehand in some respect. What we take to be *in* the imagined object or event is only what we already,

13. *Imagination Dead Imagine*, p. 7.

explicitly or implicitly, know *about* it. Imaginative experience is inherently circular in this regard, with the consequence that in imagining we cannot claim to confront anything radically new.

Theories of imagination often seem to indulge in a circularity similar to that found within imaginative experience itself. Just as the Pegasus I imagine is the Pegasus I know in advance—e.g., on the basis of reading mythology books or from being told what Pegasus is supposed to look like—so a theory about imagining draws upon preexisting knowledge of what it is to imagine in the first place. But this latter circularity is nonvicious and nonvitiating. One of its characteristic manifestations is the temptation to describe aspects of imagination by means of tautological statements such as "the imagined object is the object of the act of imagining" or "the type of possibility attaching to the imagined object is imaginative possibility."[14] And yet a tendency to give tautological descriptions of a phenomenon does not as such eliminate the possibility of giving an insightful account of that phenomenon. Again there is an instructive parallel within the experience of imagining itself: I may indeed imagine the Pegasus I know beforehand, but the precise *way* in which I do so may nonetheless generate a genuinely novel form of Pegasus that I have never before encountered. Having a generic knowledge of something does not preclude unanticipated embodiments of this knowledge in specific imaginative form. Likewise, an account of imagination as a total phenomenon, though no doubt based on preexisting knowledge, may lead to novel ways of comprehending it—or more exactly, to comprehending unsuspected aspects of it. Such an account can deepen and refine our ordinary understanding of what it is to imagine, even if it does not tell us anything we are not already acquainted with to some degree.

IV

One of the primary aims of a specifically phenomenological method in philosophy is to make more thematic what is otherwise merely implicit and taken for granted in human experience. Moreover, phenomenology places special stress on firsthand or direct description, thereby

14. Cf. the pleonastic term "imaginative image" as used by William Earle in *The Autobiographical Consciousness* (Chicago: Quadrangle Books, 1972), p. 164; and Gaston Bachelard's use of "l'image imaginée" in *La Terre et les rêveries de la volonté* (Paris: Corti, 1945), pp. 3-4. Psychologists follow suit with "imaginary image" (M. J. Horowitz, *Image Formation and Cognition* [New York: Appleton-Century-Crofts, 1970], p. 23) and "imagination image" (A. Richardson, *Mental Imagery* [London: Routledge & Kegan Paul, 1969], p. 94).

minimizing recourse to the highly mediated constructions of meta-physics, natural science, and other theory-saturated disciplines. What is sought in the implementation of such a method is an accurate description of a given phenomenon as it presents itself in one's own experience, not an explanation of its genesis through reference to antecedent causal factors. The phenomenologist's basic attitude is: no matter how something came to be in the first place, what is of crucial concern is the detailed description of the phenomenon *as it now appears*.

It is just such detailed description that is patently lacking in many previous accounts of imagination. These accounts all too often rely on scattered descriptive remarks, and on this insecure foundation they attempt to erect an intricate theoretical edifice. Perhaps the motive for this disdain of systematic description is that merely to describe something may seem pedestrian in comparison with the excitement of theory building. Whatever the motive, the consequences can be disastrous. One of them is that the reader may come to feel that what is being discussed is not at all akin to his own concrete experience. For example, although Schelling continually uses the term "imagination" (*Einbildungskraft*) in his *System of Transcendental Idealism*, the term is never securely anchored in description. As a result, it becomes practically synonymous with an exalted metaphysical insight which is most fully realized in aesthetic experience but which does not correspond in any readily recognizable way to imaginative experience outside the domain of art.[15]

More frequently, however, an inadequate descriptive basis leads to a much more specific and serious consequence: the failure to distinguish imagination in any decisive way from other mental acts. This is a failure in proper identification—in other words, a matter of descriptive confusion. Such confusion between imagination and other psychical phenomena is by no means confined to explicit theories of imagination, though they exhibit the confusion in its most egregious form. It is also present in the very way in which we use the word" imagination" in ordinary language. To take three expressions from everyday speech:

(1) My imagination was playing tricks on me when I mistook that tree over there for a man.

(2) It was just my imagination when I thought I saw a red rat in my bedroom.

15. On Schelling's theory of imagination, see Rudolf Hablützel, *Dialektik und Einbildungskraft: F. W. J. Schellings Lehre von der menschlichen Erkenntnis* (Basel: Recht und Gesellschaft, 1954). The same descriptive deficiency mars the first comprehensive discussion of imagination in modern philosophy, Johann G. E. Maass's *Versuch über die Einbildungskraft* (Halle: Ruff, 1792).

(3) In my imagination I thought that he was out to get me.
In these quotidian examples "imagination" is used to refer to three
quite different types of experience, *none of which* can be considered a
case of imagining proper. Upon even the briefest analysis, it is evident
that none qualifies as an instance of the kind of experience that is
meant when we speak of imagining Pegasus flying through the sky.
Sentence one refers to a case of perceptual illusion, where we mistake
one perceived object for another. In sentence two there is reference to
a hallucination: to the quasi-perceptual appearance of a nonexistent
object, which the hallucinated subject takes to be real. Sentence three
uses the same term, "imagination," to indicate something still different:
a fantasy or delusion of persecution. Each of these three sorts of experience differs significantly from imagining proper, which does not as such
involve perceptual error, belief in a hallucinatory object as real, or in-
dulgence in a fantasy or delusion concerning some aspect of interpersonal experience. And yet the possibility of confusing imagination with
these very different kinds of activity is inherent in the ordinary usage
of the simple English noun "imagination."[16]

V

It is above all in existing theories of imagination that one finds the
most telling instances of failure to distinguish between imagining and
other sorts of mental acts, a failure based on an underlying descriptive
inadequacy. Such confusion between distinctly different kinds of psychical phenomena is present most strikingly in certain psychological
and philosophical theories of imagining. Let us consider in summary
form how this confusion manifests itself in these theories.

PSYCHOLOGY

Under this heading I shall limit myself to brief sketches of three
representative treatments: those to be found in associationist psychology, in Freudian psychoanalysis, and in the writings of Piaget. Different
as these treatments are in matters of detail, they are ultimately allied in
that all are causal accounts that attempt to *explain* the genesis of imagination as a particular capacity of the human mind. Their common con-

16. The basis for the ambiguity of this seemingly innocent word is that it "has a
distinct idiomatic history, and forms part of an intricate and unique conceptual
tradition; it fulfills a large variety of odd job functions, severally interpretable in
different contexts" (Rodney Needham, *Belief, Language, and Experience* [Oxford:
Blackwell, 1972], p. 134).

cern for causal explanation goes hand in hand with a conspicuous lack of precise description. In no instance do we find a satisfactory assessment of how imagining is experienced by the imaginer himself. Instead, there is an effort to explain how it is that one *comes to* imagine in the first place. Valuable as such a causal account may be in its own right, it is singularly unhelpful in providing insight into the actual experience of imagining.

(a) The associationist psychology of the eighteenth and nineteenth centuries supplied the theoretical underpinnings for much of modern cognitive psychology, including the various forms of behaviorism and neobehaviorism that have been prominent in this century. In classical associationist theory all mental events that are not themselves sensations are, in Taine's phrase, merely "spontaneous repetitions of sensation."[17] Anything that is not simply and unqualifiedly a sensation is labeled an "image" in a sense so diffuse that it encompasses short-term memory on the one hand and free-floating fancy on the other. All psychical phenomena are supposedly built up from combinations of sensations and images thus defined. But since images are themselves only facsimiles of sensations, everything is ultimately traceable to sensory impressions. As a consequence, there is no way to distinguish imagination *in kind* from other mental acts, all of which also stem from sensory experience. Moreover, every "higher" act, such as imagination or memory, must obey the laws of association—i.e., contiguity and resemblance —by which complex psychical phenomena are constructed. Even when these phenomena include as their content the poet's fanciful "far other Worlds, and other seas," they must still be understood merely as combinatory arrangements of sensations and images. The world of a poem, therefore, does not differ in kind from the world of memory: all differences are differences of degree. This is to deny intrinsic differences between distinct types of experience. Each experience is determined by its position within the single continuum whose two poles are designated as "sensation" and "image" respectively.

However ingenious and economical such a theory may be, it fails utterly to account for the experimental differences between such closely related mental acts as memory and imagination. Associationists would agree with Hobbes that "Imagination and Memory are but one thing, which for divers considerations hath divers names."[18] And yet the dif-

---

17. See Hippolyte Taine, *On Intelligence*, trans. T. D. Haye (New York: Holt & Williams, 1871). The phrase quoted above is cited by Sartre in *Imagination*, trans. F. Williams (Ann Arbor: University of Michigan Press, 1962), p. 23.
18. *Leviathan*, p. 89.

ferences between imagination and memory are not accurately described as mere differences in mode of combination. Further, how is one to locate and specify the basic sensory units whose replication and subsequent combination are supposed to yield the content of all "higher" mental acts? The search for such units within conscious experience is futile, for these higher acts present themselves as seamless wholes. This is especially true of imagination, whose content is only rarely reducible to the mere juxtaposition of discrete elements: the classical example of the centaur, far from being paradigmatic, is only a limiting case. In fact, any adequate account of imagining must treat it *as such*, that is, on its own terms and not in terms of hypothetically posited elementary units, which serve only to obscure its differences from other apparently allied acts such as memory.

(b) Freud's theory of mental activity—a theory whose origins lie in associationism itself—is no more satisfactory in accounting for the felt differences between imagination and other acts, and particularly between imagination on the one hand and fantasy and hallucination on the other. Freud regards all three acts as strictly wish-fulfilling in character and thus as expressions of desires and drives stemming from the unconscious. In each case wish-fulfillment is achieved by employing the "primary process" mechanisms of condensation, displacement, and pictorial representation. Hallucinations, found most prominently in dreams, are direct products of the primary process; but fantasies and imaginings, typified by daydreams, are derivative from the same process: "The psychical process of constructing composite images in dreams is evidently the same as when we imagine or portray a centaur or dragon in waking life."[19] Consequently, imagining, fantasying and hallucinating are thrust together and regarded as varying ways of providing surrogate satisfactions of basic wishes. There are, of course, differences between the three acts in terms of the exact form of satisfaction involved in each case. These differences are introduced by the "secondary processes" under the control of the ego; yet on examination they prove to be frail and subject to dissolution. As a distinguished neo-Freudian writes: "Although fantasying is recognized (or recognizable) for what it is by the subject, through regression it can succumb to the primary process and lose its index of being 'in the imagination'; in that case it turns into a delusion or hallucination."[20] The very facility with which

19. Freud, *Standard Edition*, IV, 324.
20. Roy Schafer, *Aspects of Internalization* (New York: International Universities Press, 1968), p. 38. As a description of fantasy alone, however, Schafer's statement has considerable merit.

any one of the three acts can be converted into any other gives rise to the view that all three acts belong to the same psychical category. Nor can they be adequately distinguished by invoking special secondary process functions. For example, if imagining is of value to the ego because of its ability to project events in advance of their occurrence, fantasies and hallucinations also possess anticipatory value, e.g., in science fiction. It should be noted as well that insofar as imagination is given autonomy, it is restricted to what neo-Freudians call "secondary autonomy," an autonomy that remains genetically and structurally dependent upon the underlying autonomy of the primary process. Thus the alliance of imagining and fantasying with secondary processes does not serve to distinguish these acts from one another or from hallucination in any definitive way. The result is that it is never entirely clear where the borderlines between the three acts are to be located. Is a daydream an act of imagination or of fantasy—or perhaps even of hallucination? The Freudian model does not allow us to say which, and we are left perplexed.

(c) In the developmental psychology of Piaget we witness an attempt to subsume imagination under the symbolizing powers of mind. Imagining is seen as a mental activity arising early in life from the internalized and deferred imitation of perceived objects and motor movements. When this occurs, i.e., immediately after the "sensory-motor" period in the child's development, the way is opened to what Piaget calls "egocentric representational activity," that is, to forms of symbolizing that are manifested first and most strikingly in the spontaneous games and play of childhood. Imagining—entertaining "mental images"—aids such symbolizing to the extent that it allows the child to represent objects and situations that are not present in perception. At first purely imitative ("reproductive"), it becomes progressively more self-sustaining and wide-ranging ("anticipatory"). Yet imagining remains only a single phase of the symbolizing stage of cognitive growth, which in still later stages will no longer need to have recourse to mental imagery at all. And if imagination is regarded as a merely transitional moment in the development of the child's full cognitive capacities, fantasy and hallucination are accorded a still more diminutive importance. They are regarded as types of "secondary symbolism," that is, as offshoots of the primary symbolism embodied in children's play.[21] As with

21. "On the whole, unconscious symbolic thought [e.g., fantasy and hallucination as present in dreams] follows the same laws as thought in general, of which it is merely an extreme form, being an extension of symbolic play" (Jean Piaget, *Play, Dreams, and Imitation in Childhood*, trans. C. Gattegno and F. J. Hodson [New York: Norton, 1962], p. 212).

Freud, no basis for differentiating between imagination, fantasy, and hallucination as distinct kinds of experience is given: all three are considered simply as various aspects of a stage that is itself soon to be surpassed. Even if we grant that from the standpoint of cognitive development the three acts may overlap in significant ways, an account is still required of their felt differences in the experience of the adult, for whom they have become distinct and separately recognizable. To conceive imagining in the context of a theory of emergent cognitive powers is to confine imagination to an ultimately minor role; and the effect of this move is to make distinctions between it and kindred activities a matter of comparative indifference: all become mere signposts on the route to the "formal operations" of conceptual thought, and it is not deemed crucial to distinguish them from each other in any rigorous way.[22]

PHILOSOPHY

Imagination has fared no better in the hands of philosophers, where it suffers from the same two sorts of mistreatment that it has received from psychologists: confusion with apparently allied acts such as memory, fantasy, and hallucination; and denial of importance. The two actions are not unrelated to each other. On the one hand, because imagination is seen as secondary in significance, it is regarded as continuous with other mental acts that are held to be equally minor. On the other hand, because imagination has been falsely assimilated with other seemingly similar acts, it has come to be regarded with disdain. Furthermore, each of the two modes of mistreatment (confusion with other acts, demeaning of status) reflects a fundamental defect common to psychological and philosophical theories alike: an inadequate basic description of the phenomenon itself. Psychologists and philosophers are equally remiss in this respect; neither group has given persistent and careful attention to imagination as a phenomenon worth analyzing in its own right. The result is that many of their accounts of imagination are *truncated from below* and thus top-heavy; the descriptive detail that should precede and underlie theory building has been singularly lack-

22. In the end imagination is merely symbolic of, and thus subordinate to, the higher powers of conceptual thinking: "the image does of course persist, but merely as a symbol of the operational schema, and no longer as an integral part of it" (ibid., p. 244). For further discussion of Piaget's theory of imagination, see Jean Piaget and Bärbel Inhelder, *Mental Imagery in the Child*, trans. P. A. Chilton (London: Routledge & Kegan Paul, 1971) and Hans G. Furth, *Piaget and Knowledge* (Englewood Cliffs: Prentice-Hall, 1969), esp. pp. 68-106.

ing. Perhaps it has been assumed that such detail is not needed because of the accessibility and facility of much imaginative experience. In fact, however, detailed description is required if imagination's very elusiveness is not to baffle and confound us.

The negligence of philosophers in this regard is of long standing. At very few, if any, discernible points in more than two thousand years of philosophical endeavor have convincing and lasting distinctions been made between imagination and the group of sibling acts that would include memory, perceptual illusion, fantasy, delusion, and hallucination. Indeed, philosophical theorizing sometimes exhibits an even more extensive confusion than is found in psychological studies: a confusion not just between imagination and apparent allies, but also between imagination and quite *dissimilar* mental acts. Imagining is seen in some instances as an aspect of perception, in others as part of thought. When it *is* given a distinct role, it is characteristically that of being a mere mediator between other powers presumed to be primary in importance.

The shifting status of imagination in philosophical theory can best be indicated by singling out three representative positions, each of which illustrates a major way in which imagining has been considered in the course of Western philosophy. In their profound disparity these positions reveal the markedly ambivalent attitude toward imagination that has colored so much of philosophical reflection on the subject.[23]

Subordination

The first fully articulate philosophical theory of imagination in the West, that of Plato, placed imagination in the lowest rank of mental faculties. For Plato, imagining is an instance of *eikasia*: mere supposing, a phantom or pseudo-knowing that is analogized to the reflections cast by perceptual objects. Since perceptual objects themselves are located at the only slightly more elevated level of *pistis* or belief, the position of imagining is doubly subordinated—first to *pistis* and then to progressively more legitimate forms of knowing: *dianoia* (discursive reasoning), *epistēmē* (scientific knowledge), and *noēsis* (rational intuition). Consequently, imagining as *eikasia* is an activity to be overcome and left behind as quickly and completely as possible. Not even Plato's occasional praise of "divine madness"—which involves the free exercise

23. For a full survey of ancient and medieval philosophical theories of imagination, consult M. W. Bundy, *The Theory of Imagination in Classical and Medieval Thought* (Urbana: University of Illinois, Studies in Language and Literature, 1927). For a briefer but more comprehensive overview, see Jean Starobinski, "Jalons pour une histoire du concept d'imagination" in *La relation critique* (Paris: Gallimard, 1970), pp. 174-95.

of a poetic or religious imagination—alters his basic attitude. As the *Republic* makes clear, imagination's primary product, the image, is only "an imitation of an imitation" and is, despite its allure in art and rhetoric, to be regarded with suspicion.[24] Thus the course of philosophical theorizing about imagination is launched in a highly critical vein.

Mediation

Aristotle initiated a lengthy tradition in which imagination, instead of being pushed to the bottom of the epistemological hierarchy, is interpreted as a middle-range mental faculty. For imagining is now located *between* perception (*to aisthētikon*) and intellect (*nous*), and is even made necessary to the latter: "the soul never thinks without an image."[25] Imagination is given even higher status by being linked with memory, both being regarded as direct outgrowths of perception.[26] The linking of imagination and memory as sister faculties—one turned toward the future in expectation, the other toward the past in recollection—continues throughout medieval and Renaissance thought. It is still evident in Hobbes, who conceived both imagining and remembering as lingering remnants of sensation, and hence as occupying a middle ground between sensing and thinking.[27]

Hume did not alter this tradition of thought in any fundamental way when, following Locke, he distinguished between impressions and ideas. In Hume's view, images are low-level ideas which, being more vivid than what he calls "ideas of judgment" (although less vivid than ideas of memory), may exist in close proximity to impressions themselves.[28] A vivid image may even give rise to what Hume calls an "impression of reflection" and thus function as an intermediate mental

24. See Plato, *Republic*, Book Six (esp. 510d-516c) and Book Ten (esp. 597a-599c).

25. Aristotle, *De Anima*, 431a 16. Cf. also 431b 2, 432a 8-14. I have used the translation of D. W. Hamlyn in *Aristotle's De Anima* (Oxford: Clarendon Press, 1968).

26. See Aristotle, *De Memoria et Reminiscentia* in *Aristotle on Memory*, trans. Richard Sorabji (London: Duckworth, 1972), esp. p. 49: "It is apparent, then, to which part of the soul memory belongs, namely, the same part as that to which imagination belongs." Cf. also *Metaphysics*, I, 980b 24-25.

27. See Hobbes, passage cited above; and more fully: *Leviathan*, part I, ch. 2 et seq.

28. See David Hume, *An Inquiry Concerning Human Understanding*, ed. C. W. Hendel (New York and Indianapolis: Bobbs-Merrill, 1955), p. 63. It is to be noted that in this passage Hume distinguishes between "fictions of the imagination" and "ideas of the judgment." On the difference in vivacity between memory and imagination, see Hume, *A Treatise of Human Nature*, ed. L. A. Selby-Bigge (Oxford: Clarendon Press, 1967), pp. 8-10, 85-86.

entity that, though itself an idea, can stimulate emotions.[29] Hence Hume was led to devise a special role for imagination—a role of mediating between sheer sensory impressions and ideas of memory and judgment by enlivening the latter with a semblance of the vivacity of the former.[30]

Kant reinforced imagination's mediatory role by distinguishing between two kinds of imagining: a reproductive type, which is intimately connected with memory and perceptual apprehension, and a productive type, which is contiguous with conceptual thinking.[31] Thus imagination stands precisely midway between sensibility and understanding, the two major human faculties which together stake out the limits of Kant's topography of mind: "The two extremes, namely sensibility and understanding, must stand in necessary connection with each other through the mediation of this transcendental function of imagination."[32] The "transcendental function" referred to in this passage is effected by means of the transcendental schema, a product of productive imagination and the explicit basis for imagination's mediatory role:

> Obviously there must be some third thing, which is homogeneous on the one hand with the category, and on the other hand with the appearance, and which thus makes the application of the former to the latter possible. This mediating representation . . . is the transcendental schema.[33]

From Aristotle to Kant, then, imagination is seen as a mediating or middle-range power, as an intermediate faculty destined to shuttle back and forth between the two primary poles of sensation and intellect.[34]

Superordination

In contrast with Aristotle, Hobbes, Hume, and Kant, a number of German Romantic thinkers attempted to situate imagining in the uppermost position in the hierarchy of mental faculties. In the exuberant encomia of Friedrich von Schlegel, Novalis, Jean Paul, and Schelling, imagination became the primary creative capacity of the human mind—not only in art (where even Plato had suspected its importance)

29. *A Treatise of Human Nature*, pp. 7-8, 84-86, 275-77.
30. Ibid., pp. 265 and 371 on the vivifying powers of imagination.
31. *Critique of Pure Reason*, A100-A129, pp. 132-50.
32. Ibid., A124, p. 146.
33. Ibid., B177, A138, p. 181.
34. Coleridge sums up this tradition when he writes: "There are evidently two powers at work, which relatively to one another are active and passive; and this is not possible without an intermediate faculty, which is at once active and passive. In philosophical language, we must denominate this intermediate faculty in all its degrees and determinations, the IMAGINATION" (*Biographia Literaria*, p. 72).

but also in epistemology and metaphysics: "all powers and forces of the internal as well as of the external world must be deduced from the productive imagination."[35] The effect was exhilarating, especially for a poet-critic such as Coleridge, who introduced and refined the thesis for an English audience. Yet in the end what Kant called *Schwärmerei* (wild enthusiasm) ruled the day. "Imagination" became a mesmeric term that meant so much in general—claims concerning its powers were often so exaggerated—that it came to mean very little in particular. Lacking a basis in direct description, and despite its considerable resonance in the poetry of the period, the term lost most of its recognizable content in the more ecstatic outbursts of the *Naturphilosophen*. The supreme position so boldly imputed to imagination was all too easily encompassed and surpassed in the dialectical system of Hegel, for whom imagination was once again subordinated to thought (albeit in the guise of Absolute Knowledge). The only significant subsequent revival of the notion of imagination as the supreme human faculty is found among the surrealists, particularly in the writings of André Breton. But this revival, like its parent movement of Romanticism, also tended toward enthusiasm and exhortation rather than toward a deepened understanding of the activity of imagining itself; and Breton's insight into this activity was expressed in similarly dithyrambic terms: "la seule imagination me rend compte de ce qui *peut être*."[36]

The error of both Romantics and surrealists lay in overreacting to previous accounts and in mistaking the centrality of imagination in art for its supremacy in epistemology and metaphysics. Yet the most effective way in which to make up for former lapses is not merely to turn the tables. To claim a superordinate position for imagination is just as misguided as Plato's futile attempt to foist upon imagination a strictly subordinate role. In both cases, and in that of the mediation theorists as well, a rigidly hierarchical model of mind is presupposed. To adopt such a model is to presume that imagination must occupy some particular position within its stratified structure; and it is also to imply that there is some inherent competition between various mental activities for the honor of being accorded the topmost position.

What emerges as most disconcerting in the foregoing précis of representative philosophical theories is the highly ambiguous place of

---

35. Novalis, *Schriften*, ed. J. Minor (Jena: Diederichs, 1923), III, p. 375.
36. André Breton, from the first *Manifeste du Surréalisme*; his italics. Note also the statement of Louis Aragon: "tout relève de l'imagination et de l'imagination tout révèle" (*Le paysan de Paris* [Gallimard, 1926], p. 78). On the continuity of French Romanticism and surrealism, see Marcel Raymond, *De Baudelaire au Surréalisme* (Paris: Plon, 1934), passim.

imagination in Western philosophical thought. One and the same experience—or at least what is called by the same name—is cast into exceedingly diverse roles, ranging from that of mere understudy to that of the leading character in the drama of mind. Such variation in role-assignment is indicative of an underlying uncertainty concerning the character of imagination. Is it the pariah of the philosophy of mind or its savior? Is it an independent faculty with its own species of insight, or is it merely a parasite on other faculties? On the basis of a brief conspectus of views alone, like the one just given, we cannot provide any straightforward answers to these questions. In fact, the predominant philosophical traditions in the West do not allow us to conclude anything definite with regard to the position of imagination vis-à-vis other mental acts. Not only is it not cogently distinguished from such apparent sibling acts as memory, fantasy, and hallucination—a weakness of psychological theories as well—but it is not securely situated in regard to such decidedly different acts as sensory perception and conceptual thinking. The overall picture, then, is one of disarray.

Taken together, psychological and philosophical theories of imagination teach a similar lesson: if the mind is regarded as a mere processor of perceptions or as a graduated series of successively higher functions, imagination will be denied a genuinely distinctive role of its own. In the constrictive views of mental activity that we have considered above, imagining has almost invariably been relegated to a secondary or tertiary status in which it merely subtends some supposedly superior cognitive agency such as intellect or (more frequently) modifies some presumably more original source such as sensation. Either way, the uniqueness of imagination as a mental act fails to be acknowledged. Clearly, what is needed is an approach that respects essential, and not merely contingent, differences between mental acts and that attempts to account for each in its own right and without recourse to a preestablished hierarchy of acts. Any such hierarchy is *pre-evaluative* in the sense that it determines or expresses in advance which acts are more, and which less, important.

In order to avoid this form of foreclosure, we must remain open to what can be called the *multiplicity of the mental*. Within this multiplicity there is no strict hierarchical structure—only a proliferation of unforeclosable possibilities. An acute and continuing sensitivity to the multiplicity of the mental will allow us to acknowledge what is unique in each mental act and thus to view imagination as nonderivative, as a phenomenon to be evaluated on its own terms. As Wittgenstein remarks:

"But what is this queer experience?" Of course it is not queerer than any other; it simply *differs in kind* from those experiences which we regard as the most fundamental ones, our sense impressions for instance.[37]

If imagining truly differs in kind from other mental acts, then it calls for a careful descriptive account that will permit its specificity to emerge from the confusion and misconception in which it has been so deeply mired in Western thought.

37. Wittgenstein, *Philosophical Investigations*, trans. G. E. M. Anscombe (Oxford: Blackwell, 1967), p. 215. My italics.

PART ONE

PRELIMINARY PORTRAIT

CHAPTER ONE

Examples and First Approximations

I

PHENOMENOLOGICAL METHOD as conceived by Husserl takes its beginning not from uninterpreted givens but from carefully selected examples. Phenomenologists might well agree with Wittgenstein's comment that "we now demonstrate a method, *by examples*."[1] These examples do not have to stem from an exhaustive survey; there is no need to analyze *every* example that occurs or might occur within a given domain of experience. Typically, only the most promising are seized upon—those that exhibit an essence or essential structure with a maximum of evidential lucidity. For this reason considerable care must be taken in the preliminary choice of examples, since it is by their examination that we are to achieve eidetic insight. Just such an examination is the primary task of this chapter; but before undertaking this task let us consider further the nature and place of examples in the phenomenological enterprise.

Since eidetic insight is strictly nonempirical in character, phenomenologists treat examples neither as brute facts nor as factual illustrations of conceptual truths. Even if I decide to begin with an example drawn from the realm of fact, it is not initially chosen or subsequently scrutinized *because* or *insofar as* it is factual. Rather, by exercising the phenomenological reduction, I suspend its very factuality. In this way it ceases to be an independent phenomenon and becomes a phenomenon-for-me: i.e., an appearance whose actuality is held in abeyance and whose essential structure is revealed only in and to my conscious apprehension of it. As an integral part of a phenomenological inquiry, an example thus possesses an indeterminate status; it is neither sheer fact nor pure essence, but something distinct from and located between

1. *Philosophical Investigations*, sec. 133. My italics.

these two polar terms. Insofar as it is stressed that the example is concretely given in actual experience, it falls closer to the pole of factuality. Insofar as it is taken as an example *of* an essential structure, it draws nearer to the opposite pole of essence.

Given this view of examples, Husserl insists that it is a matter of indifference whether a given example stems from personal experience or is purely fictitious in origin. The latter possibility needs to be underlined; "fiction" in the broad sense of any nonreal product of imagination is a perfectly legitimate source of examples:

> The *eidos* or pure essence can be exhibited by examples . . . borrowed from the givens of experience, i.e., from perception, memory, etc., but also from the mere products of imagination. This is why, in order to grasp an essence in a definitive way, we may begin with appropriate empirical intuitions, but also with intuitions having no relation to [sensory] experience: non-positing intuitions which are 'merely imagined'.[2]

Thus the phenomenologist is at liberty to draw examples either from actual experience or from the active use of imagination. But it should be noted that fictitious examples enjoy a certain advantage over those drawn from fact, for they do not have to undergo a preliminary reduction of factuality. Hence Husserl claims that "free imaginings possess a privileged position with regard to perceptions" and even that "fiction constitutes the vital element of phenomenology as of all eidetic sciences."[3]

Phenomenological method takes objects, events, or acts—whether real or imagined—as *exemplifying* an essence or essential structure. In this way their basic constitution is made perspicuous, and examples become the specific vehicles or privileged media of eidetic insight. This insight does not derive from an act of pure intuition comparable to Platonic *noēsis*, in which the mind is in immediate contact with the highest objects of reason. Insight into essences is a mediated affair. But it is not mediated by either of two traditionally conceived varieties of mediation: perception or symbolic forms. On the one hand, perceptual content as such does not form part of eidetic insight; if it enters at all, it enters as already reduced and thus in a neutralized form that is ontically equivalent to imagined content. On the other hand, symbolic forms (whether mythical, artistic, linguistic, etc.) provide only an indirect or "signitive" embodiment of essential insight.[4] In the practice

2. *Ideas*, trans. W. R. Boyce Gibson (New York: Macmillan, 1958), sec. 4, p. 57. Here as elsewhere I have modified Gibson's translation.
3. Both quotations are from ibid., sec. 70.
4. On the notion of signitive fulfillment, see Husserl, *Logical Investigations*, trans. J. N. Findlay (New York: Humanities Press, 1970), II, pp. 710-18.

of phenomenology, it is the *example itself* that is the basic mediating factor; and an example *per se* is neither perceptual nor symbolic, but paradigmatic in character. As truly exemplary, it serves as an indispensable *via media* between the initial decision to search for the essence of a given phenomenon and the final attainment of insight into this essence. In Husserl's formula it is "on the basis" (*auf Grund*) of examples, and of examples alone, that the phenomenologist is able to attain eidetic insight.[5]

Such preliminary considerations point to the need for initiating a phenomenology of imagination with the presentation and analysis of several examples of the act itself. These examples will be taken from my own experiences of imagining, and this will be done despite the merit of Husserl's admonitory remark:

> Much can be drawn from examples furnished by history and, even more, by art and especially literature. Undoubtedly these [latter sources of examples] are fictitious; but the originality in the invention of forms, the richness of detail, the continuous development of motif raise them high above the creations of our own imaginations.[6]

It may be admitted that examples taken from history and literature possess a complexity and subtlety often lacking in everyday, garden-variety acts of imagining. But, by the same token, it would be naive to regard such examples as unadulterated reports of their authors' imaginative experiences, for they have almost invariably undergone significant modification (e.g., for the sake of unity of plot or theme). What is needed in a scrupulous descriptive account of imagination is the reporting of examples in an unmodified form and precisely as they present themselves to the imaginer. The examples to be given below meet this demand insofar as they represent direct descriptions of several imaginative experiences—descriptions which were written down immediately after the experiences took place.[7]

5. *Ideas*, sec. 70.
6. Ibid.
7. These examples are for the most part products of more or less attentive efforts to imagine; none is a merely fragmentary act. Yet fragmentary imagining is certainly a legitimate and perhaps even the most frequent mode of imagining; and we cannot afford to neglect it altogether. It is not, however, suitable as a point of departure for the present study: an adequate phenomenology of imagination must consider, so far as is possible, the *full* act. Accordingly, several fairly protracted examples, containing considerable descriptive detail, have been chosen in order to bring out as many of the significant essential traits of imagining as may be accomplished in a first approximation.

The fact that the following examples are drawn from firsthand experiences of imagining is thus both desirable and legitimate: desirable insofar as a more comprehensive description can be given of such experiences than of others' imaginative experiences; legitimate insofar as actual episodes of imagining are always first-person in character (there is no such thing as co-imagining in any strict sense). What Freud said in defending the analysis of his own dreams in *The Interpretation of Dreams* holds true in the present instance as well:

> No doubt I shall be met by doubts of the trustworthiness of 'self-analyses' of this kind; and I shall be told that they leave the door open to arbitrary conclusions. In my judgment the situation is in fact more favorable in the case of *self*-observation than in that of [observing] other people.[8]

II

The following three reports have been kept in the present tense in order to convey as fully as possible the vividness of the original experiences.

EXAMPLE #1

I am seated at a long library table. I close my eyes. Immediately a school of white—very white—dolphins appears. There are perhaps between five and ten of them, though they cannot be enumerated with precision. At first the dolphins just gambol in the water, shooting out of it in a playful fashion. I am mainly aware of the movements of their bodies, and only very indistinctly of their faces. Suddenly, in a second scene, which is neither strictly continuous nor yet discontinuous with the first, the dolphins approach a simple wooden boat, which is seen from above. This boat instantaneously and inexplicably changes into a larger vessel, perhaps a trawler; and then, just as unexpectedly, the larger craft is transformed into an enormous metal freighter. (All of this continues to be viewed from the same somewhat elevated point.) The dolphins then swim around and under the freighter's hull, and the scene is set for a third episode, in which the dolphins approach a desert island. They swim right up to its beach until they are practically out of the water. They disport themselves for some time near the beach, and then seem to head back out to sea. A final scene ensues, somewhat disconnected from the foregoing ones: the dolphins are playing among

8. *Standard Edition*, IV, 105. Freud's italics.

themselves. I can see them now in much greater detail than before; I notice their quizzical-clowning faces, their mocking smiles, their violent movements as they leap out of the water and into each other's path. (Only in this last episode do I feel I am fairly close to the scene of action. This proximity contrasts with the relative remoteness of previous scenes, in which I was above and, as it seemed, to the "left" of the action.) The sequence then comes to an end; I have the distinct feeling that I could continue it if I wished, but that it has now run its course.

Remarks

(1) The whole sequence was soundless, even though normally there would have been sounds in the real-life equivalent of such a situation (e.g., dolphins' cries, their splashings in the water, etc.). The term "soundless" does not refer to strict silence but to an amorphous auditory state in which no *specific* sounds were distinguishable.

(2) I am surprised that I had such a definite sense of position and perspective in relation to the events witnessed. My vantage point seemed to remain the same throughout—high up and looking down— with the exception of the last scene. I was aware of myself as witnessing the unfolding drama from a particular vantage point. Yet I was not expressly conscious of myself as an *external* observer. Rather, I felt myself to be viewing a scene of which my very remoteness of position was an integral part.

(3) I am also surprised to find how detailed a description I am able to give of this fleeting sequence. As it was originally experienced, it seemed quite compressed and inconsequential—as if its description might merit no more than a couple of sentences.

(4) Also striking was the way in which the sequence divided itself spontaneously into four episodes or scenes; these scenes formed themselves into loosely knit units, and yet in each case as if around an invisible nucleus. An intrinsic but unknown ordering principle seemed to be at work throughout.

EXAMPLE #2

Still at the library table, I begin again with my eyes closed, but instead of letting a scene unfold of its own accord, I am conscious this time of a desire to imagine something auditory and not visual alone. I find myself trying to imagine what the cry of a flamingo might sound like (a cry with which I am not familiar). In the beginning I am able to summon up only a visual image of the bird; and indeed, throughout, I have difficulty dissociating the sight of the bird from the sound it makes. But very soon I am wholly absorbed in "hearing"—or, as we shall call it, "audializing"—an animal cry; it begins on a high shrill note and descends to a low warbling. Almost immediately this movement of sound takes on a rhythmic cadence, a sort of regular swooping downward followed by a quick return to a high note. The sound itself has a fairly definite sense of locus—emanating either from the visualized bird or (when I manage to audialize without visualizing) from a quite indeterminate region of audialized space ("sound-space," as we might call it). Yet, strangely enough, there is at the same time a quasi-visual sense of the sound's shape, a kind of linear arabesque that is traced out as the sound runs its characteristic course. I now find that I can easily repeat the sound and its characteristic movement on the basis of its strongly rhythmical character.

But this repetition does not continue for long, and I discover myself wanting to imagine a different sound, one more familiar. Immediately the roar of a walrus obtrudes itself, appearing without any special effort on my part. In this case I find I can imagine the sound without being at the same time tempted to entertain a visual image of a walrus. Also, I can add the walrus roar to the already imagined flamingo cry, producing a duet of sounds that are almost, but not completely, simultaneous. I note that the walrus sound is comparatively simple compared to the flamingo sound; it is a loud, single-toned, vibratory bass note. It does not assume the undulating rhythmic pattern of the flamingo cry, but seems to sustain itself without taking on any such pattern.

As an extension of the attempt to imagine the flamingo and walrus sounds together, I try next to imagine a chorus of diverse animal sounds that are heard all at once. This is difficult to do, and I find myself halting and being easily distracted from the task. The best I can achieve is a vague cacophony in which I feel myself to be invaded by numerous and contrasting animal cries. This cacophony continues so long as I do not try to focus too definitely on any single sound or group of sounds. But the animal chorus is hard to sustain, and I notice that there is no rhythm or basic repetition of sounds which would facilitate its continuation.

Finally, I try to imagine melodies from musical compositions, and this occurs in two phases. (a) I evoke a melody with which I am fairly familiar—a main theme from Stravinsky's *Petrouchka*, the ballet I have witnessed during the past week. This theme springs crisply to mind without any difficulty, and I repeat it to myself several times without there being any significant change in its form. (b) I try to imagine a theme from a symphony written by an entirely fictitious composer.

Thus it is a question of a genuinely imaginary symphony. Audializing a theme from this fictive symphony is not easy at first. I pause and find myself again distracted by surrounding sounds in the reading room where I am seated. But suddenly a rather thin and insubstantial group of notes occurs. These notes do not seem to have any definite form or movement—not even a definite rhythm. They lead to nothing else, but seem simply to be suspended in audialized space. They fade away rapidly, although I find that they can be called back into mind with sufficient mental effort. Here the experience ends.

Remarks

(1) I find it difficult to audialize in any sustained fashion. In order to do so I seem to have to rely on one of two procedures: either introducing a rhythmic, repetitious element (as in the case of the flamingo cry) or borrowing from memory, which facilitates the continuing appearance of the audialized object or event (e.g., the *Petrouchka* theme). If neither of these procedures is available, as in the fictive symphony, it becomes difficult to maintain an imagined sound in mind for more than a brief moment; it is also more difficult to summon it back into existence. Therefore, rhythm, repetition, and memory aid not only in the first appearance of imagined sounds but also in their *reappearance*.

(2) The sequence as a whole differed in two ways from that given in the first example. First, instead of appearing in an unsolicited fashion, the imagined sounds were for the most part objects of volition. I no longer took a passive stance in which an imagined object or scene presented *itself*; instead, I set out expressly to imagine sounds of various sorts. In this example, therefore, we observe a number of instances of conscious self-inducement, in striking contrast with the nearly complete spontaneity of the previous example. Second, what was thus consciously induced was correspondingly poorer in content. Although there were several "parts" within the whole experience, they were not felt as intrinsically interesting episodes or scenes; rather, I had the sense of witnessing an unadorned and uninvolving presentation of isolated, nonsequential sounds or groups of sounds. There was no sense of active alliance between these focal objects of awareness and other items or aspects of the experience. The overall impression was one of emptiness and sterility—as contrasted with the dynamic, colorful dolphin scenes. But it should be pointed out that I, like many others, visualize much more readily than I audialize; my visual imagination is considerably more developed than my auditory imagination. Since this development is dependent, in part at least, upon contingent cultural factors, one can-

not attribute all the differences between the two examples to inherent differences between visualizing and audializing powers. The inherent differences themselves appear to arise from different ways of presenting imagined objects—either by stressing space and the spatial setting or by emphasizing time and temporal modalities.

(3) It is noteworthy that the result of attempting to imagine melodies was not significantly different from the result of imagining animal cries. In both cases a more and a less difficult sound were imagined: on the one hand, the flamingo cry and the fictive symphony; on the other hand, the walrus roar and the *Petrouchka* theme. It did not seem to make any fundamental difference that two of the sounds came from nature and two were man-made, since the exact degree of difficulty was not determined by such facts alone. A melody has to be at least faintly familiar, or possess a marked rhythmic or repetitious pattern, for it to be easily entertainable in my imagining. And the same holds for imagined animal sounds.

(4) There is no special difficulty in combining visualized and audialized aspects of imaginative experience. If anything, there is a natural tendency to do so, as when I imagined the flamingo cry as emanating from the body of the bird; only with further effort was I able to disembody the sound and to audialize it without visualizing it. But, while the audial and the visual thus form natural partners in experiences of imagining, they are also essentially dissociable. As already remarked, the dolphin sequence in the first example was soundless; and in the present example the *Petrouchka* theme appeared without any visual accompaniment. Thus these two modalities of imagining either may appear in initial separation from each other or may be separated *after* they have first appeared conjointly.

EXAMPLE #3

Settling back into my easy chair, I close my eyes and start to imagine. In this case my only express intentions are to avoid imagining animals (which have populated the two previous examples)[9] and somehow to include human beings and human speech in the imaginative presentation. Then I think to myself: why not imagine what might

9. Perhaps the appearance of these animal forms is not so accidental as it might seem to be at first glance. Bachelard, commenting on the "bestiary" in Lautréamont's poetry, speaks of *"the need to animalize* which lies at the origin of imagination. The primary function of imagination is to make animal forms." (Gaston Bachelard, *Lautréamont* [Paris: Corti, 1939], p. 51; his italics. Cf. also pp. 142-43.)

happen later today at the seminar on Rawls's *Theory of Justice*, which is being given at University College in Oxford by Dworkin, Hampshire, and Hart? (I had read of this seminar the evening before; the first meeting was to take place this afternoon at 5:00 P.M.) Thereupon I imagine that I am in a dimly lit and deeply shadowed medieval room. It is situated high above a central college courtyard. I sense that I am a member of the seminar audience along with an indefinite number of others. At first these others are almost wholly nondescript; I am barely aware of them except as an ill-defined group whose attention is focused, as is mine, on the three seminar leaders, who are seated at a long conference table covered with a white tablecloth. These figures are also indistinct; no definite features stand out—indeed, at first I have very little sense of their presence in the imagined scene other than my conviction that they *must* be there insofar as they are the leaders of the seminar. This quite indeterminate situation changes when one of them, Ronald Dworkin, stands up behind a small lectern in the middle of the table and begins speaking. Even of Dworkin, whom I have seen once before, I have only a vague impression: a somewhat squarish, bulldogish face, hair falling down into the eyes, and glasses. Glancing down at some notes, Dworkin starts by saying something like: "This is one of the most important books to appear in recent philosophical history. Accordingly, the three of us thought it opportune to offer a seminar on it. We shall alternate in presiding over meetings. . . . Today, let me begin by reviewing briefly several former theories of justice. Plato, in the *Republic* . . ." Dworkin's talk trails off. I even visualize the mark ". . ."—which seems to indicate that Dworkin is going over very familiar territory. He does not stop speaking at any precise point, but drones on a decidedly pedantic manner.

After a certain lapse of time, I think to myself, why not insert a fourth leader, someone who is not a philosopher, a legal scholar, or a lawyer? This wish is instantaneously fulfilled by the felt presence of a fourth leader, seated somewhere in the front of the room, though without any definite features at all. Frustrated by this featurelessness, I try to bring all the faces of the leaders into sharper focus. I visualize Hampshire as looking something like Bertrand Russell in middle age, Hart as a benign and balding scholar with glasses, Dworkin as described above, and the new figure as a ruddy, smiling, fortyish person who seems very lively and willing to contribute to the discussion. Following this, I attempt to visualize the other members of the audience, but with less success: I apprehend a number of students, including some eager, serious, short-haired Americans busily taking notes. The audience evidently fills the room; there are no empty seats. Perhaps because there seem to be so many auditors, I cease trying to visualize them.

Dworkin finishes his talk, which has somehow continued through all of this. He asks if there are any questions. Someone looking suspiciously like myself (he is wearing a red sweater like mine and is about my age—yet I continue to observe him from the same vantage point I have maintained throughout the whole sequence) rises and asks, "Is it really worth the trouble to study this book after all?" There is polite but embarrassed laughter all around. Then one of the leaders, seemingly Hampshire, replies that "Yes, in fact it *is* worthwhile." At this, the seminar breaks up. I drift away with most of the others—gliding swiftly down into the courtyard below and then onto an indistinct street nearby.

Remarks

(1) This was the most smoothly sequential of the three examples of imagining. It was neither strictly episodic (as was the first example) nor markedly discontinuous (as was the second); instead, it involved a more or less steadily unfolding scene punctuated only by trivial developments which corresponded to changes in my attention. As in the second example, I was quite aware of having initiated this relatively protracted sequence; I was also aware of my ability to redirect its course at any given point (e.g., when I decided arbitrarily to add a fourth leader-figure). But the sequence also exhibited a measure of spontaneity, unfolding with a momentum of its own that was lacking in the second example.

(2) My own role in this sequence was more complex than in the previous examples. I continued to be the witness of all that happened (since there was nothing hidden which I could not apprehend) and to retain a fixed vantage point throughout. But I seem to have witnessed *myself* as well when I visualized the Casey-like figure who asked an impertinent question. There was thus an ambiguous mixture of observation and action—not unlike those dreams and daydreams in which the subject is both spectator and participant at once.

(3) We have already remarked in regard to the second example that audial and visual aspects of imagining may occur either separately or together. The present example suggests that this initial claim should be qualified: when it is a matter of the *human* voice which is audialized, it is almost always apprehended as emanating from a visualized human body. For it to appear as disembodied would require a special effort of imagination—one that would normally be stronger than that required to imagine the disembodied flamingo cry. For humans themselves, the voice seems to be intrinsic to the human body and not just an accom-

paniment of it. Also, the language that is imagined as being spoken by an imaginary figure is directly continuous with one's own "inner speech": what the imagined person is saying is precisely what the imaginer is thinking. (This may account for the relative rapidity of imagined speaking and thus for the difficulty in restating it word for word.)

(4) It will be noticed that in this last example elements both of memory and of anticipation are present. I had seen and heard Dworkin on an earlier occasion, when he was lecturing at the Yale Law School. And the whole sequence was anticipatory of an actual seminar which was to be held later in the day and which I planned to attend. But the undeniable presence of these two particular factors does not undermine the imaginative status of the sequence. It only shows that imagination may enter into close alliances with kindred acts such as memory and anticipation: the imaginer can draw on memory just as he can enact imagining in the context of anticipating. The possibility of such alliances demonstrates, not that imagination is dependent upon memory or that it is fundamentally anticipatory in function (other parts of the same sequence were independent of memory and anticipation), but that it is sufficiently encompassing to incorporate mnemonic and anticipatory elements while retaining its own specific character.

(5) The sequence as a whole is representative of many protracted daydreams in which we project before ourselves a situation or event that might happen—that even seems likely to occur. The result is a curious shadow-event, which appears to serve as a substitute for an actual event that is wished-for, feared, or merely a subject of curiosity. Unlike the previous two examples, then, we have to do here with an imaginative experience that is essentially linked with other, nonimaginative experiences having definite positions in past or future time.

III

In this section I shall single out several of the more prominent features of imagining as it was experienced in the foregoing examples, though I will not attempt to furnish full descriptions of these features. The purpose of this provisional picture is to make visible a set of traits of basic importance in any adequate assessment of imagination's eidetic structure. The traits themselves will be taken up in the order in which they emerged in the course of reflecting on the examples at hand. No supervenient form has been imposed on the traits, nor has there been any effort to relate them to each other in terms of some single generic feature. It will be noticed, however, that the six traits described subdivide into three pairs. These same pairs will supply the basis for the division of chapters in Part II, where the phenomenon of pairing will itself be further discussed. For now, it is merely a matter of gaining a preliminary acquaintance with the individual members of these pairs.

1. A first pair of traits distinguishes itself from the very beginning: *spontaneity* and *controlledness*. Every one of the experiences of imagining reported above, as well as every episode within these experiences, is classifiable as spontaneous or controlled—or both, though not both simultaneously. By "spontaneous" I mean first of all, and most crucially, arising in an unsolicited manner. The dolphins in the first example, and the walrus roar in the second, presented themselves without express effort on my part. It was as if they thrust themselves on my imagining mind without being willed or wished into existence. They appeared, as it were, of their own accord. Such a sense of effortless appearing is to be distinguished from still other aspects of imaginative spontaneity: its instantaneous character and its ability to surprise. The dolphins, being unexpected, surprised me by their initial appearance, even if the surprise was in fact a mild one. Moreover, each of the dolphin episodes developed quite quickly and without any sense of drawn-out duration. Throughout, there was a feeling of unhindered development, as if the dolphin sequence was somehow generating itself without being the mere fulfillment of conscious intentions.[10]

Such intentions were of critical importance in the other examples, which involved volitional elements in varying degrees and thus an attempt at control on my part. Sometimes the effort at control expressed itself in quite general terms, as in the Rawls seminar sequence, and sometimes in a more pronounced form, as when I attempted to audialize a flamingo cry or the wholly fictive symphony. A factor of control was evident not only insofar as such experiences were self-induced to start with, i.e., were generated in order to provide examples of imagining. It was also manifest in the way in which control was continually exerted during the course of certain of these experiences, as in the willed repetition of the flamingo cry or in the prolonging of the music of *Petrouchka*. I also experienced a basic controlledness whenever I broke off

10. Whether I intended them *unconsciously* must remain an open question. This is of course possible, and a psychoanalytic investigation of my seemingly innocuous imaginings might very well reveal a basic wish or unconscious fantasy acting as a primary motivating force behind them. Even so, however, such an investigation would not undermine the *felt* spontaneity of the above experiences. Whatever a causal or genetic analysis might reveal—and however great its intrinsic interest or predictive power might be—in a phenomenological inquiry we are concerned exclusively with what is actually *experienced* by the imagining subject.

a given sequence of scenes or episodes in a willful way—or even when I felt that I *could* terminate the sequence merely by wishing to do so. The controllable character of imagining seemed to be present, then, at three critical moments during its course—at its inception, at any given point throughout, and at (or rather, *as*) its termination.

2. Less evident than spontaneity and controlledness is a second pair of traits: *self-containedness* and *self-evidence*. Both the act and the content of the imagining exhibited in the above examples were self-contained in the strict sense of their not directly referring to or implying other acts or contents. Each experience was self-contained *as an experience*, that is, as a single, self-enclosed, monadic unit. When I imagined the sequence of dolphin scenes, it did not present itself to me as calling for completion by further imaginings or by nonimaginative mental acts. Instead, it presented itself as self-contained in two basic ways: first, by virtue of being divided into discrete episodes, each of which constituted a fully formed scene; second, by virtue of the whole formed by the entire sequence of episodes. In contrast with this was the Rawls seminar, where there was a sense of self-enclosure as a whole but no series of self-contained episodes. In the instances of auditory imagination, given sequences possessed a weaker sense of closure in themselves, while each sound or group of sounds *within* a sequence was experienced as a self-contained unit: e.g., each rhythmical repetition of the flamingo cry, each walrus roar, and even the animal cacophony. Thus self-containedness may occur in several forms—forms that will be explored more fully in chapter four—but it appears to be present in *some* form in every imaginative experience, however open-ended and unrestricted this experience may be in other respects.

Self-containedness forms the basis for the presence of the closely allied feature of self-evidence. To be experienced as self-contained in imagination is to be experienced as not needing clarification or supplementation by subsequent experiences. In other words, the self-contained act and content of imagining are present to the mind of the imaginer in a pellucid way—so unmistakably and transparently that no *additional* evidence is called for in determining their character or structure. The evidence given in a self-contained imaginative experience is of such a sort and of such a degree that it makes this experience unmistakably *self*-evident. Thus the dolphins in the first example were, despite the rapidity of their movements and their facelessness, unquestionably dolphins and not some other kind of animal. Their swimming motions were distinctly dolphin-like; and the ship's hull they swam around and under was indubitably just what it presented itself as being, and this was so although the ship itself had just been transformed from a trawler into a freighter: the certainty of my apprehension was unshakable. The animal cries and musical melodies in the second example possessed the same sort of incontrovertible evidence, though in certain instances the imagined sound was manifestly more difficult to summon up than in others. Even if a given sound did not appear immediately, when it *did* appear, it was undeniably just the kind of sound that was sought: no extra evidence was required to strengthen this sense of appropriateness. Finally, the seminar sequence was lucidly presented—or more exactly, it was as lucidly presented as was requisite for an unquestioning grasp of the developing scene. In none of the examples, then, do we find intrinsically dubitable or even corrigible evidence; each was experienced as strictly self-evident.

3. The final pair of traits, *indeterminacy* and *pure possibility*, differs markedly from the previous pair. For this pair, it is not a matter of two features which, reinforcing each other, serve to delimit imaginative experience and to close it in upon itself. Indeterminacy and pure possibility do reinforce each other, but to a quite different end. Instead of acting to circumscribe and enclose imaginative experience, they *open out* this experience, endowing it with a fluidity and freedom that it would not otherwise possess. Despite this difference, however, these last two pairs of traits are not incompatible with each other, for indeterminacy and pure possibility open up imaginative experience *from within*; and they do so precisely from within the limits established by the same experience's self-containedness and self-evidence.

By "indeterminacy" is meant a lack of strictly specifiable form or content. The examples reported above exhibited two types of indeterminacy. Evident first of all was a radically indeterminate background or aura surrounding particular imagined objects. Unlike its perceptual counterpart, which typically possesses considerable determinacy of detail, the imaginative backdrop seems to lack determinacy of any significant sort. For instance, around the arabesque of sound traced out by the imagined flamingo cry there was a nebulous region without determinate character or definite limit. The same kind of characterless region wrapped itself around the patch of sea through which the dolphins swam. And in the Rawls seminar situation, the classroom and the courtyard below did not connect up with any outlying zones of imagined space, but were instead set within almost wholly amorphous surroundings.

A second sort of indeterminacy characterized the imagined objects themselves. They never presented themselves as determinate wholes— as substantial, well-rounded entities, each of whose parts is also determinate. Although I recognized the imagined dolphins *as* dolphins, their faces were at first almost entirely indefinite; only later, when I had made an explicit effort to focus on these faces, did they take on any determinateness of form. And the words of Dworkin's imagined lecture, to which I was half-listening and which I thought I understood and could reconstruct in part, were imbued with so much vagueness that it would be difficult to determine exactly *what* he was saying after his opening remarks. The fact is that he might have been saying any number of things, though all of them fell within the context of a course on Rawls's *Theory of Justice*. Such indefiniteness within given limits exemplifies the openness that the element of indeterminacy introduces into imaginative experience.

The same openness is manifest in the "thetic" or posited trait of pure possibility. Everything that was imagined in the examples was experienced as purely possible in character. I did not take the dolphin episodes, the various imagined sounds, or the Rawls seminar to be *actual* objects or events unfolding before me. I was not tempted to place the least credence in them as real appearances or occurrences. Nor did they present *themselves* as actual or existent—as competing with perceived objects or events for my attention. In no instance could their ethereal presence be given a fixed position within the spatio-temporal matrix of nature or history. Where did the imagined dolphins swim? In an imagined sea, of course. But where then was this sea? Certainly not in physical space. In psychical space then? We cannot say for sure. The same difficulty holds for the temporality of imagined content, which appears in a time difficult to specify. All that I can claim for certain is that what I imagine exhibits a purely possible space and time. Likewise, the objects or events "in" such space and time are things which *might be*—might just conceivably be—but which in fact *are not*. Thus, the swimming white dolphins appeared to me as sheer imaginative possibilities. Along with their purely possible spatio-temporal positionings, they were experienced as independent of the character and constraints of empirical existence, hence as open to infinite variation. This sense of unimpeded possibility was inherent even in imagined objects that had a basis in previous experience. Although I had seen Dworkin before, I regarded his presence in the seminar sequence as merely co-possible with the presence of the other figures, whom I had never seen. Of each imaginative presentation I experienced, it could be said that in it *anything* was possible; no particular object or event *had* to appear there in the first place, or to appear there in any specific way. The latitude introduced by the factor of pure possibility brings with it a sense of endlessness—of open development, which is limited only by the particular content of a given presentation.

CHAPTER TWO

Imagining as Intentional

I

THE RESULTS of the previous chapter are undeniably tentative. An examination of several examples has yielded a group of six fundamental features, and in this way a beginning has been made toward a full description of the phenomenon of imagining. But this beginning is *only* a beginning. The features as described thus far are distinctive but not definitive; indeed, their only claim to our attention is that they stand out in a preliminary analysis. More importantly, taking up these features in simple serial order has not allowed us to discern how they are related to each other as *jointly structuring* the activity of imagining itself. Here we must ask: is there an ordering principle for imaginative experience in its entirety—a principle by means of which various essential traits might be correlated with one another as *co*-essential instead of being regarded as strictly separate items? Such a principle must be found if we are to provide a basis for more coherent and more complete descriptions of imagination than have so far been given.

Intentionality is precisely such a principle. To claim that mental activity is intentional in structure is to claim, at the very least, that it is composed of two distinguishably different phases, which we shall designate as the "act phase" and the "object phase." In and through an act —"act" in the strict sense of mental act or act of consciousness—the mind directs itself onto and absorbs itself in a specific content. What is most remarkable in this self-transcending movement of mind is that what is aimed at in the content, the intentional object, need not be existent. In fact, such an object is always "intentionally inexistent": intended and yet not (qua intended) existent. In Brentano's celebrated description:

Every mental phenomenon is characterized by what the scholastics of the Middle Ages called the intentional (or mental) inexistence [*Inexistenz*] of an object, and what we might call, though not wholly unambiguously, reference to a content, direction toward an object (which is not to be understood here as meaning a thing) or immanent objectivity. Every mental phenomenon includes something as object within itself, although this does not always occur in the same way.[1]

For Brentano, intentionality thus conceived is the single most distinctive structure of all mental acts, their "general distinguishing characteristic."[2] In effect, Brentano is proposing a classical Aristotelian definition by genus and specific differentia. The genus is that of phenomena of every sort, the differentia is intentionality, and it is the possession of intentionality that distinguishes mental from physical phenomena. Or to put the same point in a different way: physical phenomena are incapable of being the subject-terms of intentional relations; and the object-terms of non-mental relations *must* be existent.

If Brentano is correct, intentionality is a universal feature of every mental phenomenon, and thus does not as such tell us what is peculiar to imagining as opposed to other mental acts. But if the basic structural properties of intentionality are to be found in mental acts other than imagining—even, as Brentano proposes, in *all* mental acts—this does not mean that every such act is intentional in exactly the same way. Specificity occurs in terms of the particular mode of intentionality present in each case. And, for our purposes, the primary value of an ordering principle such as intentionality resides not in the degree to which its application is universal but in the effectiveness with which it allows us to discern the unique intentional structure of imagining. The aim of this chapter, accordingly, is to indicate precisely how imagination incorporates and illustrates intentionality. I shall first sketch the skeletal structure of imagining regarded as an intentional act and then show how this structure provides a unifying framework for the essential traits isolated in the preceding chapter.

II

Insofar as imagination is intentional in character, it is analyzable into an act phase and an object phase. These two phases, while distinguishable for the sake of analysis, require each other's presence in

1. From Franz Brentano, *Psychology From an Empirical Standpoint*, ed. O. Kraus, trans. A. C. Rancurello, B. B. Terrell, and Linda McAlister (London: Routledge & Kegan Paul, 1973), p. 88.
2. Ibid., p. 91. I have slightly altered the translation here.

imaginative experience. Each calls for the other within a continuous intentional arc: to speak tautologically, we may say that there can be no intentional object without an act which specifically intends it, and no intentional act without an intended object. There is, further, a dovetailing between particular aspects of the two phases: elements of the act phase answer to factors in the object phase, and vice versa. But this is not to claim a strict parallelism with regard to *all* aspects of each phase, as in Husserl's notion that to every "moment" of the *noesis* corresponds a precise moment of the *noema*, and conversely.[3] In this chapter and those that follow we shall find ourselves constantly shuttling back and forth across the primary division of imagination into act and object. The possibility of, and need for, such oscillating movements will serve to remind us that the act/object division is not an absolute and inviolable one. Act and object are distinct from each other, both in experience and in analysis; as Ingarden says, "no real element (or moment) of the act is an element of the purely intentional object, and vice versa."[4] Yet such distinctness does not preclude the presence of significant continuities and overlappings, as we shall see illustrated by the fact that several of the original six traits are to be found in *both* phases.

ACT PHASE

Although in principle this phase is no more important than the object phase—both being equally essential to any complete mental act—in the case of imagination the act seems to assume a special importance. Imagining is a mental act that often appears to reveal itself more crucially in its performance than in any particular product it may bring forth. Its frequently instantaneous enactment—its rapid consummation and equally rapid evanescence—only serves to underscore the prominence of its act phase. And when imagining occurs spontaneously, it seems to consist almost wholly in its enactment. Yet, even in the most accelerated and exhilarating acts of imagining, we still imagine *something*: a content is apprehended, however fleeting. Indeed, no act of imagining can be utterly contentless; there is always an imaginative presentation of some kind, even when our imagining dazzles us with its

3. See Husserl, *Ideas*, sec. 88. I shall not adopt Husserl's terminology of *noesis* and *noema* because these terms carry with them an enormous burden of detailed theory which would clutter and confuse the present analysis, an analysis seeking to lay bare only the most elementary intentional structures.

4. Roman Ingarden, *The Literary Work of Art*, trans. G. Grabowicz (Evanston: Northwestern University Press, 1973), p. 118.

celerity. Therefore, although the act phase of imagination is sometimes more conspicuous than its object phase, it cannot exist without the latter, and is in fact always closely correlated with it. Hence neither phase can claim priority over the other.

There are three primary ways in which we can imagine, i.e., three main forms in which imagining as a mental *act* may occur: imaging, imagining-that, and imagining-how. Let us consider these in order.

Imaging

To "image" is to form an imaginative presentation whose content possesses a specifically sensuous—an "intuitive" or "imagistic"— form. It is to entertain imagined entities or events whose description would include predicates denoting qualities of color, tone, kinesthetic feeling, and the like. This means that imaging occurs in the specific modalities of visualizing, audializing, smelling in the mind's nose, feeling in the mind's muscles, tasting with the mind's tongue, and so on.[5] There is, accordingly, no such thing as imaging in general—i.e., sensory-neutral imaging—since imaging always and only occurs in at least one of these particular sensory modalities. To image, then, is to imagine in a sensory-specific way. (This is not to deny that the imaginer may combine several sensory modalities in a single but complex imaginative presentation, e.g., a visualized-and-audialized presentation; but the various components of such a presentation remain readily distinguishable from one another in terms of their diverse sensory qualities.)

The specification of imaging into particular sensory modalities was evident in all of the examples presented in the last chapter. In the first of them I imaged dolphins in terms of a certain color, body shape, and movement; here the imaginative presentation was a strictly visualized one. The second example, that of imaged sounds, was primarily audialized; for the most part, I was hearing with my mind's ear. In the third example there was a combination of sensory modalities: I imaged Dworkin's lecturing as at once 'seen' and 'heard'. Such imaging in more than one modality at a time did not present itself as an experience of a significantly different *kind* from imaging in a single modality—only as somewhat more complex. Indeed, it is evident that, whether sensuously simple or complex, the imaging that occurred in each example was experienced as perfectly appropriate, i.e., as being a suitable sensuous embodiment of the particular content in question.

5. The expression "smelling in the mind's nose" comes from Gilbert Ryle, *The Concept of Mind* (New York: Barnes & Noble, 1949), pp. 252-53. To retain continuity with the examples given in chapter one, I shall restrict discussion in what follows largely to visualizing and audializing.

Imaging, therefore, is one of the basic ways in which we imagine. It is perhaps even the most customary and frequent form of imagining, especially when it occurs as visualizing, to which we normally have ready recourse. In fact, in common parlance "imagining" and "visualizing" coincide to a significant degree, and there is thus a temptation to mistake a particular mode of imaging for imagining as a whole—as if, in order to imagine, one *has* to summon up an imaginative presentation that is intuitively given in some specific sensory guise, above all a visual one. Yet this is not the case; imagining cannot be reduced to imaging, much less to a particular form of imaging. There are at least two other kinds of imagining, each of which is importantly different from imaging and hence, *a fortiori*, from simple visualizing.

Imagining-that

When we imagine, we not only envision or project objects and events in imagistic form and as distinct from one another in their sensory specificity. We may also imagine *that* individual objects or events together constitute a circumstance or situation: a "state of affairs."[6] States of affairs can emerge just as well among imagined objects or events as among empirically real ones. For particular *imaginata* can be posited as standing in a number of possible relations— e.g., temporal precedence, spatial contiguity, causal connection, and modification or qualification of various kinds. When we imagine things as standing in such relations, we imagine that these relations *obtain*; we suppose that something is the case, and in this way a given state of affairs forms the specific content of our imaginative presentation. A nexus of relations, not objects or events in their separateness, is intended.

6. The term "state of affairs" and also the equivalent expressions "affair complex" and "objective complex" designate the sort of imagined content whose description in words would take the form of a complete sentence. A state of affairs is the intentional correlate of a non-simple act of intending—a correlate whose expression in language has both a nominative and a verbal element: (I imagine that) 'the Washington monument is walking'. The state of affairs imagined here involves an internal, reciprocal relationship between what is designated by the nominative component ('the Washington monument') and the verbal factor ('is walking'). In contrast with the intentional correlate of simple imaging, an imagined state of affairs is therefore always complex in character, since it involves the conjunction of the designata of both nominative and verbal components. The nominatively designated component can be an object (a physical object, a person, etc.) or an event (e.g., 'the winning of the war'). Also, imagined states of affairs can be embedded in other imagined states of affairs (e.g., [I imagined that] 'he was able to feel that he was back in Paris') or form part of intentional correlates answering to imperatives or optatives ([I imagine that] 'I command you to deliver the mail in time', [he imagined that] 'he wished that he was in Paris again'). For an exposition of states of affairs in the approximate sense in which I shall be using the term, see Ingarden, *The Literary Work of Art*, pp. 128-44.

The single most striking feature of imagining-that is that what we imagine as constituting a state of affairs *does not have to assume a sensuous guise*. Of course, it may—and often does—come clothed in sensory detail. But it need not, since we may equally well imagine-that in a nonsensory way. There are, consequently, two species of imagining-that; imagining-that sensuously and imagining-that nonsensuously.[7] Each of these species is represented in our original examples. (a) On the one hand, I imagined that the visualized dolphins were swimming in a quite concrete way: I 'saw' them swimming with my mind's eye, taking in their movements not just one by one or in a static *tableau* (as I would do if I were merely to image them), but as forming an internally complex state of affairs built up out of a number of coordinated swimming movements. In other words, I imagined that a certain set of relations obtained between the presented objects, however dimly these objects themselves were apprehended. The result was the imagination of an evolving objective complex which might be linguistically transcribed as: (I imagined that) 'an indefinite-number-of-dolphins-were-swimming-in-a-group-through-the-sea'. (b) On the other hand, I also imagined-that nonsensuously. Thus, in the third example I began by 'listening to' Dworkin's lecture in front of a seminar, but soon afterward I visualized different scenes within the seminar room. Nevertheless, throughout these later visualizings I continued to imagine *that* Dworkin was still lecturing: that he was standing and speaking before the class. Such imagining was not sensuously specified, but it was nonetheless a genuine case of imagining-that: I imagined that a certain state of affairs was obtaining continuously even though I was not in fact apprehending it in a concretely sensuous form.[8]

It may be concluded, therefore, that both imagining-that sensuously and imagining-that nonsensuously are essential possibilities of imaginative experience. Yet, whether considered singly or as a pair, they do not constitute an essential *necessity* of this experience, as Ryle implies in

7. Note that I am using the terms "sensory" and "sensuous," as well as their negations, as equivalents. "Sensory" will generally be used in adjectival expressions, "sensuous" in adverbial constructions. But both refer to the quasi-perceptual aspect of what we apprehend in imagination, memory, and other acts: to their "imagistic" or "intuitive" character.

8. Nonsensory imagining–that is in certain instances extremely difficult to distinguish from intellection. In Descartes's familiar example, when I "conceive" a chiliagon I am manifestly not imaging the figure (I cannot do so unless I possess extraordinary imaginative powers). But I do seem to be imagining *that there can be such a figure*: I entertain it as a possible object of thought. In conceiving of this figure, am I then indulging in imagination or in intellection? I am inclined to say *both*: I am both imagining–that nonsensuously *and* thinking in accordance with a rule.

his claim that "imagining is always imagining that something is the case."[9] Imagining is no more invariably imagining-that than it is invariably an act of imaging: it is just as mistaken to reduce all imagining to imagining-that (as does Ryle) as it is to consider it always to be a form of imaging (as in the characteristic British empiricist view). Each of these reductive moves—one put forward for sophisticated philosophical reasons, the other claiming to reflect common sense—imposes a premature closure upon the diversity of ways in which the act of imagining may take place.

Imagining-how

A further way in which we can imagine is quite similar to imagining-that—indeed, so similar that it may appear at first glance to be merely another species of the latter. But there are crucial differences between the two types of imagining, and imagining-how represents a genuine alternative both to imaging and to imagining-that. For we are capable not only of imaging (objects and events) and imagining that (states of affairs obtain), but also of imagining *how* to do, think, or feel certain things, as well as how to move, behave, or speak in certain ways. Imagining-how is easily overlooked because it frequently occurs in conjunction with some *other* kind of mental activity. It is often employed, for example, in what John Dewey called "dramatic rehearsal in imagination," that is, when we anticipate how a certain task is to be performed or a given goal achieved.[10] This was precisely what happened in the imagined seminar on Rawls: in anticipation of a certain event that was to take place later that day, I imagined *how* such a seminar might occur. But imagining-how need not be anticipatory in function: I also imagined how a flamingo cry might sound without in any way anticipating a concrete event in which that cry would occur. More generally, I can imagine how it is to experience something even when I have not undergone, and am not about to undergo, the experience in question: e.g., how it was to participate in the California Gold Rush.

Imagining-how possesses two significant similarities to imagining-that, but in each case the similarity is accompanied by a distinctive difference. First of all, *what* we imagine how to do, think, feel, etc. is usually presented in the form of a state of affairs. The content of an act of imagining-how typically consists of a dynamic complex of various items, and the imaginer is more concerned with the relations that ob-

9. Gilbert Ryle, "Imaginary Objects," *Proceedings of the Aristotelian Society*, suppl. vol. XII (1933), p. 43. Cf. *The Concept of Mind*, p. 256, for a similar claim.
10. *Human Nature and Conduct* (New York: Random House, 1957), pp. 190-91.

tain within this complex than with the individual terms (whether these be objects or events) of these relations. To imagine-how is, at the minimum then, to imagine *what it would be like if such-and-such a state of affairs were to obtain*. In this case, imagining-how, though not identical with imagining-that, is still *accomplished* by means of the latter. Here we imagine-that so as to provide specific content for imagining-how; I imagine how it would be to land on Uranus by imagining *that* I am landing in a certain space ship, at a certain point on the surface of the planet, etc. Yet this is not the whole story. There is an active aspect of imagining-how not found in imagining-that proper. To imagine-how is to imagine what it would be like *to* do, think, or feel so-and-so, or *to* move, behave, and speak in such-and-such ways. This kind of imaginative activity is not realized by projecting an unfolding scene of which the imaginer is the mere witness, but rather by entertaining an imagined state of affairs in which he (or a figure who stands proxy for him) is envisaged as *himself an active and embodied participant*. Thus I might imagine how to lace a certain sort of boot by imagining *myself lacing* the boot, that is, by conjuring up a state of affairs in which I am actively lacing up a boot or in which I imagine the sort of kinesthetic sensations involved in the action of boot-lacing. Similarly, I may imagine how it feels to experience a certain sort of grief by so fully identifying myself with a real or fictitious grief-stricken person that I seem to become that person, experiencing in imagination his or her grief as if it were mine. In other words, there is a sense of *personal agency*, of the imaginer's own involvement in what is being imagined, which is lacking or at least muted in instances of sheer imagining-that. To imagine-how is to project not merely a state of affairs *simpliciter* (i.e., one in which the imaginer is not a participant) but a state of affairs into which the imaginer has also projected himself (or a surrogate) as an active being who is experiencing *how* it is to do, feel, think, move, etc. in a certain manner.[11]

11. By the terms "action," "activity," "agent," etc. I do not mean to imply that the content of imagining-how is always a form of action in which the subject (here the imaginatively projected subject) *takes the initiative*. This is often so in imagining-how, but there are also cases of imagining how to suffer, to be imposed upon by others, etc. Thus the central notion of "personal agency" includes a broad spectrum of ways in which the imaginer becomes implicated via self-projection or by proxy in his own imaginative presentation, and some of these ways include adopting a passive stance within the state of affairs contained in the presentation. For a general treatment of the sense in which passive postures can be regarded as forms of action, see Roy Schafer, "Action: Its Place in Psychoanalytic Interpretation and Theory," *The Annual of Psychoanalysis* (1973), I, 176-92. For a helpful discussion of imagining-how in terms of central vs. peripheral placement of the imagining self, see Richard Wollheim, "Identification and Imagination" in *Freud*, ed. R. Wollheim (Garden City, N.Y.: Doubleday, 1974), pp. 177-80.

Imagining-how resembles imagining-that in a second respect—namely, in that it enjoys the same option of occurring either sensuously or nonsensuously. But there is a basic difference in the ways in which these alternatives present themselves in the two types of imagining. (a) On the one hand, when I imagine-how in a sensory way—e.g., by envisioning myself lacing a boot or by imagining how it would be to land on Uranus—I experience an ongoing, *internally developmental* quality that is absent from cases of sensuous imagining-that. I am, after all, imagining how a certain action takes place as viewed from the perspective of an agent who forms part of the scene of action. When I merely imagine *that* a certain state of affairs appears sensuously, the projected state of affairs does not develop with the same sense of inner movement, and it is witnessed from a position external to the state of affairs itself. In short, it does not unfold dynamically as does imagined action or activity in which I as the imaginer am involved. (b) On the other hand, when I imagine-how nonsensuously, I notice a comparable difference from nonsensory imagining-that. In the latter I posit a sensuously unspecified state of affairs as obtaining in a certain static fashion: as simply being the case. In nonsensory imagining-how, by contrast, it is a matter of imagining a state of affairs that, though also unspecified sensuously, possesses a rhythm and movement with which I as agent identify. One can, for example, imagine how to solve a certain problem in mathematics without any recourse to sensuous detail. This is done by running through a certain indefinite number of steps in one's mind, projecting what these interrelated steps might be like without actually taking them or thinking them through. Any such sense of development internal to the mind of the imaginer, in which he plays an active part by carrying out consecutive might-be operations in imagination, is absent from nonsensory imagining-that.

Having now surveyed the three primary forms in which the act of imagining takes place, we must ask ourselves: how do these forms relate to each other? Their interaction occurs both empirically and structurally. Let us consider each way in turn.

Empirically considered, the interaction appears in the form of various contingent combinations that arise in the course of imaginative experience. Thus, I might begin by imaging, say, the god Jupiter in isolation from all other content, as clothed in a certain way, and as standing in a certain fixed pose. But I can also image the same Jupiter as speaking, thereby adding an audialized dimension to my visual presentation, or again as moving, which adds a kinetic element to the same presentation. In all of this I am still *imaging*, despite the increasing complexity of the imaged content. Now, however, suppose that I imagine Jupiter in the company of other gods—all of whom, let us say, are lounging around an elegant Olympian pool. In this case I am *imagining that* a certain state of affairs obtains, namely, 'that-Jupiter-and-other-gods-lounge-around-an-Olympian-pool'. This tranquil scene can become much more dynamic if I proceed to imagine 'that-these-gods-begin-to-fight-among-themselves'. Or I can imagine something strictly nonsensory concerning the same gods, perhaps 'that-they-are-envious-of-each-other'. Further, staying with the same figures, I can *imagine how* it would be to act like one of these gods in any of the situations just described, e.g., 'how-it-is-to-walk-as-a-god', 'how-it-is-to-envy-other-gods'. In these instances of imagining-how, I have placed 'myself—my imaginatively projectable self—within the scenes that formed the content of imagining-that, taking an active (though strictly imagined) role in such scenes and experiencing them from within.

In such a sequence of imaginings, we see how closely implicated the three primary forms of imagining can become, one following upon another with relative ease. Moreover, these forms may directly overlap, as when the originally imaged figure of Jupiter is taken over into the content of imagining-that, and the latter is in turn enveloped in imagining-how. Hence there may be a borrowing or sharing of results among different modes of imagining; insofar as this is the case, we can speak of their collaboration within a single imaginative sequence—a sequence which may be quite complex and prolonged. (The prolongation may be practically indefinite, since at any moment we can return to prior points and start anew by initiating variant strains of the same scene or sequence.) Only one possibility is excluded: the simultaneous occurrence of two or more forms of imagining. At any given moment I am either imaging *or* imagining-that *or* imagining-how, but not more than one of these at a time. A given state of affairs may have formed the original content of an act of imagining-that; yet if I am now imagining *how* (to do x, feel y, etc.) within this state of affairs, I can no longer be expressly imagining *that* the state of affairs happens as a situation which I am merely witnessing. (Or to be more exact, the act of imagining-that is now absorbed into the content of a supervenient act of imagining-how, providing the setting for the action or activity that forms the focus of this latter kind of imagining. This is not to exclude the converse situation, whereby an experience of imagining-how furnishes the content for an act of imagining-that.)

Structurally considered, the three forms of imagining are related in a quite different way. Instead of forming contingent combinations within a given sequence of imaginings, they are related by virtue of their occupying one or more places within the following schema:

sensory status / type of content	sensory	nonsensory
single object or event	imaging	
state of affairs *simpliciter*	imagining-that (sensuously)	imagining-that (nonsensuously)
state of affairs involving the imaginer (or surrogate) as agent	imagining-how (sensuously)	imagining-how (nonsensuously)

As determined by its two primary parameters (type of content and sensory status), this schema provides a cross-classification of types of imagining. It also suggests that imaging, which is sometimes taken to be a paradigm or prototype for all imagining, is in fact the most circumscribed type. Occurring as it does in a strictly sensory form, it does not display the versatility of which imagining-that and imagining-how are capable as a result of their bivalent, sensory/nonsensory character. Also, the content entertained in these latter two forms of imagining is correspondingly more complex and thus able to exhibit more nuance and subtlety than does imaged content proper.

Imaging, imagining-that, and imagining-how are, therefore, three distinctly different forms, three alternative ways, in which we imagine. They are presented here without any attempt to describe them fully, either in themselves or in their relationship to each other. Nor am I claiming that these particular modes of imagining are the *only* forms the act of imagining may take. Perhaps we can imagine in still other ways—e.g., by imagining-*as* or by imagining-*with-respect-to*—and in any event rigid limits should not be placed on the possible forms that imagining may assume. What has been discussed above concerns only certain crucially characteristic ways in which the act of imagining occurs within human experience.

OBJECT PHASE

As has already been observed, when we imagine, we always imagine something in particular; we apprehend, however dimly, an imaginative presentation having a certain content. Imaginative experience always involves an object phase or "intentional correlate"[12] that answers to the act of imagining. For the sake of simplicity, we might say that, qua intentional act, imagination is the act of imagining an imagined object. Such a near tautology might seem to be self-evident and noncontroversial. Yet Ryle has flatly denied the existence of imagined objects: "there are no such objects."[13] This claim can be countered only by careful description. But even if one might agree that Ryle's judgment is much too peremptory, an examination of the object phase of imagination gives rise to considerable difficulties. Some of these difficulties, e.g., those concerning the ontological status of imagined objects, will be avoided altogether at this point. (See chapter five.) For the present, it is mainly a matter of laying bare the primary features of the object phase. *What*, then, do we imagine?

What we imagine is a total imaginative presentation. This presentation does not play a unitary role in imagining. As we have just seen, it can enter into imaginative experience in at least two different ways: in sensory or in nonsensory form. But precisely what is it that thus appears sensuously or nonsensuously? We know that the imaginer may intend two basic sorts of thing: objects proper (i.e., entities and events) and states of affairs. But is this all that is imagined? Here the analysis must be extended by pointing to two other factors—i.e., the imaginal margin and the image—which together with imagined content constitute the object phase as a whole.

Imagined Content

The content of what we imagine is that aspect of the total imaginative presentation upon which our attention focuses. It is *just this* that we imagine and not something else—where "just this" means what is thematized in the imaginative presentation. As such, it possesses a form of identity specific enough to be referred to by a name or by a descriptive clause or phrase: e.g., 'John's face', 'John when he was young', 'John running to first base'. Hence imagined content is the strictly specifiable aspect of the imaginative presentation—i.e., the presenta-

12. For a discussion of the term "intentional correlate," see Ingarden, *The Literary Work of Art*, p. 118.
13. *The Concept of Mind*, p. 251, p. 254: the statement is made twice as if to underline Ryle's insistence on this point.

50 IMAGINING

tion insofar as it can be indicated with some degree of descriptive precision. This content is normally specified by what one *says* one has imagined—that is, by the actual description one gives, or would offer if asked, of a given imaginative experience. In the case of the examples in chapter one, it would correspond roughly to what was contained in the written accounts that were supplied just after the experiences themselves took place. But such accounts cannot claim to describe the *complete* content of what I imagined in these examples; inevitably, certain details have been omitted or overlooked.

When we attend to the specific content of acts of imagining, we see it to be describable first of all in terms of the entities, events, and states of affairs with which we are already familiar from our preceding consideration of the act phase. Such specifiable factors constitute the core of what we imagine—its "noematic nucleus" in Husserl's term.[14] But a closer scrutiny reveals other components of imagined content as well, components on which the imaginer typically does not focus but which are nonetheless nonthematically present to his imagining consciousness. These non-nuclear components of imagined content constitute what we shall call a "world-frame" for particular imagined entities, events, and states of affairs. For none of these latter appear or occur in an experiential vacuum. They present themselves as positioned, however indeterminately, in an immediately surrounding zone of presentation.

In its severely delimited and delimiting character, the world-frame is unlike the continuously unfolding and ultimately unlimited *world* of perception. The perceived world is a massive, all-inclusive whole—so encompassing in fact that there is finally only *one* such world. This world persists throughout our many perceivings of it, and can never be exhausted by any finite series of such perceivings. It is a world to which we return again and again as an abiding *fons et origo*.

No such originative and stable world underlies the specific content of imagining. No single experiential plenum persists from one imaginative presentation to the next, linking such presentations as presentations of one all-encompassing world. Rather, each presentation carries with it its *own* special situatedness. Such situatedness is so shifting and unstable that it cannot even be regarded as constituting a *field*, at least insofar as "field" implies a persisting plane that underlies and extends beyond the particular items that appear in it. Unlike, say, a perceptual

14. The "noematic nucleus" (or *Sinn*) is the group of essential properties that enable us to identify a given entity, event, or state of affairs as precisely *this* entity, event, or state of affairs. It is the core-character of a phenomenon, around which cluster all secondary characteristics. Cf. Husserl, *Ideas*, secs. 90-91, 99.

field, the world-frame of imagination has no enduring extensiveness: it appears always and only as the *proximal* locale of imagined content, as its *immediate* context. Thus the world-frame is sketchy and schematic in character, offering to the imaginer patches of space and stretches of time instead of a single coherent spatio-temporal continuum. Because of its noncontinuous and nonlasting nature, the world-frame cannot be considered as presenting the imaginer with a world in any sense comparable to the perceived world.

In view of its discontinuity and fragmentariness, we might be tempted to apply to the world-frame Sartre's graphic term "anti-world."[15] But this is to go too far. Although the world-frames of imaginative presentations lack the depth, breadth, and persistence of the perceived world, they do present themselves as evanescent constellations of specific imagined contents, as momentary mini-worlds of imaginative experience. Thus if world-frames do not count as worlds in any strict sense, they are at least world*like* insofar as they provide suitable and fitting frameworks for what we imagine.

Despite their ephemerality (they perish at the end of each act of imagining), world-frames function in a worldlike way by *situating* imagined content—giving it, if not a name, at least a local habitation. This situating capacity derives from the spatializing and temporalizing powers of world-frames, that is, from their ability to establish a specifically *imaginal space* and *imaginal time*. Such space and time lack the universality of the *a priori* space and time that, as Kant endeavored to show, serve to make the perceptual world intuitively present to the senses and yet infinite in extent. But this does not mean that imaginal space and time are merely "quasi" in character, as Husserl claims.[16] They are not posited *as if* they were the space and time of perception— which is to imply that they are nothing *in themselves*. Nor do they represent a strictly "unreal" sense of time and space.[17] Rather, each of these dimensions of the imaginative presentation has its own distinctive character and plays a special role in implementing and specifying the world-frame. For it is due to this character and this role that the world-frame becomes a genuinely framing factor within the imaginative pres-

---

15. *Psychology of Imagination*, p. 194.

16. "The object of imagination is present to consciousness as temporal . . . but its time is a *quasi-time*" (*Experience and Judgment*, trans. J. S. Churchill and K. Ameriks [Evanston: Northwestern University Press, 1973], p. 168). By "quasi-" Husserl means two things: on the one hand, it designates the "as-if" character of imaginal time (p. 169); on the other, it denotes "a time without actual, strict localization of position" (ibid.).

17. "The time of unreal [i.e., imagined] objects is itself unreal; it has no characteristics whatever of perceptual time" (Sartre, *Psychology of Imagination*, p. 169).

entation, enabling each specific item of imagined content to occupy
a certain position within the presentation. Let us look at imaginal space
and imaginal time more closely.

IMAGINAL SPACE

My imagined dolphins swam in a surrounding sea, and approached
a ship's hull and a beach; in doing so, they were not nowhere but were
situated in an open and fluid spatial medium that included the sea as
well as the sky in which I as witness of the scene seemed to be stationed.
Even the imagined flamingo cry traced out a kind of trajectory in imagined space, thus suggesting that there is an audialized space ("sound-
space," as we called it) which can surround, and sometimes coincide
with, an imagined object. In the seminar sequence there was a distinct
sense of closely confined space, accentuated by the external position of
the courtyard outside and below the seminar room. Each of these
three types of imagined space was uniquely self-determining and self-
enclosing; in no way did they interconnect to form a single world-space
that could be revived or reinhabited in subsequent experiences of imagining. In some instances, e.g., that of the imagined sounds, there was
a notable absence of a coherent spatial spread even within a *single* experience: the space of the flamingo cry differed from that of the other
sounds apprehended later in the same sequence. But in spite of their
diverse and often truncated character, these varieties of spatial expanse
were nonetheless intrinsic elements of the imagined content in every
case, serving as a basis for the peculiar sense of locus possessed by individual imagined entities, events, and state of affairs. For all such items
of specific content are invariably presented as *localized*, if not strictly
located, within imaginal space.

IMAGINAL TIME

Also contributing to the felt presence of an immanent world-frame
was the experience of time in each example. It is true that the seamless
temporal continuum subtending and permeating perceived and remembered objects was conspicuously missing. Not only was there no single
temporal matrix extending throughout the three examples in question,
there was also no sense of genuine duration within any given example:
e.g., the rapid time-sense established by the repetitive character of the
flamingo cry contrasted with the adagio quality of the wholly fictive
symphony. Nevertheless, in each instance there was present a vague
positioning of given items of content within a time span at least ample
enough to allow for the emergence of loose rhythmic patterns. Thus, a

measured pace was as distinctive of the Rawls seminar as an abrupt, episodic temporality was characteristic of the dolphin sequence. There was also a sense that I, as the imaginer of the unfolding events, was caught up in the same imperfectly rhythmical time-sense; yet, as in the parallel case of imagined space, I felt for the most part that I was viewing things from a somewhat removed temporal position, thereby creating a sense of slight *décalage* vis-à-vis the temporality of those things that I was witnessing.

Taken together, then, the temporal and spatial frameworks of imagined content constitute an immanent, discrete, and self-enclosing structure which acts to frame and to position (though only approximately) the various items that make up imagined content in its specificity. But neither imaginal space nor imaginal time represents a coherent all-inclusive matrix in which reidentifiable particulars—i.e., items that persist in time and are extended in space—could be given determinate locations. No such matrix and no such particulars are to be found in imaginative presentations. What we do imagine as situated in such presentations is neither extended nor persistent, and as such it does not form part of an overarching world-space or world-time with precise positions determined by a system of universally applicable co-ordinates.

Imaginal Margin

By "imaginal margin" is meant the fading fringe found at the outer limit of specific imagined content. Unlike the world-frame of this content, it is not immanent in what we imagine. Neither is it present as a distinct factor which is external or transcendent to imagined content. For, being almost entirely featureless, it cannot be given any definite location; indeed, it seems to defy exact description of any kind, since it is not only unthematized (as are imaginal space and time) but *unthematizable*. It is so unspecific and formless that the imaginer tends not to notice it at all most of the time and must intensify his mental gaze to make it out. Since it does not inhere in imagined content, it was not expressly mentioned in the descriptive accounts of the three examples explored in chapter one. This is only to be expected, since an imagining consciousness focuses almost exclusively on imagined content —primarily on imagined objects, events, and state of affairs, secondarily on their world-frame.

It is only by an unusual diverting or redirecting of attention that the imaginer becomes explicitly aware of the imaginal margin as a particular component of the total imaginative presentation. Yet he is always at least tacitly aware of it; for there is nothing in a given imaginative presentation of which the imaginer is not to some degree conscious. Such a presentation can *conceal nothing*, as there is no way in which anything in it can be hidden from the imaginer's all-seeing mental gaze. Everything in the presentation, including the imaginal margin, is in some sense apprehended, since the presentation itself is nothing *beyond* what it is apprehended as being. But by using the term "imaginal" instead of "imagined," I have acknowledged that we do not explicitly *posit* the margin as such. At most, it might be said that we imagine it through a kind of lateral or tandem consciousness.

What, then, *is* this margin? How does it present itself? We lack the precise terms of description that might provide fully satisfactory answers to these questions. All that can be ventured is the following brief account, which is more notable for what it does *not* tell us than for what it does. At a certain ill-defined point in the outer or extra-focal part of the imaginative presentation—a "point" which is no point at all because it does not possess any locus, not even the indefinite locus of imagined content—all distinctness of detail ceases. The presentation seems to trail off into an almost wholly inchoate nebulousness, an undifferentiated limbo. No object or state of affairs can be picked out from within this nimbus of nonactuality; no entities or events occupy it, not even fragmentary ones. Thus, around the imagined seascape of swimming dolphins was another "sea," but this latter sea, like Plato's Receptacle, contains no determinate qualities of its own.[18] All that we can say is that it seems to surround the specific imagined content and its world-frame like a loose-fitting, but wholly nondescript, garment. Or we might say that it *is* this content *as it fades into indeterminacy*. Much the same kind of shadowy marginal zone was present in the other examples as well: as an aura surrounding the second example's audialized sounds (i.e., at the outer fringe of their peculiar sound-space) and, in the last example, as the sense of something strictly amorphous that lay just beyond the visualized seminar room and courtyard. Although resisting precise delineation, this radically indefinite margin remains part of the total imaginative presentation and cannot be eliminated from a thorough account of it. Nor can it be considered as a mere aspect or extension of imaginal space or time, for it is distinguishable from either of these dimensions of the world-frame by its radically indeterminate character. We cannot say of the imaginal margin either that it *is*, or that it is *not*, spatial or temporal; indeed, nothing definite

18. Cf. Plato, *Timaeus* 50c-51b.

can be said of it at all—in this respect or in any other particular respect.[19]

The Image

By "image" I mean the mode of givenness pertaining to the total imaginative presentation. This presentation always appears in a certain way—or, more exactly, in certain *ways*. For an imaginative presentation appears to its imaginer in several different forms or modalities. Let us single out three of them for comment. First, a given presentation may appear in differing degrees or types of *clarity*, ranging from the way a single salient object may emblazon itself unambiguously upon the imaginer's consciousness to the dimness with which a barely discernible imagined presence may be felt. The flamingo cry I imagined, once present to my consciousness, was given with a special clarity of tone, melody, and ryhthm. But the animal cacophony imagined just afterward was a jumble of confused sounds. The kind or degree of clarity can differ even within a single imaginative sequence. Thus, though the color of the visualized dolphins was given as a certain bright hue of white, the bodies of these animals were given with considerable ambiguity as to specific shape and size, and their faces were almost completely indistinct. Second, there is a felt difference in what we may call the *texturality* or surface quality of the imaginative presentation. A presentation's textural character can vary from the comparative coarseness and unevenness of the dolphin sequence (in which the choppiness of the imagined sea established the textural sense for all of the episodes) to the relatively smooth and even quality of some of the imagined sounds. Differing contents thus bring with them differing surface qualities, that is, contrasting kinesthetic, tactile, and visual properties of the given texture of the presentation. A third way in which the mode of givenness may vary concerns the degree of *directness* with which the imaginative presentation is given. The figures of Dworkin and the other imagined seminar leaders were presented to me at first straightforwardly. I felt as if I were confronting them, and they me. But later in the same sequence, when I envisioned myself walking away

19. If the imaginal margin is recognized at all in descriptive accounts of imagination, it is typically misconstrued by being described in terms which belong to the description of imagined content proper. For Sartre "each image [i.e., imaginative presentation] presents itself as surrounded by an undifferentiated mass which posits itself *as an imaginary world*" (*Psychology of Imagination*, p. 217). But if the presentation possesses any sense of world, it is to be found *within* the imagined content —not in the margin, which cannot cohere even as a world-frame, much less as a world.

from the seminar and into the street below, these same figures seemed only remote presences, i.e., given as back-at-the-seminar-room and not as directly in front of me.[20]

The image or mode of givenness is, therefore, a highly variable but nonetheless constituent feature of the full object phase. It is, in briefest terms, the *manner* of presentation, that is, the specific way in which imagined content and the imaginal margin are together given to the imaginer's consciousness. This is not to say that there is only one such manner or way—or only the three described above. No doubt there are still other significant modes of presentation. What matters at this point, however, is only to underline the indispensable role of the image in any adequate analysis of the object phase of imagining. A description of this phase would not be complete if we spoke only of imagined content and of the imaginal margin, which must be given or presented to the imaginer's consciousness *in some specific fashion*. Without this factor of *Gegebenheitsweise* (as Husserl calls it), there would be no difference between consciousness and content in imagining— a difference that is demanded precisely by the intentional structure of all imaginative experience.

If the test of "free variation" were to be applied at this point, it would show that each of the three major components of the object phase—imagined content, the imaginal margin, and the image—is an essential part of this phase.[21] In other words, a complete intentional correlate of an act of imagining has to include the presence of all of them in some form or other. In being thus essentially *necessary* to the object phase, they differ in type of essentiality from the three forms of the act phase. As has already been indicated, each of the latter is only essentially *possible*: we are able to imagine either by imaging, or by imagining-that, or by imagining-how, where the "or" is exclusive in character. Thus, on any given occasion we are free to imagine one way *or* another; but, choosing one way, we exclude the others. In contrast, we are not similarly free to imagine a contentless imaginative presentation, or one with no imaginal margin, or one with no mode of givenness whatever. The object phase of imagination *must* contain at least these three factors, and in this regard there is no meaningful choice to be made. Whereas there are options with respect to precisely how we

20. There is a correlation between direct givenness and the intuitive or sensory character of the presentation, and between indirect givenness and a nonintuitive or nonsensory character. This correlation is not accidental, since sensory forms of imagining are themselves ways of achieving directness of presentation.

21. On the technique of free variation in imagination, see Husserl, *Ideas*, secs. 4, 23, 70 and *Experience and Judgment*, secs. 39-40, 82, 96.

shall realize the act phase of imagination, the only comparable latitude within the object phase is found in relation to the *particular* content we imagine, the *particular* way in which the imaginal margin fades away from imagined content, or the *particular* way an imaginative presentation is given. Such particularities of content, margin, and mode represent essential possibilities, though always in the sense of variations in the detailed expression of structural invariants. It is these invariants, and not their concrete embodiments, that are necessary in character.

The structure of the object phase of imagining has proved to be somewhat more intricate and ramiform than the structure of its act phase. We might, therefore, attempt to draw together the above discussion by means of the following diagram:

Object Phase, or Total Intentional Correlate of Imagining	
imaginative presentation: what we imagine	*image:* how what we image is given
(1) *imagined content* proper	
a. specific content—the particular entities, events, and states of affairs that we imagine	a. clarity—of degree or type
b. world-frame of imaginal space and time	b. texturality
(2) *imaginal margin*	c. directness
	et al.

When the object phase is schematized in this way, we become aware of its structural complexity—a complexity which forbids us to reduce it to what Ingarden calls the "imaginational object" *simpliciter*.[22]

To stress thus the inherent complicatedness of the object phase invites us to rejoin our point of departure: the intentionality of imagination. Imagining is an intentional act insofar as it has an object phase, and *has it in every case*. Yet no matter how complex this phase proves to be—no matter how tempted we may be to consider it as a strictly separate aspect of imagination—we should remind ourselves constantly that every object phase is the intentional correlate of a particular act of imagining and does not spring into being *ex nihilo*. The fundamental correlativity of act and object phases is what establishes imagining as ineluctably intentional. Whatever we imagine, however bizarre

22. See *The Literary Work of Art*, p. 228.

it may be in terms of specific content, and no matter how intricate it is in its detailed structure, is correlatable with a concrete *act* of imaging, imagining-that, imagining-how, or perhaps still another mode of imagining. One phase presupposes the other. Moreover, the correlation between the two phases is so close that in an ordinary, unreflective experience of imagining they form an undivided unity. It is only upon analysis that the two phases gain distinctness from each other. But if analysis is to reflect the original experience accurately, it must treat both intentional phases as of equal importance, since it is the coordinated activity of the two together that brings about imagination as a single experiential whole, that is, as a coherent psychical phenomenon.

III

It remains only to indicate the relationship between the foregoing intentional analysis of imagination and the earlier eidetic analysis of six of its primary essential traits. The two analyses are closely intertwined, as becomes evident when we realize that intentionality itself may be considered an essential feature of imagining. Yet it is not a distinctive, special trait in the way that spontaneity and controlledness, self-containedness and self-evidence, indeterminacy and pure possibility all are. Each of these latter six traits characterizes imagination in some quite specific manner. Thus imagining is spontaneous when (and only when) it arises in an unexpected and unbidden manner; it is indeterminate in certain respects but not in others, and is self-contained with regard to other acts but open in respect to its own possibilities of development. Similar restrictions apply to the other eidetic traits, each of which is local and limited in character. The intentional nature of imagining, in contrast, shows no such localization or specialization in its occurrence: *imagining is intentional through and through,* in all of its aspects and avatars. No element or part of imagining fails to belong in some respect to its overall intentional structure; every element or part belongs to its act phase, to its object phase, or to both. Hence intentionality pervades imagination as a whole: it makes no sense to say that imagining is partly intentional, partly nonintentional. It is intentional altogether or not at all.

This chapter has sought to disclose precisely the pervasiveness of the intentional factor in all imagining. But now we must consider an important implication of what has been uncovered. If the intentionality of imagining is genuinely pervasive, then it is capable of serving as a general framework for more particular and more partial eidetic traits—a framework within which these traits can assume determinate positions. The possibility thus arises of constructing an intentional grid for the express purpose of comparing and classifying—i.e., of ordering—such essential traits in relation to each other. By "intentional grid" I mean a chart or table in which a basis for correlating specific eidetic features is provided by the overarching structure (or more exactly, structures) of intentionality.

Eidetic Traits / *Intentional Structures*	Con-trolled-ness	Spon-taneity	Self-contain-edness	Self-evidence	Indeter-minacy	Pure Possi-bility
Act Phase						
1. imaging	C	n	n	n		
2. imagining-that	C	n	n	n		
3. imagining-how	C	n	n	n		
Object Phase						
1. imagined con-tent (including world-frame)	n	C	n	n	n	C
2. imaginal margin	n	C	n	n	C	n
3. image or mode of givenness	n	C	n	n	n	n

n = normal appearance or occurrence   C = conspicuous appearance or occurrence

This table reveals several significant patterns of correlation. Four of the original six eidetic traits characterize *all* of the intentional structures of imagination. Of the four, two (self-containedness and self-evidence) manifest themselves in these structures with approximately equivalent emphasis: each act phase of imagining is self-contained and self-evident, and so in equal measure are all aspects of each object phase. The other two traits (spontaneity and controlledness) are also present at every step, but with differing degrees of emphasis. Controlledness is more conspicuous in the act phase than in the object phase, since we are capable of self-inducing acts of imagining in order to bring about the imaginative presentations we seek. (This is not to deny that we can also control *what* we imagine; but we tend to do so precisely by controlling the act itself of imagining.) Spontaneity, in contrast, is more strikingly present in the object phase, occurring most typically when an imaginative presentation emerges suddenly and in unsolicited fashion. The act which subtends such a presentation may also emerge spontaneously, but it tends to arise in a less conspicuous manner than the presentation itself: for the most part our attention remains riveted to the latter.

The final two eidetic traits, indeterminacy and pure possibility, are confined in their appearance to the object phase. The act of imagining is neither indeterminate nor purely possible; precisely as an *enactment*, as a specific performance on a given occasion, this act is at once determinate and actual. But the intentional correlate of the imaginative act is both indeterminate and purely possible. It is indeterminate in that no aspect of the imaginative presentation or image exhibits perfect, lapidary definiteness. The imaginal margin is most radically indefinite, but some degree of indeterminateness always infects imagined content and the image as well. Pure possibility, on the other hand, is displayed least equivocally in imagined content, for what we imagine is more conspicuously posited as purely possible than the image or the imaginal margin.

What is perhaps most significant in these initial findings is that each of the eidetic traits identified in the last chapter inheres in imagining regarded as an intentional phenomenon. Despite differences in frequency and conspicuousness of appearance, all of these traits have a place within the act/object framework furnished by imagination's intentionality. Or more exactly, all have *places* within this framework, for in no case is the position of a given trait limited to a single locus on the intentional grid. This multiplicity of locus itself reflects what we have earlier called "the multiplicity of the mental," that is, the mind's proclivity for expressing itself polymorphically, resisting reduction to monistic schemes and structures.

Yet the multiple positioning of imagination's eidetic traits does not entail an undifferentiated multiplicity, a chaotic proliferation of psychical activity. As the grid itself illustrates, the multiplicity in question is an *ordered* one, expressing itself in a plurality of positions that are correlated in a regular and not a merely random way. The exact nature of this regularity will be explored further in the next part. Here we need only observe that a meaningful ordering of eidetic traits of imagining is possible and that the principle of such an ordering is provided by the various intentional structures of imagination. If this is so, the eidetic features we picked out initially and seemingly *au hasard* can no longer be regarded as a mere congeries of disparate and disjunctive items. They are truly co-essential, not only insofar as they form pairs but also as occupying particular positions within the network formed by imagination's intrinsic intentionality. At this point eidetic analysis and intentional analysis merge.

PART TWO

DETAILED DESCRIPTIONS

CHAPTER THREE

Spontaneity and Controlledness

I

IN THE COMPARATIVE ANALYSES offered at the end of chapter two
spontaneity and controlledness emerged as essential traits of imagination in both of its basic intentional phases. In these analyses we saw
that all three forms of the act of imagining and all the constituents of
the intentional correlate of this act are subject to the imaginer's control
—and yet all these forms and constituents may also, on different occasions, arise spontaneously. This striking alternativeness—in which each
trait appears only in the other's absence—does not represent a meaningless clash of unrelated or only contingently connected factors. For
the two essential traits not only contrast with but also *complement* each
other: what is lacking in spontaneity is found precisely in controlledness, and vice versa. This is not merely to claim that the two traits are
abstractly or conceptually complementary to each other. Rather, their
complementary character emerges within imaginative experience itself.
The imaginer senses directly, without any supplementary act of infer-
ence or recourse to reasoning, that the controlled features of imagining
complement its spontaneous features—the former seeming to compen-
sate for what is missing in the latter, and conversely. Thus, in the
original dolphin example the spontaneous initial upsurge of the sequence was counterbalanced by the element of control inherent in its
episodic units, each of which had a more or less distinct beginning,
middle, and end. But both traits need not actually appear in the course
of the same experience; the *potential* presence of the lacking trait also
supports the imaginer's conviction that the two traits complement
each other. Hence, although my imagining of a certain flamingo cry
was highly controlled, I felt that something spontaneous *could* have
intervened in this experience at any moment: such spontaneity remained an essential, albeit unrealized, possibility.

It is just at this juncture that a first expansion of previous descriptions must be made. A more complete analysis shows that each of the two traits in question may be considered in either of two ways: as actual or as potential. Potentially, all of imaginative experience is controll*able*. Actually, in a given case only certain aspects will be in fact controll*ed*. The same duality holds for spontaneity, though there is no comparably convenient way of verbally demarcating the two possibilities, which we might designate for the moment as spontaneity$_p$ (spontaneity qua potential) and spontaneity$_a$ (spontaneity qua actual). As a consequence there are two kinds of complementary relation between the traits at issue, as may be expressed in two different dyadic forms. In the first of these forms, i.e., *controllability-spontaneity$_p$*, it is entirely a matter of what *might* be the case, and thus the two complementary terms do not exclude each other. Insofar as something is not actually being imagined in the present, it may be regarded as *both* controllable and spontaneous$_p$ in the sense that it is indifferently one or the other, and it may enter imaginative experience either as controlled or as spontaneous$_a$ (where the "or" is inclusive). By contrast, in the second dyadic form, i.e., *controlledness-spontaneity$_a$*, the relationship between the two terms is one of mutual exclusion. For whenever we actually imagine, our experience cannot be characterized by both terms: it has to be either controlled *or* spontaneous$_a$ (where the "or" is exclusive). In other words, the effect of actualizing a possible imaginative experience is to require that a choice be made between two alternatives which, in their potential state, are capable of coexisting equanimously with each other.

From this we may infer that spontaneity$_a$ and controlledness cannot coexist, at least not in the strict sense of existing at the same time and in regard to the same aspect of imagining. Only if all reference to a specific time of appearance or occurrence is removed—as when both traits are considered as purely potential—can they be considered coexistent features. But since temporal specificity can be eliminated only from nonactual imaginings—the *enactment* of a given mental act is always specifiable in terms of date of occurrence—in any analysis of imagining in terms of its actuality qua act, exclusivity will dominate the relationship between the two traits. And if this is so, we may leave aside any further analysis of the dyad controllability-spontaneity$_p$ and concentrate our attention on the dyad controlledness-spontaneity$_a$, which we shall henceforth designate by the simplified formula "controlledness-spontaneity."[1]

1. The term "controllability" will be used when attention is to be drawn to a capacity or disposition upon which the imaginer draws. But when the phenomenon

If the spontaneous and controlled features of imagining remain complementary despite their inability to coexist at a given moment and in a given respect, there must be some way of indicating the unitary whole that they form as complements of each other. It is precisely the newly designated dyad controlledness-spontaneity, regarded as a single unit, that stands for such a whole. Now, this dyadic unit qua *unit* is essentially necessary in status. As the table at the end of chapter two illustrated, one or the other of its complementary components *must* characterize every intentional structure of a given act of imagining. Consequently, the essential necessity embodied in the dyadic unit qua unit may be stated thus: there is no aspect of any imaginative experience which is not describable as *either* spontaneous *or* controlled in character; but, at the same time, no aspect of this experience (insofar as it is actual and not merely potential) presents itself as *both* spontaneous and controlled at once and in the same respect.

The antithetical character of spontaneity and controlledness does not entail their incompatibility under all conditions. There are at least two ways in which they may become compatible with each other. First, the two traits may occur in *close proximity* in an actual experience of imagining. For example, I may be expressly controlling a given stream of imaginative presentations when suddenly something unexpected, which I had not consciously intended, springs up spontaneously. Or conversely, I may fasten onto something that first appeared spontaneously and then proceed to direct its course. The proximity between the two features of imaginative experience may be so considerable that one seems not only to precede the other but to *give rise* to it: e.g., as when controlled imagining provides the occasion for an outburst of spontaneous imagining that appears to protest the element of control itself. In this way there may be a sense of quite intimate interaction between the two traits in question. Second, it is a notable feature of imaginative experience that within a single simultaneous cross-section of this experience controlledness and spontaneity may characterize *different* aspects of the experience. Thus I might be in the process of controlling the temporal course of a given imagined content when a spontaneous change in its mode of presentation unexpectedly occurs. I suddenly 'see' the content in some significantly new way. Despite the possibility

---

of control is considered in its specific relationship with spontaneity, it will be designated by the term "controlledness" in order to indicate that it is a question of whether a given act of imagining is *actually* controlled or not. The single term "spontaneity" will have to do double duty—serving to denote both the essential trait of spontaneity *simpliciter* and this trait as it relates to controlledness—since it would overburden the text to distinguish continually between spontaneity$_p$ and spontaneity$_a$.

that spontaneity and controlledness may dovetail in these two fashions, however, it is still the case that only *different* aspects of imagining taken at a single moment or distinctly *different* moments of a single imaginative experience can be described in both of the complementary terms at once. Consequently, the two traits remain incapable of achieving strict co-presence in imaginative experience and are in this basic sense mutually exclusive of each other.[2]

The relationship between spontaneity and controlledness is not only mutually exclusive but also jointly exhaustive. Spontaneity and controlledness, considered as genuine complements, are coextensive with that particular domain of imaginative experience they serve to specify—a domain that invites description by the use of terms indicating the presence or absence of control, e.g., "activity," "passivity," "effort," "ease," etc. These terms designate the degree to which the imaginer is, or is not, in a position of dominance in regard to a given imaginative experience. In this perspective, controlledness signifies that pole of the domain of control at which the dominance of the imaginer over his own acts is most effectively expressed and experienced. Spontaneity, in contrast, signifies the opposite pole, where imaginative acts and presentations appear in an irrepressible and sudden upsurge. Each trait is thus representative of strikingly divergent aspects of imaginative experience—as is reflected in the fact, already remarked upon, that controlledness appears more conspicuously in the act phase and spontaneity in the object phase.

To sum up: controlledness-spontaneity is a dyadic unit of imaginative experience which embodies what we may call an "option-necessity." As mutually exclusive, and yet jointly exhaustive, the traits contained within the dyad present the imaginer with a choice between competing though complementary alternatives. Option-necessity obtains precisely to the extent that one is not always able to say in advance *which* of the two dyadically related traits, spontaneity or controlledness, will occur and be experienced in a given case of imagining. In contradistinction to this situation, one can always say which *singular* (i.e., non-dyadically related) essentially necessary traits will occur and be experienced in a

---

2. This brief consideration of the two primary manners—i.e., successively and simultaneously—in which controlledness and spontaneity come together in imaginative experience demonstrates that we cannot afford to overlook the ways in which different essential traits combine in concrete cases of imagining. These modes of combination are themselves essential possibilities of imagination, representing different basic forms of hybridization of essential traits. Each such mode occupies a legitimate position in a comprehensive eidetic analysis of imagination, an analysis that must account for essential traits not only in their distinctness but also in their primary combinatory states.

given instance: e.g., self-evidence, self-containedness, indeterminacy, and pure possibility. Thus, while the latter four traits exhibit what we can call "trait-necessity"—i.e., a straightforward essential necessity always inherent in the phenomenon at hand—the option-necessity attaching to the dyadic pair controlledness-spontaneity involves a forced choice between alternative traits, one *or* the other of which must characterize the phenomenon. Moreover, as the only available options, controlledness and spontaneity together stake out the limits of that sector of imaginative experience which we shall call "freedom of mind."[3]

II

In comparison with controlledness, *spontaneity* has been invoked much more frequently in previous descriptions of imagination. Since Kant in particular, the link between imagination and spontaneity has become a familiar theme in the philosophy of mind. Throughout the nineteenth century and down to the present day, a parade of thinkers has explored, or at least presupposed, this link—without, however, clarifying its nature. For Sartre, who in many ways culminates this line of thought, spontaneity is one of the four primary "distinctive characteristics" of imagining: "an imagining consciousness . . . presents itself to itself as an imagining consciousness, that is, *as a spontaneity*."[4] But this statement tells us very little as to specifically *how* spontaneity is characteristic of imagining. What is most questionable in Sartre's approach is found in his assumptions that (a) *all* acts of imagination are spontaneous, and (b) they are all spontaneous in the same manner. We have already encountered reasons for doubting the truthfulness of (a): spontaneity cannot be said to characterize every act of imagining if it is only one of two options available to the imaginer at any given time. As to (b), imagining exhibits itself as spontaneous in several descriptively different (though ultimately closely related) ways, as will be shown in this section.

In attempting to describe the spontaneity of imaginative experience, we may take a first clue from a phrase Kant uses in a seminal discussion of spontaneity in *The Critique of Pure Reason*. According to Kant, a spontaneous process is one that "begins of itself."[5] It is the formula

3. For further dicussion of freedom of mind, see chapter eight.
4. *Psychology of Imagination*, p. 17; my italics. I have altered the translation here as in other citations from this poorly translated text.
5. The full statement is: "[there is] an *absolute spontaneity* of the cause, whereby a series of appearances, which proceeds in accordance with laws of nature, begins *of itself*" (*Critique of Pure Reason*, A446 B474, p. 411; Kant's italics).

"of itself" (*von selbst*) that is most important for our purposes. A spontaneous process is one that begins of itself in the strict sense that it begins *by* itself, that is, through its own internal agency and not through external causation—i.e., by the specific action of some other agency. Thus, a truly spontaneous phenomenon initiates *itself* rather than being initiated by other phenomena: it is *autogenous.*

We do not encounter genuinely autogenous phenomena in the perceived world. What we perceive typically presents itself as arising from a concatenation of causally connected factors: e.g., the shadow I perceive as stemming from the sun's illumination. Hence we are astounded when a perceptual object or event appears which seems to belong to no existing chain of causes, as when a fire apparently starts on its own. Strenuous efforts often ensue to find the appropriate causal series for such a recalcitrant "exception," so that it may finally become explicable and intelligible as a *bona fide* member of the perceived world.

In experiencing spontaneous imaginative acts and presentations, in contrast, the human subject is confronted with an essentially different situation. Here, it is as a matter of course, and not merely as an exception, that a given entity or event resists being located in a well-ordered, causally concatenated series, for a spontaneous imaginative experience does not present itself as embedded in any such series. Instead of emerging from a nexus of causally efficacious factors, it arises suddenly, in a psychical vacuum. To be sure, *upon reflection* the imaginer may succeed in locating the spontaneous imaginative appearance within a certain causal context, but this context does not as such enter into the specific content of his experience. What is experienced is rather an imaginative act-*cum*-presentation, which presents itself as unconnected with preceding or surrounding circumstances, including even those circumstances provided by former acts of imagining. This act-presentation appears *of and by itself*, as quite independent of the imaginer's immediate practical situation (a situation that may even include particular plans and projects for imagining). It is as if this situation, though undeniably present, were irrelevant to the spontaneity of imagining. In order to understand more fully what such spontaneity consists in, let us consider in some detail three basic characteristics of all spontaneous imagining.

Effortlessness

A first distinctive feature of spontaneous imagining is its effortless character. This feature stood out in our original analysis of selected examples in chapter one. There I pointed to the effortless character of the dolphin sequence, which seemed to unfold on its own initiative.

No express effort to direct or control the sequence as a whole was evident; my mind was content to follow the imaginative presentation as it progressed in a free-flowing form. The object phase in particular seemed to generate itself without calling upon my inherent powers of initiation or guidance. For this reason I was led to describe such spontaneity as appearing more prominently in the imaginative presentation than in the act of imagining: the spontaneity of *what* we imagine is often more striking than the spontaneity of the act itself. Yet, despite this tendency, the act of imagining can also arise quite effortlessly. We "just find ourselves imagining"—that is, we suddenly realize that we are already, without having made any preparatory effort to do so, engaged in an act of imagining. The clearest examples of such effortless imagining are found in acts of ordinary reverie. Frequently we realize that we are engaging in these acts only *after* we have been indulging in them for some time. By a sort of psychic repercussion, we find ourselves caught in their midst—*in medias imagines*, as it were. Indeed, it is difficult to initiate or direct such acts as these if the attempt is too explicit.

We may conclude that both of the primary intentional phases of imagination may appear with free facility. Each phase, and each aspect of each phase, may arise of its own accord. What is common to the effortlessness of act and object phases is the felt sense that *the imagining subject contributes nothing* to the emergence of either phase. Whatever the *ultimate* role of the imaginer may be (and only an explanatory account would be able to determine this), he plays no immediate or explicitly conscious role in bringing about spontaneously appearing imaginative acts and presentations.

Surprise

All intentional acts, including imagining itself, are potentially fulfilling in character. They are capable of bodying forth, of presenting, the proper intentional objects of such acts. The designs or wishes of the imaginer may or may not be explicitly conscious. When they are explicitly conscious, as in controlled imagining, their fulfillment does not surprise, for then one experiences the fulfillment of intentions that one already knows one has. But in spontaneous imagining the imaginer is not expressly aware of the designs or wishes that animate his experience, and thus what he imagines takes him by surprise, as if it were an unexpected gift. Although such surprise is not overwhelming in nature—it rarely, if ever, amounts to the sense of shock that may occur in hallucinating or even in ordinary perceiving—it is nonetheless a more than merely occasional feature of imaginative experience. Hence we are forced to disagree with Sartre's contention that in imagining "I know where I am going and what I want to produce. This is why no development of the image can take me by surprise."[6]

It is doubtless true that *all* spontaneous objects or events, perceived or imagined, are surprising to some degree. But where surprise may approach stupefaction in a case of perceived self-generation (e.g., when we witness what is significantly called "spontaneous combustion"), in experiences of spontaneous imagining our reaction is rarely this extreme: in such cases we are "taken by surprise," but we are not swept away by it. We retain our basic composure because nothing has appeared that undermines or threatens ingrained beliefs concerning causal action or interaction; indeed, when we imagine, such beliefs are put out of play from the start. By the same token, our basic stock of knowledge is not altered since we cannot be said to learn anything entirely new from imagining. Nevertheless, even though a spontaneous imaginative experience represents no threat to knowledge or to belief, it is still capable of surprising us because of the way in which it subverts certain expectations as to its course or outcome and because it fulfills intentions of which we were not previously aware. It does not matter that our surprise is subject to variation, ranging from the mild (as in much uneventful imagining) to the upsetting (as when an imagined scene depicting what I should have done, but failed to do, springs to mind). The point is that an element of surprise, however minimal, accompanies all cases of spontaneous imagining. When such surprise is absent altogether, we have to do with imagining that is no longer spontaneous but controlled in character.

Instantaneity

Appearing hand in glove with this last feature is a third characteristic of spontaneous imagining: its instantaneous nature. Where controlled imagining may occur gradually and even with considerable delay, spontaneous imagining always occurs *at once*, taking place as if it were a miniature mental explosion. An entire imaginative act-*cum*-presentation presents itself *tout d'un coup*, as a single simultaneous totality. But it is imagined content as such that is most conspicuously instantaneous, for, to the extent that what we imagine appears spontaneously, it exhibits no sense of distended development in time. As in the dolphin example, imagined content tends to be merely episodic in form, expressing itself in discontinuous and rapidly disappearing *tableaux*. Thus each dolphin episode arose in an instantaneous upsurge,

6. *Psychology of Imagination*, p. 168.

and not in any continuously developmental fashion. A closer analysis of the first dolphin episode, for example, shows that, although the creatures were initially apprehended as swimming, they were not experienced as swimming *through* any definite stretch of water, i.e., from one particular point to any other particular point. Hence their movements, traversing no specifiable spatial interval, were not experienced as enduring through any lasting temporal period. And, lacking significant duration, the episode could not be said to *develop* in any strict sense. Instead, it presented itself, *all* of itself, at the very moment of its spontaneous upsurge in my mind. Moreover, even when the imagined action was more definite—e.g., in those episodes in which the dolphins swam around and under the ship's hull or toward the beach—there was a similar sense of something happening all at once and lacking any genuine duration.

From these considerations we may conclude that when one speaks of the evanescent or fleeting character of imagination, one is implicitly referring to the instantaneous nature of spontaneous imagining. But we should bear in mind that not all imagining is instantaneous and that we are able, through our inherent capacities of control, to prolong the sense of time lapse within a given imaginative experience. Precisely insofar as we do so, however, we are no longer imagining in a spontaneous way.

These three characteristics of imaginative spontaneity may further be regarded as varying expressions of a single basic feature of all spontaneous imagining: its *self-generativity*. Kant pointed to this feature when he defined spontaneity as "the mind's power of producing representations from itself."[7] Spontaneous mental acts generate themselves, bring themselves into being. In the case of spontaneous imagining, such self-generativity is not merely another particular characteristic to be ranged alongside the other three characteristics just described: it is rather a generic trait, in relation to which these characteristics can be seen as aspects or even as species. To be self-generative may mean any or all of the following: not subject to external coercion or control, but instead bringing *itself* about (thus the "self-" of "self-generative" refers not to the imagining subject but to the imaginative act or presentation itself); arising from an apparent lack of cause, motive, or reason; appearing in a way that is unsolicited and unpremeditated by the imaginer and emerging without any express effort on his part; appearing in such a way as to surprise; operating by means of its own self-propelling forces,

7. *Critique of Pure Reason*, A51 B75, p. 93.

being wholly self-determinative in this respect; and generating itself all at once, *totum simul*, without any significant prolongation or sense of steady development.

The notion of self-generativity also encompasses that aspect of imaginative spontaneity discussed above in terms of independence of causal series. Self-generative phenomena arise, or at least they appear to arise, apart from any explicit explanatory context, especially one that is conceived in terms of efficient, push-pull causality (whether external or internal to the subject). Even if such a context can be shown to be present, it is not experienced as continuous with, or as intrinsic to, the spontaneous imaginative act or presentation for which it provides an explanatory matrix. Indeed, self-generative imaginative acts and presentations arise independently even of *other* imaginative acts and presentations. As if *sui generis*, they occur in disregard not only of the circumambient perceived world but also of past or future imaginings.

III

Controlledness characterizes the situation in which the imaginer assumes conscious and practically complete control over the course and content, and especially over the act, of imagining. Like spontaneity, controlledness is analyzable into a cluster of characteristics. In the present case, however, these characteristics are not so much constituent or inherent features as they are different forms or "moments" of imaginative activity. We shall begin with a description of these moments, and then proceed to discuss various implications of this description.

DESCRIPTION PROPER

When Aristotle remarked that imagining "is up to us when we wish"[8] and Wittgenstein observed that "images are subject to the will,"[9] both philosophers were underlining the considerable control we can bring to bear on our own imagining. Yet neither thinker specified precisely how such control is exerted in imaginative experience. Accordingly, our task in this subsection is to provide a description of the primary ways in which control over imagining is achieved by the imaginer himself. These means or modes of control are found in three basic

8. *De Anima*, 427b 16-17.
9. *Zettel*, eds. G. E. M. Anscombe and G. H. von Wright (Berkeley: University of California Press, 1967), sec. 621.

forms, namely, the initiation, the guidance, and the termination of the imaginative act-*cum*-presentation.

Initiation

We might just as well have termed this form of control "self-inducement." For this particular mode of controlledness concerns one's ability to induce imaginative activity of a certain kind by the mere desire to do so. At any time I wish, so long as I am awake and undistracted, I can initiate an imaginative act or presentation of my choice, no matter what my immediately preceding state of consciousness has been. Although I remain bound by certain minimal limitations (to be discussed below), *within* these limitations I can bring about any given act or presentation that I wish. Let it be a scene in which an Abyssinian Abuna (about whom I know only what a dictionary tells me) is officiating in a religious ceremony: no sooner have I proposed such a scene to myself as a possible imaginative project than it begins to appear before my mental gaze. In this case the initiation is comparatively easy; the only effort involved, if it can be called effort at all, is found in the initial proposing of the subject matter to be imagined. In other cases the effort is somewhat more concerted: e.g., in imagining an Abuna as President of the United States. But no matter how complicated or bizarre the subject matter may be, I can almost always initiate the particular imaginative experience that I propose to myself. As imaginer, I possess an inherent and inalienable power of initiation. *Why* I possess this remarkable power is not a matter of concern in a phenomenological account of imagining. What does matter is only *that* I can call upon it when I wish and that I can describe how it manifests itself in imaginative experience.

The self-induced initiation of an imaginative experience may occur in such an effortless and sudden way as to be mistaken for a case of spontaneity. This happens particularly when one is only dimly aware of the original idea or project that spurs the initiation of imagining. My thought of an Abyssinian Abuna may be so "idle" or "passing"—not to mention lacking in precise knowledge—that I cannot speak of this thought as explicitly aiming at the figure who is the patriarch of the Abyssinian Church. Moreover, the content of the thought may be so enmeshed within a complex constellation of memories, fantasies, and other mental acts that it is difficult to extricate it in any strictly imaginal form. The more obscure my awareness of the seed-thought, the more likely that its appearance in imaginative form will be experienced as spontaneous; and there are in fact borderline cases where it is difficult to say with complete certainty whether a given imaginative act or presentation has arisen spontaneously (i.e., without any express intention or volition on my part) or from my own initiative.[10]

Guidance

Not only are we capable of initiating our own imaginative experiences, we are also able to direct these experiences in whatever manner we wish once they have been initiated by us. Such "guidability" is found even in instances of imagining that we have *not* ourselves initiated. These non-self-initiated acts of imagining fall into two classes: those which have arisen spontaneously in previous imaginings, and those which have emerged from strictly nonimaginative experiences such as perceiving or remembering. Both types of act begin outside the imaginer's immediate control—either as spontaneous imaginings preceding the actual application of this control or as proceeding from a different kind of experience altogether (e.g., perception or memory). What is remarkable is that we can at will bring experiences of either type under our own control by deciding to direct their *subsequent* course. If an imaginary interstellar creature suddenly and without having been expressly induced appears in my mind's eye, I can assert control over this spontaneous appearance by contriving to imagine the creature in any number of subsequent situations. And if the initial experience is a particular perception or memory, I can isolate the specific content of this experience and imagine its further course as my fancy dictates. Such acts of guided continuation are not restricted to embroidering on the original perception or memory in the manner of, say, apprentice composers, who limit themselves to writing variations on the music of their masters. For I am free to disregard the original experience in its perceptual or mnemic reality, that is, as an actual event which is to be imitated or varied in imagination. Once the content of the initial experience has been "imaginified," I am at liberty to control its future course in any way I choose, including even the possibility of allowing the imaginative experience to become once again a perceptual experience. I might begin by perceiving Hertford College through the window of the Bodleian Library, transform the college in imagination into a fantastic Temple to the Sun, and end by letting the perception of Hertford itself reemerge and reoccupy my conscious attention. Such

10. Such borderline cases present a difficulty not of description—for they can still be described in considerable detail—but of classification: they perch precariously on the thin, yet normally discernible, line that is to be drawn between spontaneous and controlled imaginative phenomena. Such a difficulty in exact classification does not render the intrinsic differences between spontaneity and controlledness any less important: on the contrary, it makes their determination all the more crucial.

vacillations are perfectly possible, although it must be recognized that they are effected between essentially different kinds of act: continuation *in* imagination does not mean that the initial perceptual experience has become continuous *with* imagination.

Because of the endless possibilities to which it gives rise, guidance exhibits the imaginer's capacity for control in its most impressive and extensive form. Here, especially, one is tempted to view imagination as sovereign in its own sphere. For insofar as the imaginer remains within this sphere, he is able to direct and redirect imaginative experience with practically unlimited latitude. It is just this latitude upon which the artist relies in his characteristically unhindered use of imagination and in his search for plasticity of expressive means. Literature in particular is exemplary of imagining's diversified directive powers. In literary works the artistic mode of imaginative guidance may be obsessively rigid (as exemplified by the deliberately repetitive nature of many of Samuel Beckett's novels), smoothly and predictably continuous (as in a number of Jane Austen's works), radically discontinuous (as in James Joyce's *Ulysses* and *Finnegans Wake*), or suppressed and mute (as in Ernest Hemingway's action-oriented fiction). But the multiform guidability of imagining is not restricted in expression and in exfoliation to particular works of art. For the most part, imaginative guidance takes place within the mind's private proscenium, where we entertain and indulge ourselves alone. Whether or not the results of controlled imagining are made available to others through everyday discourse or artistic expression, we experience *ourselves* in the moment of guidance as in a position of unfettered control. Upon the merest of whims, we can alter our present course of imagining and move it in a different direction with respect to its content, mode of presentation, time sense, and spatial character; and we can also freely change the specific form the act of imagining takes: from, say, imagining visually to nonsensory imagining-that. It is precisely such a readily available capacity to take the course of imagining in new directions—whatever its ultimate origin or eventual outcome—that helps to instill in us the conviction that as imaginers we possess powers of control without parallel in other mental acts.

Termination

This conviction is strengthened when it is realized that the imaginer can annihilate the very act-*cum*-presentation that he has initiated and perhaps also guided. No matter what its intrinsic interest may be, he can always call a halt to it. Such "terminability" lies easily within his grasp, and it may be actualized in two different ways. On the one hand, he may choose simply to cease imagining altogether. This decision in turn can be enacted in two manners: either by attempting to empty one's mind of all its specific imagined content—a difficult procedure that may require special training, e.g., certain specialized techniques of meditation—or by becoming engrossed in a wholly *different* kind of activity, such as doing sums in one's head. On the other hand, a given imaginative experience can be replaced by another distinctly different *imaginative* experience: here one deliberately initiates a new experience of imagining to take the place of the former experience. In effect, the initiation of the new experience *is* the termination of the old one; because of differences in content, mode of presentation, etc., one cannot go on imagining both together.

The controlled termination and initiation of imaginings possess several traits in common. Both tend to be short-lived, typically occurring in what Whitehead calls the "rush of immediate transition"[11] rather than in a prolonged fashion; in both there is a sense of abrupt change (whether from a state in which the act or presentation is present in mind to one in which it is not, or the reverse); and in neither case do we normally encounter the kind of complex and convoluted development possible in imaginative guidance proper. But a decisive difference remains insofar as the initiation of a train of imagining is accompanied by a feeling of being *productive* (albeit in a minimal, non-Romantic sense), while the termination of an imaginative experience is characterized by a sense of *annihilative* power. In terminating imaginative acts or presentations, we do away with what has become, if only for a brief moment, an intimate part of our mental life; in initiating them, we bring about, or add to, a basic dimension of this life. Of the two, termination is the more inclusive power: one can always terminate what has already been initiated in imagination, but only rarely can what has been terminated be reinitiated in precisely the same form. To reimagine a certain *imaginatum* is intrinsically more difficult than banishing that same imagined content from mind in a single act of expulsion.

One might object to these claims concerning an inherent power of termination by citing the familiar case (discussed briefly in the Introduction) in which we are told '*not* to imagine a black bear'. It is undeniable that in a case such as this it is difficult to prevent the interdicted object from arising in consciousness. But it is just as true that one remains capable of expunging the persistent presentation from the mind at any point *after* its appearance or reappearance there, e.g., by

11. Alfred North Whitehead, *Process and Reality* (New York: Harper, 1960), p. 181.

allowing oneself to become distracted. Thus the capacity to terminate does not in fact fail; all that differs from the normal case is that here the termination may not be as effective or as enduring as usual, but must (if the imagined bear keeps coming back to mind) be continually reenacted. There may be a rapid oscillation between the successive appearances of the bear and their attendant mental annihilations, but such oscillation, even if it comes to border on obsession, does not disprove one's power to terminate *any given* imaginative act or presentation. This power remains intact, however necessary it may be to *re-exercise* it in certain circumstances.[12]

IMPLICATIONS AND QUALIFICATIONS

The finding that the imaginer's capacity of control is such that he can initiate, guide, and terminate imaginative acts and presentations at will implies a still stronger claim, which appears to follow directly from it and to which allusion has already been made in the Introduction: the imaginer can imagine what, how, and when he wishes to. Insofar as this is the case there would seem to be no effective limits to one's imaginative powers. A further claim implicit in the foregoing discussion is that the imaginer *cannot fail* to realize his imaginative projects; his success seems to be virtually assured and to be built into the very character of imagining. Combining these two claims, we arrive at the following preliminary formulation: the imaginer cannot fail to imagine what, how, and when he wishes to. Stated in such a bald and blatant way, this assertion may seem unwarranted, especially in view of the widespread assumption that imagination is one of the frailest and feeblest of human mental activities. This assumption, which informs commonsensical as well as philosophical thinking, is articulated in R. G. Collingwood's declaration that "the extent to which we can control our imagination by a deliberate act of will is very limited."[13] In the face of such skepticism the question becomes: how are we to give due credit to

12. For further discussion of cases of obsessive imagining, along with a denial of their terminability, see P. F. Strawson, "Imagination and Perception" in *Experience and Theory*, eds. L. Foster and J. W. Swanson (Amherst: University of Massachusetts Press, 1970).

13. *Principles of Art* (Oxford: Clarendon Press, 1938), p. 179. That skepticism concerning powers of imaginative control remains in force is indicated in the following more recent statement: "of course all thinking has this mixture of being purposive and directed and of experiencing thoughts cropping up, but in the case of seeing images . . . there is an added element of something beyond our control" (Hide Ishiguro, "Imagination" in *Proceedings of the Aristotelian Society*, suppl. vol. 41 [1967], p. 53).

the imaginer's inherent powers of control while at the same time accounting for the everyday belief (frequently reflected in philosophical theory as well) that imagination is quite constricted in its operations?

To begin with, it must be admitted that the above assertion—viz., "the imaginer cannot fail to imagine what, how and when he wishes to"—cannot survive critical scrutiny without being qualified in certain ways. Stated without qualification, it simply claims too much. In particular it does not acknowledge three basic sorts of limitation upon one's capacity to control imagining. Let us examine these limitations in succession.[14]

(1) The first and most crucial kind of limitation is *conceptual* or *logical* in character. There are certain things that we cannot imagine because they are formed from the combination of contradictory concepts. Two sorts of such strictly unimaginable things may be distinguished. On the one hand, there are those objects which are unimaginable insofar as they are formed from the conjunction of certain characteristics and the simultaneous *absence* of those very same characteristics. In this instance we attempt to imagine something as such-and-such (e.g., as existing, as colored in a certain way, etc.) and yet also and at the same time as *not* such-and-such. We find out quickly that we cannot succeed in this venture, for no object (real or imagined) can be characterized by the presence of certain properties and the absence of these same properties. As Husserl says, "this [imagined] house, the same, is thinkable as *a* and as *non-a* but, naturally, if as *a*, then *not at the same time* as *non-a*. It cannot be both simultaneously. . . ."[15]

On the other hand, there are objects that cannot be imagined because they are formed from the combination of two or more *incompatible* characteristics. Here it is not a question of the presence or absence of various properties but of certain properties that by their very nature cannot co-specify the same object in the same respect at the same time. Take the classical case of the 'square circle'. I cannot imagine an object which is at once circular and square in shape, because no single object can be altogether circular *and* altogether square at one and the same time. Circularity and squareness exclude each other as defining properties of the same total object. Their mutual exclusion stems not from an antithesis between presence and absence but from

14. The limitations in question apply *a fortiori* to spontaneous imagining as well. For whatever limits efforts at control must also limit what occurs spontaneously. But we shall concern ourselves with the three limitations in question only insofar as they are specifically pertinent to controlled imagining.

15. *Experience and Judgment*, p. 345. Husserl's italics.

an incompatibility of type or character. The effect, however, is the same: strict unimaginability.

Of course, one can always *attempt* to imagine objects of the two sorts just described; in so doing, one can come up with varying results —some more, some less satisfactory. But no matter to what extent one's imaginative powers are stretched in this effort—drawing out one's capacities of control to their utmost—whatever one does succeed in imagining will not qualify as a *bona fide* instance of the object in question.

Nevertheless, it would be mistaken to assume that this essential limitation of imaginative powers testifies to their inherent weakness or fallibility. For *nothing*, real *or* imagined, can exemplify objects of the two kinds that have just been discussed. These objects are composed of such conflicting concepts (i.e., *a* and *non-a*, *a* and *b* where *b* is incompatible with *a*) that they are *eo ipso* impossible—which is to say, logically impossible. And as Paul Weiss asserts, "the logically impossible [is] that which *could not be in any sense*."[16] Successful instantiation of any kind—whether in imagination, perception, memory, or wherever— is ruled out of court from the very start, since contradictory concepts cannot ever be simultaneously exemplified in the same object and in the same respect.

Such an impossibility of successful instantiation or exemplification, an impossibility which is established *a priori* (i.e., by the very nature of the concepts involved), means that one cannot talk, strictly speaking, of failure. Where there is *no possibility* of success, it is difficult to speak of failure to achieve success; or, if we can still be said to fail, it is in a nonignominious and noninjurious sense. Therefore, even if it is true that we cannot succeed in imagining certain conceptually contradictory things, we do not fail in any significant sense to imagine these things. This inability to fail flagrantly, which is a function of the logical limits of success, may be given expression by adding a first qualification to our initial formula: the imaginer cannot fail *in any significant sense* to imagine what, how, and when he wishes to.

One might object at this point that the imaginer can at least bring forward a *representation* of an object that is formed from incompatible concepts. Even if I cannot imagine a 'square circle' as such, am I not capable of bringing forth something that represents, i.e., 'stands for', such a circle? I might, for example, summon up the following shape: ◯ and claim that it represents a square circle. And yet it is clear that this figure (whether purely imagined or depicted graphically) is

16. Paul Weiss, *Modes of Being* (Carbondale: Southern Illinois University Press, 1958), p. 106. My italics.

not an *adequate* representation of the impossible object. To be adequate such a representation would have to correspond point by point with the impossible object as defined by the phrase 'square circle'. The above figure—and any other figure of our devising, no matter how detailed or ingenious it may be—fails to satisfy the criterion of strict isomorphism, since only certain parts of it (namely, the corners in the present case) correspond to a circle and only certain other parts (i.e., the sides) to a square. It is true that the figure in question may be taken in a very loose sense as a "symbol" of a square circle. But this is only to say that it may be taken as an empty sign, that is, as a figure which stands proxy for an object that cannot itself be instantiated or even adequately represented. In this loose sense (which eliminates all requirements of isomorphism), almost anything may be taken as a symbol of the impossible object, and the choice becomes arbitrary in the end. The question remains, however, whether any product of imagining can be said to represent the object in any rigorous sense, namely, in such a way as to be both circular and square at once and in all respects. To this question the answer must be resoundingly negative: we cannot conjure up in imagination (or depict on the basis of imagining) any such representation.

We may generalize this point by reverting to prior terminology: we cannot *image* impossible objects; that is, we cannot imagine them in a sensuously specific way. For in the present context "representing" and "imaging" involve very much the same effort to provide a sensory guise for a particular content. But then the further question arises: if an impossible object cannot be imaged, perhaps it can nonetheless be imagined in *some other way*, e.g., by imagining-that. Can I imagine *that* there is such an object? Ingarden seems to claim precisely this:

> Thus, for example, there is no real 'wooden iron' or ideal 'round square', whereas purely intentional objects with such contents are quite possible, even though they cannot be *intuitively* imagined. If the conscious subject wishes to move in the framework of the intuitively imaginable . . . he is bound by the determinate limits that are drawn by the *what* of the content. If he abandons this resolve, however, the limits of his freedom are extended, so that, for example, he can move freely within the limits prescribed by a special *type* of objectivity (e.g., that of 'real' objectivities).[17]

Here we must be cautious, however. The only sense in which I can imagine that there is a round square is by *supposing* that there is such

17. *The Literary Work of Art*, pp. 123-24. His italics.

an object. Such supposing—as opposed to the "sheer supposing" which is involved in imagining proper[18]—is a form of postulating, not of imagining. I may postulate—i.e., posit in thought—the existence of a round square without committing myself to a belief in its existence and, more importantly, *without even entertaining the possibility of such a thing.* To imagine that there is a round square, on the other hand, would be to entertain the possibility of this object; yet that is just what I cannot do, since this object's possibility—its 'could-be' character—is precisely what is eliminated in the nature of the case. I cannot imagine as possible what is inherently, i.e., conceptually, impossible.

As a consequence, I cannot be said to imagine *that* a particular impossible object exists. And if this is so, it follows that there is no significant sense whatsoever in which I can imagine such objects, since I can neither image them or imagine that they exist.[19] This is a conclusion, moreover, with which Ingarden's statement quoted just above is in agreement, appearances notwithstanding. For what this statement actually claims is that when I *image,* the content of my imaging has to accord with the essential characteristics (the "what") of the object I image. If these characteristics are self-contradictory then I simply cannot image ("intuitively imagine") such an object. And if I am imagining nonintuitively or nonsensuously, I am still bound by certain limits, those established by the *type* of object I imagine. If this type is in turn self-contradictory by nature, then I cannot imagine *it either,* not even by trying to imagine that such a type of object exists. Our previous finding, then, remains in force: I cannot, whether by imaging or by imagining-that, conjure up in imagination an object formed from contradictory concepts.[20]

(2) The second kind of limitation is *ontological.* When I imagine something and just insofar as I imagine it, I do not make that something exist if it does not already exist; nor can I, by imagining alone,

18. For a discussion of sheer supposing, see chapter five, section III.

19. It is clear that imagining-how is also excluded here. Since there is no sense of personal agency involved in the content which we are trying to imagine in the case of impossible objects, there is no way in which imagining-how would be able to represent such objects.

20. Throughout the foregoing discussion, the term "impossible object" has done triple duty. Taken narrowly, it denotes any object or singular entity conceived in self-contradictory terms, e.g., 'round square'. But there are also impossible events (e.g., a simultaneous movement of one part of a single object in two opposite directions) and impossible states of affairs (e.g., the coexistence of two contradictory modes of interaction between the members of a given class of objects). The same strictures as stated above apply to such events and states of affairs: we cannot imagine them in any significant sense.

make it cease to exist if it already exists. An act of imagining *as such* cannot bring about either of these extreme results. In other words, imaginative activity is incapable of creating or eliminating empirically existent things or events. Imagination has no genuine ontological power, that is, no power to make real what is nonreal or the reverse— where by "real" is meant having a determinate and intersubjectively ascertainable status within an enduring spatio-temporal framework.

To deny such ontological power to imagining is not to deny that it may be causally efficacious in certain ways. For example, by imagining various forms a projected building might assume, an architect may be able to determine which form he will actually give to the building. Or, more simply, imagining how a certain movement of my body might occur may facilitate or even give rise to this very movement.[21] In addition, by the use of biofeedback techniques, one can imagine something in such a way as to change the pattern of one's brain waves and thereby induce an altered state of consciousness.[22] But for imagining to be causally efficacious in any of these demonstrable ways is not the same thing as for it to create or annihilate existent objects or events. Imagining a possible painting may represent a stage in the realization of an actual painting. Still, an actual painting is created only when other factors (e.g., brushes and brushstrokes, paint and canvas) are involved. So too an architect must have recourse to builders and building materials in order to construct the building he has imagined; likewise, I must rely upon my musculature to accomplish even the simplest bodily movements and upon my brain to achieve actual changes in my state of consciousness. Thus, it is one thing to acknowledge that a particular act of imagining may function as a contributory factor, linking up with a group of other such factors to establish a situation in which a given effect or result is realized. It is quite another thing to claim that imagining itself, the sheer act taken in isolation from any surrounding or superordinate causal nexus, is capable of adding to or subtracting from the actual constituency of the empirically real. And precisely in this way imagination comes up against an ontological limit

21. The "Feldenkrais method" is based in part on this efficacy of imagining in the facilitation of physical movement. One can, by imagining oneself rotating the upper body in a certain way, make such rotation easier and more extended when it is actually undertaken. Cf. Moshé Feldenkrais, *Body and Mature Behavior* (New York: International Universities Press, 1950), passim.

22. See in this connection Durand Kiefer, "Meditation and Biofeedback" in John White, ed., *The Highest State of Consciousness* (Garden City, N.Y.: Doubleday, 1972), pp. 322-30; Joe Kamiya, "Operant Control of the EEG Alpha Rhythm" in C. Tart, ed., *Altered States of Consciousness* (New York: Wiley, 1969), pp. 507-517; and J. C. Eccles, "The Physiology of Imagination" in T. J. Teyler, ed., *Altered States of Awareness* (San Francisco: Freeman, 1972), pp. 31-40.

that it cannot trespass. To express this limitation upon imaginative activity we should add a further qualification to the formula with which we began: the imaginer cannot fail to imagine what, how, and when he wishes, *though his act of imagining cannot by itself make what he imagines exist or cease to exist as empirically real.*[23]

(3) The third kind of limitation, and perhaps the least important, is *empirical* or *contingent*. It consists in the given, particular limits within which one can presently direct the course and content of one's imaginings. Such limits reflect the undeniable fact that, from one person to another, there are discernible differences in the exact extent to which one can control one's imaginative activity. It is these differences that express the empirical limitations upon the ongoing experiences of individual imaginers and thus serve to distinguish these imaginers from each other.

Yet contrasting performances among individual imaginers should not be overstressed. Despite discrepancies—say, in the facility with which one can visualize or audialize certain things and not others—the *general* scope of human imaginative activity remains remarkably constant from one imaginer to the next. A special weakness, e.g., in imaging as such, is often compensated for by a corresponding strength, e.g., in nonsensory imagining-that. Moreover, one's given imaginative powers are capable of being trained, through disciplined exercises, to overcome marked deficiencies or to strengthen further one's already existing capabilities.[24]

In fact, this basic educability of imaginative powers, which allows

23. A skeptic might respond to the foregoing discussion by claiming that *no* mental act qua act is capable of existence-creating or existence-destroying power. Can perceiving something or thinking of it make it exist or cease to exist? Of course they cannot. The point, however, is that there is a special temptation to regard imagining as ontologically efficacious because of its seemingly unlimited scope, as in Schlegel's claim: "one must realize that the imagination *through which the world first originated* for us and that through which works of art are created are the same power" (A. W. Schlegel, *Vorlesungen über schöne Literatur und Kunst*, ed. J. Minor [Stuttgart, 1884], II, 84; my italics). It is just this sort of extreme assertion that a recognition of imagination's inherent ontological limitation renders implausible.

24. Such "educability" of imagination obtains except in cases of severe brain damage or extreme psychiatric disturbance. Many years ago Francis Galton observed that "there is abundant evidence that the visualizing faculty admits of being developed by education." (*Inquiries into Human Faculty*, p. 73. A study supporting this point is cited on the same page.) More recently, Robert H. McKim has observed that "almost everyone can learn to experience and to use some form of mind's eye imagery. What needs to be compensated [for] in a majority of educated people is a default in their education" (*Experiences in Visual Thinking* [Belmont, Calif.: Wadsworth, 1972], p. 84).

them to stretch beyond present empirical limitations, serves to support the original claim that we cannot fail to imagine what, how, and when we wish. For if, on any given occasion, we fail to imagine as we wish, it is always in principle possible to train ourselves to complete the particular imaginative task successfully—unless doing so entails transcending the logical or ontological limits described above. Insofar as it is possible to overcome specific empirical limitations legitimately, our powers of imaginative control cannot be said to fail. In other words, one may admit a circumstantial, momentary lack of success that is due to shortcomings in aptitude, desire, or experience *without* having to concede strict or total failure. It is true that what counts as "momentary" allows for considerable variation from case to case. For example, if I attempt to visualize a thirty-sided polygon, I may not succeed even after repeated efforts to form an image of such a figure. Still, I cannot be said to have failed utterly until I have exhausted all of my imaginative resources. Since there are no absolute limits on these resources (save again for logical or ontological limits), I can never say for certain that I have exhausted my imaginative capacity—that I am precluded from *ever* carrying out the project in question. I remain capable of making still further exertions and hence of succeeding at some future point: what matters is not precisely *when* this realization will occur but *that it still can occur*. This is why lack of immediate or instantaneous success is not tantamount to complete and final failure. Here we may observe that while instantaneity is an essential concomitant of spontaneity— there being no such thing as *deferred* spontaneity—it is by no means essential to controlledness. A successful outcome of controlled imagining may elude us for a very long time, and yet we have not failed definitively until we give up making renewed efforts at control. And to recognize the possibility of such postponed success leads us to propose still another qualification of the initial formula: the imaginer cannot fail to imagine what, how, and when he wishes to, *even though his efforts may have to be prolonged into the indefinite future in order to succeed.*

Subject to the foregoing three qualifications, our success in controlled imagining remains remarkably assured. Our powers of imaginative control are such that we are able to realize success in almost every instance. If we fail, we do not fail in any discreditable way but only as a function of the limitations that have just been discussed. For the most part, however, we succeed. Our success seems guaranteed or, more exactly, *self*-guaranteed, and it is self-guaranteed because it is *self-incurred*. Controlled imagining succeeds inasmuch as it realizes projects of our own devising, within situations of which we are the temporary mental masters. We ensure our own success by ushering it in ourselves.

But it must be stressed that such assurance of success, which goes hand in hand with an inability to fail significantly, does not obtain for imagining as a whole. It is a characteristic belonging to controlledness alone because only in controlled imagining is there an effort or project which can be said to succeed or to fail. In a description of spontaneous imagining, by contrast, terms such as "success" or "failure" have no meaningful application.[25] Since spontaneous imagining does not represent the accomplishment of an express intention or objective, such imagining cannot count as success *or* failure. A spontaneous act or presentation just appears or happens, without our being able to say that it appears or happens successfully or unsuccessfully: judgments as to its success or failure simply do not apply.[26]

Nevertheless, even the foregoing admission of limits to controlled imagining will not satisfy the skeptic who doubts that our powers of imaginative control are as extensive as has been claimed in this chapter. Such a skeptic is impressed less by the inbuilt success of most imagining than by its "essential poverty": i.e., its frequently barren quality, the lack of luxuriancy in many of its everyday expressions. This skepticism may be countered, and at the same time partially accommodated, by the following line of consideration. By controlledness has been meant the production of the imaginative act or presentation which the imaginer desires or intends—at least this, but by the same token *no more*. To be sure, what is brought forth from one's own imaginative resources is usually satisfactory, barring exceptionally difficult or impossible cases. But it is typically *just* satisfactory; it meets the minimal requirements for satisfying the original imaginative intention— yet without fulfilling this intention in any richer or more complete way than is demanded in order to count as a successful fulfillment.

We may therefore grant that success in controlled imagining is for

25. Thus it is not accurate to claim that "to imagine" is always both a "performance verb" and an "achievement verb," as does Ishiguro. Only in controlled imagining can we be said to be at once performing a mental act and achieving specific results by this performance. Spontaneous imagining involves performance, but not achievement: hence the inappropriateness of speaking of success or failure in this case. For Ishiguro's discussion, based on Ryle's original distinction between two kinds of verbs, see her article "Imagination" in *British Analytical Philosophy*, eds. B. Williams and A. Montefiore (New York: Humanities Press, 1966), p. 163 and pp. 168-70.

26. This is so even though, as was pointed out in footnote 14, spontaneous imagining remains subject to the same three limitations pointed to in this section. It cannot trespass certain definite conceptual and ontological limits, and it too embodies contingent empirical limitations belonging to a given imaginer. Still, staying within all three types of limitation, it does not succeed or fail in its intrinsic action.

the most part certain, yet also recognize that it rarely, if ever, brings with it an embarrassment of riches. Normally, we do not "succeed beyond our wildest dreams" because the very factor of control, which serves to bring about success, also acts to eliminate what is unexpected or excessive. In other words, the price paid for the self-incurred success of controlled imagining is that this success tends to be modest, minimal, and even pedestrian—as is testified by the banality of most of one's quotidian imaginings. Recall in this connection the unexciting and uninspired imagined sounds (e.g., the monotonous flamingo cries) that I conjured up in the second example reported in chapter one. Even a more complex imaginative presentation, such as the Rawls seminar sequence, was mostly flat and insipid. An honest assessment of one's self-controlled acts of imagining would reveal numerous examples of the same dull stripe. If flamboyance and extravagance do sometimes appear, they almost always emerge in the context of spontaneous imagining: the most exotic of my original examples was the dolphin sequence, which was also the most spontaneous. Not even spontaneous imagining, however, can be counted on for richness of content; it too is often trivial and lifeless.[27]

As a result of these reflections, we must make a final addition to our original formula, and thus arrive at a conclusion to this chapter:

> The imaginer cannot fail, in any significant sense, to imagine what, how, and when he wishes to—even though his efforts may have to be prolonged almost indefinitely and will never, even when successful, make what he imagines exist or cease to exist. But whatever the imaginer does succeed in imagining by virtue of his capacity for imaginative control is typically *just* what he intends and no more.

27. From these remarks we may infer that since the content of an act of ordinary imagining, spontaneous or controlled, is so often devoid of unusual interest, it will rarely merit aesthetic status by itself. Such content does not possess the intrinsic fascination that would make it worthy of aesthetic attention; it lacks what Berenson calls the "intransitive" character of works of art. Thus it is uncommon for an ordinary reverie to be recounted *as such*, without modification, in a short story or poem. This is not to deny that such a reverie may provide the occasion and even some specific ingredients for a given work of art. Nor is it to deny that an artist can discipline his or her imagination so as to make it into an indispensable ally in artistic activity. But none of this occurs in the everyday imagining that is our primary object of inquiry. In such imagining, the imaginative presentation is typically Spartan in simplicity and does not hold our attention as it might if it possessed greater internal complexity and richness of content.

CHAPTER FOUR

Self-Containedness and Self-Evidence

I

EACH SUCCESSIVE PAIR of essential traits under consideration in this part exhibits a different form of necessity. Thus, as we now know, spontaneity and controlledness embody an option-necessity in which the two traits are mutually exclusive yet jointly exhaustive. This means that one trait or the other, but only one at a time, may characterize any given aspect of imagining. In the case of self-containedness and self-evidence, in contrast, we have to do with a straightforward trait-necessity, that is, with the requirement that both traits characterize *all* aspects of every imaginative experience. Whereas it is an open option whether a given feature or phase of imagining will be spontaneous or controlled, the two traits presently in question always characterize every feature and phase of a particular experience of imagining. Moreover, instead of witnessing a situation in which two essential traits are complementary to each other and together compose a dyadic unit of essential necessity, we now confront a circumstance in which there is no such complementariness and thus no formation of a unified dyad. For each of the new traits is *by itself* characteristic of all of imaginative experience; each possesses, on its own, an inherent trait-necessity that extends to the phenomenon of imagination in its entirety.

This is not to claim, however, that self-containedness and self-evidence are wholly unrelated to each other. One of the two traits acts as a necessary condition for the other: to be self-evident is to presuppose a state of self-containedness. Unlike the relation of complementariness, though, this particular relation is not reciprocal: to be self-contained is not necessarily to be self-evident. Yet, despite the fact that self-containedness and self-evidence are closely linked with each other in this fashion, they are still not interrelated with the same stringency as are spontaneity and controlledness. They do not form a dyad which is essentially necessary qua binary unit. Rather, they remain a loosely knit pair of non-exclusive traits, each of which is separately essential to imagining as a whole.

II

The *self-containedness* of imagining manifests itself in a group of three distinctive characteristics: self-delimitation, discontinuity and unexplorability.

Self-Delimitation

As self-contained, imagining takes place within a psychical arena whose immediate boundaries are traced out by the imagining subject's own activity. Such boundaries serve to define a field within which imagined content may appear. This imaginal field reflects the particular interests or intentions of the imaginer; we might even say that it is *nothing but* the expression of these interests or intentions within a given imaginative presentation. The result is a phenomenon that may be called "the imaginal arc": what we imagine arises within a field of possible action determined by the activity of imagining itself. Activity and field of activity are co-extensive, each being the reflection of the other.[1]

Such strict self-determination of the proximal range of possible action is not found in other kinds of human experience. In perceptual experience, for instance, it is primarily the object or event perceived, not the perceiver, that determines the character and dimensions of the present field of action. The perceived object or event takes the lead, as it were, and the perceiving subject must follow this lead insofar as he continues to perceive. When I perceive a building, it is the building itself that establishes the immediate limits of the field of possible perceivings, which are constituted more crucially by the building than by my particular designs as a perceiver. Consequently, *what* is perceived assumes priority over the *act* of perceiving by virtue of determining the content, direction, and scope of this act.

In imagining, the situation is reversed. Here the act is primary inasmuch as its very realization marks off the boundaries of a particular imaginative experience. This is so in two ways. First, as just mentioned,

1. "Field" is here used metaphorically to indicate a range or spectrum of possible actions. It is not a spatial or quasi-spatial factor within imaginative experience as such—thus it forms no part of the imaginative presentation's world-frame of space and time.

my desires and designs as imaginer determine the field of possible imaginings open to me at a given moment; this field is a function of whatever is projected by my imaginative intentions. Second, the product of my imagining will possess certain general features that my imaginative activity imposes on it: the imaginal margin, the world-frame of space and time, etc. These features will be found to qualify *anything* that I imagine. Thus it is not the content (the "what") that is determinative in imaginative experience but the activity of imagining *per se*. This activity lays out the spectrum of possible ways in which a given *imaginatum* may appear. At the same time, nothing external to this activity determines in any *positive* way its immediate boundaries or range of maneuver.[2] In the absence of external determination we can only speak of a *self*-delimitation, a delimitation of imaginative experience *from within* by the consciously imagining self. Such delimitation by the activity of the imaginer himself provides us with a first characteristic of imagination's self-containedness.

Discontinuity

A second, and perhaps still more basic, aspect of imaginative self-containedness is found in the way in which the act of imagining is experienced as discontinuous with other mental acts.[3] This discontinuity is evidenced, to begin with, in that independence of causal context first discussed in the preceding chapter. Above all, the act of imagining is felt to be independent of *efficient* causation by another act; we do not experience it as either pushed or pulled into being by any other act or group of acts. This is not to deny that in certain cases a prior act may seem to provide the *occasion* for a given imaginative act. Even in such cases, however, there typically remains an absence of felt continuity between the occasioning and the occasioned act. And in most instances there is a distinctive *dis*-continuity, a sense of disconnection, between imagining and other acts. This discontinuity may vary in the degree of intensity with which it is felt, but it gives itself to us as something that is intrinsic, and not adventitious, to imaginative experience.

In perception or memory, by contrast, a given act is normally experienced as flowing into another act and thereby as forming part of a

2. I say "positive way" because the general limitations discussed in the preceding chapter serve as negative determinants of (i.e., specific constraints upon) imaginative activity. They designate what this activity *cannot* accomplish, whereas the activity itself determines precisely what *can* be accomplished within such limitations.

3. The term "act" in this section is to be understood in the generic sense of "mental act" and not in the narrow sense of act phase. Thus "act of imagining" will here be equivalent to imaginative experience as a whole, i.e., to what we have called the "act-*cum*-presentation" or "act-presentation."

series of intimately linked acts: e.g., as in the interconnected and over-lapping views we gain of a perceived object while walking around it.[4] No such series of strictly continuous, closely dovetailing acts is to be found in imaginative experience. Not only do individual acts of imagining tend to arise abruptly and disjunctively, but we cannot claim that any group of such acts constitutes a continuing apprehension of *one and the same* imagined object. Since no strict criterion of sameness—such as reidentifiability over time—is applicable to the ever-changing objects of imagining, no group of imaginings can achieve the continuity that links together various apprehensions of a selfsame perceived or remembered object.[5]

The discontinuity exhibited by self-contained imaginative experiences is of two basic sorts. (a) On the one hand, a given act of imagining is felt to be essentially discontinuous with strictly nonimaginative acts, e.g., acts of perception, memory, or sheer intellection. None of them joins forces with imagining as coordinate components of some larger synthetic whole, e.g., 'imagining-and-perceiving-X'. However close together in time they may occur and despite their similarity of content 'imagining X' remains distinct from 'perceiving X'. (b) On the other hand, a given act of imagining is also felt to be discontinuous with *other acts of imagining* that precede or follow it. At the most, several imaginative acts may form a loose sequence of the kind that was found in at least two of our original examples (i.e., the swimming dolphins and the Rawls seminar). But such a sequence does not represent an intrinsically interconnected *series* of phenomena. There is present here a contrast that can be expressed in the following formalistic fashion:

A. *Series* of (perceptual, mnemonic, etc.) acts:

$x_1 - x_2 - x_3 - x_4 - x_5 \ldots$

B. *Sequence* of (imaginative) acts:

x y z . . .

4. To be consulted here is Aron Gurwitsch's account of the essential continuity within a series of linked perceptual noemata. Cf. *The Field of Consciousness* (Pittsburgh: Duquesne University Press, 1964), pp. 234-45. See also Hubert Dreyfus, "The Perceptual Noema: Gurwitsch's Crucial Contribution" in L. E. Embree, ed., *Life-World and Consciousness* (Evanston: Northwestern University Press, 1972).

5. In fact it may be said that only material entities are strictly reidentifiable and thus are selfsame objects of continuous, connected apprehensions. In support of this view, see P. F. Strawson, *Individuals*, 2nd ed. (London: Methuen, 1965), part I. Consequently, we must be skeptical of claims as to the sameness or self-identity of imagined objects, as in the following assertion of James Kuehl: "Successive image-noemata appear and can be noemata of the *same* object" ("Perceiving and Imagining," *Philosophy and Phenomenological Research* [1970], XXXI, p. 217; my italics).

[The dash between letters indicates an experiential (though not necessarily causal) connection; the reiteration of the same letter as in x_1, x_2, etc., indicates the possibility of aiming at the *same* object or event by successive acts of the same type; and a different letter indicates a unit of experience which is discontinuous with other units in character and content.]

The discontinuity of imagining may seem to be only partial in view of the undeniable fact that the specific content of what we imagine is sometimes borrowed from other types of mental presentation, especially those of a perceptual or mnemonic nature. Moreover, in a given case there may be several such borrowings: to imagine a unicorn is typically to draw upon memories of perceptions of pictures of the mythical beast and perhaps also upon previous imaginings of the creature. Nevertheless, the hybrid *origin* of such content does not eliminate the discontinuity between the appearance of this content in a given imaginative presentation and its appearance elsewhere. For this presentation in its unique patterning—as constituted by a particular world-frame, imaginal margin, and mode of givenness—is not experientially continuous with other imaginative or nonimaginative presentations. Whatever the particular provenance of imagined content, once this content has been incorporated into a full imaginative presentation it is not experienced as a strictly separate feature of this presentation. Each successive imaginative presentation appears as fully "totalized"—as possessing a single inclusive gestalt. Consequently, the borrowing of specific content does not overcome the felt discontinuity between a given imaginative experience and other experiences, including those from which the specific content itself has been taken.

Unexplorability

When we perceive something, we often follow up an initial and incomplete perception by a series of further perceivings in and through which we explore the perceived object or event in increasing detail. The very nature of what we perceive makes such exploration possible, and this is so even if it does not always actively provoke it. What we imagine, in contrast, discourages exploration by its very nature. This stems from the fact that the imaginative presentation, and thus its specific content, is *given all at once* to the imaginer. To be given all at once is to lack concealed, still-to-be-disclosed aspects and hence to render exploration superfluous. Why explore what is given immediately and in its entirety?

One might counter that some perceptual objects are also given all at once: e.g., a cube of transparent glass. Do we not see at a glance all the explorable features of such an object? Even if we do, though, a crucial distinction between perceived and imagined objects remains. A perceptual object, no matter how fully or clearly it may be given, always presents itself as open to *further* exploration because, at the very least, the perceiver may assume successively different positions from which to view it. As a perceiver of the glass cube, I am able to station myself at various new vantage points so as to become more thoroughly acquainted with the cube, however limited or unprofitable such further acquaintance may be. In imagining, there is no such displaceability of standpoint. When I imagine something, I cannot, strictly speaking, take up different successive views of a single, self-identical, and enduring object, and thus become better acquainted with it. This means that I cannot come to apprehend the "other sides" of such an object by changing my standpoint. An imagined object is not the sort of object that *has* other sides to be revealed in subsequent viewings. For what I imagine has an irrevocable *frontal* character: it is always given as facing me (and I it) and as lacking that depth or three-dimensionality necessary for the exploration of full-bodied objects.[6] An imagined entity is ineluctably front-sided, and in this respect it might be compared to a movie set that is meant to be seen from one side alone. Unlike the movie set, however, it *cannot* be seen from the other side. Being strictly depthless, an imagined object possesses no sides or surfaces other than those which it expressly proffers within a given imaginative presentation.

What we imagine lacks depth in two senses. First, it has no *exterior* depth. By this is meant that it is not positioned in a spatial field in such a way that I could determine its actual distance from my own position as its observer. In other words, there is no recession in depth— no ordered succession of progressively more remote spatial planes or sectors. Second, an imagined object does not present itself as having the sort of strictly *interior* depth that is the basis for the palpability and plenitude of perceived objects. Lacking any sense of inherent mass or solidity and thus any *bona fide* lateral or rear surfaces, the imagined object is constrained to appear in a somewhat flattened and foreshortened manner and as situated in a shallow, quasi-planar space.[7]

6. As Maurice Merleau-Ponty has said, "the imaginary has no depth, and does not respond to efforts to vary points of view [upon it]" (*Phenomenology of Perception*, trans. C. Smith [New York: Humanities Press, 1962], p. 323).

7. By using the term "quasi-planar," I am deliberately stopping short of the claim that the imaginative presentation is comparable to the strictly flat surface of a geometrical plane. For one thing, the imaginative presentation as a whole is not even strictly *two*-dimensional: it has no actual spatial dimensions in the Euclidean

The compression of what we imagine into unexplorable frontal surfaces represents the strongest sense of self-containedness in imaginative experience. In every instance, though most dramatically in visual imagining, this experience exhibits a frontality within which there is nothing more to explore than what is given. And what is given is given in such an immediately accessible and self-enclosed way that it can be taken in at a single apprehension. Frontality and unexplorability, then, are intrinsically linked; to be given as irrevocably and only frontal is to be given as incapable of further exploration. To attempt such exploration—say, to become clearer about a certain detail in a particular imaginative presentation—is perforce to summon up a *different* presentation, a presentation with its own unique configuration. In attending to this new presentation, we cannot claim to be exploring exactly the same imagined object or event that appeared in the initial presentation. Thus, exploration in any significant sense—i.e., in any sense in which we can be said to discover something genuinely new and previously unknown in what we imagine—is precluded. A necessary condition of exploration is the presence of undiscovered aspects (parts, sides, surfaces, etc.) in the object or event being explored. But there is *nothing new to be discovered* in the content of any given imaginative presentation, since there is nothing *in* such content beyond what we already know *of* it. It lacks that not-yet-disclosed character which is a precondition of discovery.[8]

---

sense, possessing instead its own sense of spatial dimensionality. Furthermore, in some imaginative presentations there *is* a certain delimited feeling of depth—a "pseudo-depth," as we might call it. The imaginer feels that he can penetrate just beyond the immediately presented frontal surface of the presentation. Unlike perceptual depth, however, this shallow imaginal depth resists active exploration, since it does not *remain* to be explored by our mental eye or ear.

8. To claim this is not, however, to argue that there is nothing new to be discovered in an imaginative presentation *because* it is we as imaginers who have made it what it is: in other words, that imagined content in particular contains only what we put into it. (This view is put forth by Sartre in *Psychology of Imagination*, pp. 11-13; it can also be found in S. J. Todes, "Comparative Phenomenology of Perception and Imagination: Part II, Imagination," *Journal of Existentialism* [1966], VII, pp. 5, 9.) This is essentially a causal argument; it attempts to *explain* why there is no significant sense of exploration or discovery in imagining. Such an argument may be perfectly plausible on its own terms. But it can form no part of an intrinsically descriptive account. The latter concerns itself only with what is experienced or experienceable in imagination—that is, with *how* we imagine and not with *why* we do so in the way that we do. Thus it cannot argue in the form: 'we experience such-and-such *because* such-and-such else is the case'. Whether or not the imaginer is *ultimately* (i.e., causally) responsible for all imagined content, the phenomenological point is that he experiences this content, and indeed the entire imaginative presentation, as radically frontal and unexplorable. It is this experience, and this alone, that forms the basis of a properly phenomenological analysis.

III

Self-evidence in the sense to be described here presupposes self-containedness. For something to be self-evident in imagination it must be given as self-contained—that is, as delimited by the imaginer's own activity, discontinuous with other acts and presentations, and essentially unexplorable. These basic subfeatures of self-containedness help to bring about a situation in which the self-evidence of imagining becomes possible. Such self-evidence can occur only insofar as an imaginative experience has freed itself from its surrounding circumstances to the extent of being able to present its *own* evidence. For it to lack self-evidence in this sense would mean being forced to draw upon evidence stemming from *other* experiences. The self-containedness of imagining, then, eliminates the need for extraneous evidence and allows the imaginative act-*cum*-presentation to be experienced as genuinely self-evident. If I image, say, a five-legged turtledove, I am presented with something that is at once self-contained and unambiguously just the object I set out to imagine. I do not need to seek for further evidence to strengthen my conviction that I am in fact imagining such a creature.

From these preliminary observations we may infer the strict *irrelevance of other kinds of evidence* to a given imaginative experience. Precisely insofar as this experience is contained within itself, evidence from other sources—whether from perception, memory, or thinking, or even from other instances of imagining—does not bear directly upon the experience in question. Each imaginative experience, in short, is evidentially self-sufficient.

The self-evidence of imagining possesses two distinctive and closely related characteristics: non-corrigibility and apodicticity.

Non-Corrigibility

Traditionally the term "incorrigible" (i.e., not subject to correction) has been applied by Western philosophers to two quite different kinds of thing: on the one hand, to what rationalists call "truths of reason" (including, and often as a paradigm, analytic *a priori* truths); on the other hand, to sensory experience (especially in the form of "sense-data"), wherein we are presumed to be in immediate contact with what is directly given to the senses. Because of their persistent concern with incorrigibility in these two forms (and sometimes in still others as well), Western philosophers have been accused of exhibiting an almost obsessive "quest for certainty"[9] in their unremitting "pursuit

9. Cf. John Dewey, *Quest for Certainty* (New York: Putnam, 1960), passim.

of the incorrigible."[10] Whether this accusation is merited or not, one thing is difficult to deny: philosophers have rarely, if ever, sought incorrigibility in the realm of imagination. When Aristotle said that "imaginings are for the most part false,"[11] he assumed, as most philosophers of mind after him have continued to assume, that imagination is essentially corrigible. Moreover, not only is imagining held to be subject to correction; it is also seen as error-*prone*, as characteristically *needing* correction. As the most misleading of faculties, imagination is considered to be predisposed to untruth. Pascal, echoing an entire tradition, called imagination "the mistress of falsehood and error."[12]

Yet this traditional view of imagination is on the wrong track. Closer consideration shows that imagining is strictly *non*-corrigible in character. To be "non-corrigible" is not to be subject to truth *or* error in the conventional, correspondential sense of these terms. As such, non-corrigibility differs both from corrigibility (which allows for both truth *and* error) and from *in*corrigibility (which is concerned exclusively with truth). Consequently, we cannot say that imaginative experience is always true—as if its evidence were incorrigible. By the same token, however, we also cannot say with Aristotle that imagining is "for the most part false." But since Aristotle's claim has a perennial appeal, its unsoundness must be shown in somewhat more detail at this point.

As non-corrigible, imagining is not subject to untruth or falsehood of any sort: it cannot be wrong or mistaken if there is no way for it to be in error. As J. E. R. Squires writes concerning this aspect of imagining, "There is no room for being fooled by the appearance of a mental image in the way that we can be fooled by the appearance of a stick in water or taken in by a conjuror's sleight of hand."[13] How is this so? In the examples of perceptual illusion mentioned by Squires there is an existent or "true" state of affairs against which illusory appearances and mistaken judgments can be measured. In imagining, by contrast, there is *nothing with respect to which* the imaginer can be said to be mistaken, for there is no extra-imaginal state of affairs with which to compare the imaginative presentation: imagining is in this regard all appearance and nothing but appearance. All that is evidentially relevant is given within imaginative experience itself. This experience, revealing itself totally, contains nothing that might be mis-apprehended

10. See J. L. Austin, *Sense and Sensibilia* (Oxford University Press, 1962), p. 104.

11. *De Anima*, 428a 9-10.

12. *Pensées*, ed. L. Lafuma (Paris: Seuil, 1962), p. 54.

13. "Visualizing," *Mind* (1968), XXVII, pp. 60-61. What Squires calls "mental image" I would call "imaginative presentation."

or mis-taken. How could we mistakenly apprehend what is given all at once and without residue?[14]

As imaginers, we are always already at one with what is imagined because of the perfect match between it and our own activity of imagining. What we think we are imagining and what we are indeed imagining form a mutual fit. And if this is the case, there is no way in which we can *mistake* the course or content of our own imaginative experience. In perceptual experience, in comparison, there can very well be mistaken apprehensions and thus also a correction of these misapprehensions: we can rectify our misperception of a stick in water or learn the basis of a magician's trick because the discrepancy between the misperception and the existent state of affairs can be determined with precision. In imagining no such discrepancy can occur in the first place; hence it is senseless to speak of "correcting" it.

Should we say then that imagining is *self*-correcting? Is it correctable by its *own* evidence? Tempting as such a notion might be, it is still incompatible with imagination's intrinsic non-corrigibility. For if imagination cannot be said to be mistaken, it cannot be said to need correction of *any* kind, not even a correction that it would make in regard to its own operations. Here the critical question is: *in terms of what* would it correct itself? In imagining there is nothing to which to appeal other than imaginative experience itself. And this experience, being essentially evanescent and disjunctive, cannot engender or embody a constant, objective standard in terms of which it might correct itself were it somehow to go astray.[15]

No experience of imagining, in sum, can be falsified by appeal to additional evidence: *there is no additional evidence* to bring to bear upon this experience. Thus falsifiability must be ruled out. But if imaginative experience is thus non-falsifiable, is it in any sense *verifiable?* The response to this question must also be negative. For verifiability requires the possibility of intersubjective confirmation, and in imagining any such confirmation is excluded in the nature of the case. Presenting itself to the imaginer alone, imagining is ineluctably first-person in

14. In fact we do not even grasp or "take" what we imagine, at least not in any sense comparable to what Chisholm calls "sensible taking." (See R. M. Chisholm, *Perceiving* [Ithaca: Cornell University Press, 1957], pp. 85 ff.) We must also deny to imagining any element of "interpretation," as in Heidegger's notion of the "existential-hermeneutical 'as'." (Cf. Martin Heidegger, *Being and Time*, trans. E. Robinson and J. Macquarrie [New York: Harper, 1962], pp. 188-203.)

15. Such a standard implies rule-regulatedness—that is, a basis for grouping together diverse instances under the aegis of a single rule. But as Kant said, the products of imagination are "determined by no assignable rule" (*Critique of Pure Reason*, A570 B598, p. 487). Lacking rules in any strict sense, and thus a standard of truth, imagining cannot be said to be self-correcting.

character. I can, of course, make specific claims concerning what I experience, but it would be futile for others to consult *their* imaginings to determine if what I say of *my* imagining is true. Since they cannot confirm my claims, their responses to such claims must take the form either of believing me or of suspecting that I am being deceitful in my verbal reports. As R. S. Benjamin says; "No first-person statement that asserts an inner experience like the possession of an image . . . can be corrected by a third person. It must be accepted as true or rejected as a lie; it cannot be shown to be mistaken."[16]

But in what sense can we legitimately speak of first-person reports of imagining as "true"? We may grant that these reports cannot rightly be called true in terms of whether they correspond to others' reports of their own firsthand experiences. Nor does it make sense to refer to a "veridical" state of affairs to which all such reports (mine and others') might correspond. Yet the correspondence model of truth, which is operative in such misplaced analyses, is not the only model at our disposal. In fact, the very specialness of imaginative experience casts suspicion on the idea that the traditional correspondential model adequately reflects the range of the human experience of truth. Without attempting to set forth an alternative model here,[17] I shall simply suggest that there is a distinctively non-correspondential and non-verificationist sense in which first-person reports of imaginative experience may be said to be true. This is the sense in which the imaginer is capable of making a nondeceitful report to others concerning his own authentic experience of imagining.[18] In other words, in making a true report of one's imaginative experience, one is *not* reporting what was not experienced and *is* describing what was experienced. But the kind of truth that is obtained in this way is considerably constricted in scope, for it is mainly a question of not misleading others. Truth in imagining is thus a truth of nondeceit; it is a matter of truthfully reporting to others the imaginative experience one has had oneself. Yet *the evidence for this experience remains non-corrigible.* It is unmistakably self-evident to

16. "Remembering" in *Essays in Philosophical Psychology*, ed. D. F. Gustafson (Garden City, N.Y.: Doubleday, 1964), p. 174. Cf. also the statement on p. 175: "the important logical difference between statements about one's inner and private experiences and statements about the external and public world [runs] along the gap separating claims that may be true, mistaken or deceitful, and those that can only be true or deceitful."

17. For a discussion of such an alternative notion, see my articles: "Man, Self, and Truth," in *The Monist* (1971), LV, esp. 246-54; and "Truth in Art," in *Man and World* (1970), III, pp. 351-68.

18. By an "authentic experience" is meant an experience that the imaginer actually has had and not one that he merely pretends to have had or one that he has been deceived into believing he has had.

the imaginer himself, whatever he may say or claim about it to others. In short, the imaginer may deceive others (and be deceived by them in turn), but *he cannot deceive himself* concerning his own imagining.

Apodicticity

Philosophers have traditionally discussed apodicticity in terms of the state of certainty that is attendant upon the grasping of logically necessary truths. Kant, for example, writes that "geometrical propositions are one and all apodictic, that is, are bound up with the consciousness of their necessity."[19] In imagining, we have to do with possibility, not with necessity—with what might be rather than with what has to be. Nevertheless, imaginative experience induces in the imaginer a state of certainty that is at least analogous to the certainty with which logical truths are grasped. The analogy consists in the common conviction that what we apprehend in the two cases is strictly indubitable. Just as I cannot doubt the validity of a syllogism in Barbara form, so I cannot doubt that what I imagine is appearing to me precisely as it presents itself to me. My certainty is unshakable with regard to what arises in imaginative form. However contingent or uncertain its origins or future course may be, once it appears and just insofar as it appears, it becomes an immediate object of unassailable certainty on my part.

Apodicticity is an inherent feature of self-evidence of any kind. When we experience an object, event, or state of affairs as self-evident, we experience it as an indubitable presence, something that we cannot reasonably doubt. The intimate link between apodicticity and self-evidence is implicit in Husserl's description of self-evidence as "the quite pre-eminent mode of consciousness that consists in the *self-appearance*, the *self-exhibiting*, the *self-giving*, of an affair, an affair-complex (or state of affairs), a universality, a value, or other objectivity in the final mode: 'itself there', 'immediately intuited', 'given *originaliter*'."[20] To be presented with such complete and unmediated givenness is to be furnished with indubitable evidence of what one experiences. That something appears in such a self-revealing way to consciousness rules out any uncertainty as to its qualities or structure. This in fact is just the situation which obtains in imaginative experience. In undergoing this experience, the imaginer finds himself to be in possession of incontrovertible evidence concerning the nature of the particular act-*cum*-presentation of which he is conscious at a given time.

19. *Critique of Pure Reason*, B41, p. 70. Cf. also the passages at B47, p. 75, and at A75, p. 110.
20. *Cartesian Meditations*, trans. D. Cairns (The Hague: Nijhoff, 1960), p. 57. Husserl's italics.

The entire imaginative experience, then, appears transparently through the evidence with which it is given—or more exactly, it appears *with* or *in* this evidence. Because such evidence illuminates all aspects of the experience without remainder, it is true *self*-evidence, evidence which is apodictic in status.

We must be careful, however, not to confuse apodicticity with *adequacy*. Evidence that is genuinely apodictic is evidence given *totum simul*. Adequate evidence, in contrast, is given only gradually and partially, never fully. Such evidence finds its paradigm in perceptual experience. Whenever we perceive, we are presented with evidence that is always more or less partial—hence more or less *in*adequate in terms of the full presentation of what is perceived. Perceiving, writes Husserl, carries with it

> a multiform horizon of unfulfilled anticipations . . . [Perception's] imperfect evidence becomes more nearly perfect in the actualizing synthetic transitions from evidence to evidence, but necessarily in such a manner that no imaginable synthesis of this kind is completed as [perfectly] adequate evidence: any such synthesis must always involve unfulfilled, expectant, and accompanying meanings.[21]

Thus, even though we can collect considerable evidence bearing on a perceived object or event, we can never know this object or event with perfect adequacy: evidential completeness here remains a regulative, and not an actually attainable, ideal. The result is that the perceiver cannot claim strict certainty and must constantly ask himself: Is this *all* of the evidence? Is there not *still more* to come?

In imaginative experience such questions do not arise. When we imagine, we are not concerned with the adequacy of existing evidence. Indeed, in imagining there is no *collection* of evidence in the first place. For imaginative evidence is acquired *tout d'un coup* or not at all. Although this all-at-once and all-or-nothing evidential character is also found in the apprehension of logically necessary truths, it is still more strikingly present in the experience of imagining. Where there must typically be extensive preparation for insight into logical truths—even if the insight itself may come in a flash—in the case of imaginative experience there need be no such preparatory stage. Instead, by the sheer activity of imagining, the imaginer finds himself to be immediately in possession of whatever insight he seeks, since the evidence escorting this insight to consciousness comes without fail and without delay. Just as the act of imagining cannot (in any significant sense) fail to occur

21. Ibid., p. 62.

as the imaginer intends it to, so the imaginer cannot fail to be presented with evidence that, being wholly and transparently given, cannot be doubted.

Let us suppose that I am looking at the "artificial mountain" in the garden of New College, Oxford. As first perceived from the garden gate, this massive object gives itself to me as a protuberance arising from surrounding flat areas. If I do not know the history of the garden, I take the protuberance to be a small hill—a part of nature that has always been in just this place. So far, there is no reason to question this presumption, and yet I cannot claim to have adequate evidence concerning *precisely what* has appeared to me. In fact, I must walk around, perhaps climb to the summit of, and possibly even dig into the hill before I can ascertain more exactly the character and structure of the object before me. In becoming more familiar with this object, I may at last come to suspect that it is man-made, despite its unartificial appearance. In any event, I cannot claim that my initial perception was a sufficient basis for determining the true nature of the hill. No matter how unambiguous this perception may have been, it was no more than a starting point for the collection of increasingly adequate evidence, evidence that may or may not confirm my first impressions. For the certainty with which I initially perceive any object, however familiar or obvious it may be, is only a relative certainty which is subject to modification or cancellation at some later point.

When I imagine, quite a different situation arises. Here my initial apprehension *is* decisive—so decisive that it takes only a single mental glance to garner all the evidence required for strict certainty. No recourse to further evidence is called for. Nor is it even possible. How can this be? Let us suppose that I now *imagine* an artificial mountain, one with a different shape, size, and setting from the actual mound in the New College garden. The imaginative presentation I thereby conjure up gives itself to me totally and with self-evidence. There is no means of gaining an additional, much less an improved, view of *this* presentation or its content. It is true that I can manage to summon up *another* presentation with seemingly the same content. Yet this second presentation cannot be said to be the second member of a series of apprehensions that afford me a progressively more intimate acquaintance with a given object. There is no augmentation of insight as my mind moves from one imaginative presentation to the next and thus no way of acquiring increasingly adequate evidence through successive acts of imagining.

Therefore, every new imaginative presentation gives me *an* (not *the* or *the same*) imagined object in transparent self-evidence. The evidence with which each successive content is given presents itself not only all at once but *once and for all*: I cannot supplement it in any significant way. As a consequence, the apodicticity of imaginative evidence is at once a distinguishing mark and a delimiting factor. The evidential givenness of other mental acts, particularly of perception, does not allow for the same degree of certainty combined with the same completeness of presentation. At the same time, other acts are capable of profiting from the accumulation of evidence in past or future experiences. Imaginative evidence proper is limited to what can be apprehended at the very moment of imagining, that is, to what a single and unrepeatable experience yields.

The foregoing remarks allow us to appreciate the truth in Husserl's otherwise enigmatic claim that *"adequacy and apodicticity* of evidence *need not go hand in hand."*[22] In the case of imagination this claim may even be strengthened: the two kinds of evidence not only need not, but *cannot*, go hand in hand. For the notion of adequate evidence has no place within imaginative experience. Which is not to say that imaginative evidence is to be considered *in*adequate. The evidence we encounter in imagining is *neither adequate nor inadequate.*

This conclusion is strikingly similar to that reached in our earlier discussion of the non-corrigible. Just as the non-corrigibility of imaginative evidence means that such evidence cannot be described as true *or* false (in any traditional sense), so the apodicticity inherent in the same kind of evidence renders it resistant to description in terms of either adequacy *or* inadequacy. In fact, the two conclusions are not merely parallel to each other; they also indicate two coordinate ways of distinguishing imagining from perceiving. On the one hand, in perceiving it is the possibility of gaining increasingly adequate evidence that provides a basis for making (correspondentially) true statements about what we perceive and for correcting past statements: adequacy and corrigibility are here closely linked. On the other hand, in imagining there is no correlation between having more evidence and being more correct in one's claims concerning what is imagined. While the question of truth as correctness (and of adequate evidence for such truth) arises unavoidably in perception, it does not arise at all in experiences of imagining: here evidential adequacy and corrigibility are both ruled out of court. The result may be expressed thus:

perception		corrigibility	adequacy
imagination		non-corrigibility	apodicticity

22. *Cartesian Meditations*, p. 22; his italics.

It is precisely through the combination of apodicticity and non-corrigibility that imagining becomes a self-evident experience which cannot deceive us in any significant fashion. If imagining reveals itself to the imaginer totally, there is no possibility of concealment or dissimulation. And to be unconcealing and undissimulating in this manner is to be a genuinely self-evident act.

Self-contained and self-evident, imaginative experience is in both respects a self-sufficing experience, an experience that takes place exclusively within the psychical interface lying between the imaginer and his own autonomous activity. Such activity suffices for itself, being contained within its own self-prescribed boundaries and showing itself with pellucid self-evidence. As self-determining and self-aware, this activity fully discloses itself in its self-enclosed and self-enclosing character. As self-transparent, what is imagined on any given occasion is at one with the mind of the imaginer. Nowhere else within the spectrum of mental acts do we discover such complete concrescence of mind with the products of its own activity.

CHAPTER FIVE

Indeterminacy and Pure Possibility

I

As THE FINAL eidetic traits of imagining, indeterminacy and pure possibility may be differentiated in two ways from the pairs of traits treated in preceding chapters. First of all, they stand in a different relation *to each other* than the previously considered pairs. As we know, spontaneity and controlledness are mutually exclusive of each other while at the same time jointly exhaustive of the domain of imaginative experience they serve to specify. Self-containedness is related to self-evidence as a necessary condition of the latter. Indeterminacy and pure possibility, on the other hand, are neither mutually exclusive (since both can characterize the same aspect at the same time) nor jointly exhaustive (since they do not as a pair constitute a single coherent domain of imaginative experience). Nor does one function as a necessary condition for the other, as there can be pure possibility in the absence of indeterminacy and vice versa. Rather, they are related to each other in a significantly different way: as *mutually facilitating*. The more indeterminate something is or appears to be, the more it will tend to present itself as purely possible; and the more purely possible something is or appears to be, the greater the tendency for it to be indeterminate in form.

A second distinguishing characteristic of indeterminacy and pure possibility is found in the fact that they exhibit a special kind of *essential necessity*. As contrasted with spontaneity and controlledness, these traits do not form an option-necessity dyad in which one or the other (but not both) must characterize every aspect of a given imaginative experience. Rather, each of the new traits embodies a straightforward, non-optional trait-necessity. Yet, as distinguished from self-containedness and self-evidence, they do not possess a general trait-necessity pertaining to both of imagination's intentional phases (and to all aspects of each phase). Instead, indeterminacy and pure possibility exhibit a *partial* trait-necessity, characterizing only certain structures of the full phenomenon of imagination. For we have to do with two traits which inhere in the object phase alone and which are not present with equal prominence even within this particular area of imaginative experience. The following table sums up this form of comparative assessment:

Type of Essential Necessity	Essential Traits
(1) option-necessity (general in scope, applying to all aspects of imagination)	controlledness-spontaneity (regarded as dyadic unit)
(2) trait-necessity	
(a) general—i.e., as applicable to both intentional phases and to all components of each phase	self-containedness, self-evidence
(b) partial—i.e., as applicable to the object phase alone (and differentially to the various components of this phase)	indeterminacy, pure possibility

II

Although only rarely singled out in previous psychological or philosophical accounts, *indeterminacy* is one of the most crucial of the essential features of imagination. What we imagine is intrinsically indeterminate in character. It is indefinite in such a way as not to allow for an increase in definiteness, much less for the achievement of constant or complete definiteness. This is not to claim that what we imagine is *entirely* indeterminate; if it were, we could not then be said to imagine anything in particular—i.e., anything nameable or otherwise specifiable. Yet we always find ourselves imagining specified or specifiable objects or states of affairs, and this is the case whether our imagining occurs in a spontaneous or in a controlled fashion. Indeed, my claim in chapter three concerning the strict inability of controlled imagining to fail presupposes that what we imagine has a certain definiteness, however minimal it may be. Without *some* definiteness, we would have no basis for judging whether a given imaginative presentation successfully fulfills a particular intention or not. If I set out to imagine a hippogriff, what I succeed in imagining must have sufficient form or shape to be recognizable *as* a hippogriff, or else I cannot claim to have imagined any such mythical beast. In spontaneous imagining it is not a question of fulfilling explicit intentions, but what is imagined must still possess enough coherency for it to count as the *specific* content of an imaginative experience. In fact, I cannot claim to have imagined *at all* unless I can be said to have imagined *something*. However thoroughly indeterminate this "something" may be, it must be specifiable in some respect or other if it is to serve as the intentional correlate of my act of imagining.

As essential indeterminacy was unmistakably present in the original examples cited in chapter one: e.g., the indefiniteness of the dolphins' faces and of their swimming motions; the vagueness of the background surrounding the imagined flamingo cry; and the indistinctness with which the seminar leaders were presented in the Rawls sequence. But let us consider a fresh example that will bring out more clearly the peculiarities of imaginative indeterminacy.[1]

I decide suddenly to imagine a mermaid. So as to avoid undue influence from standard depictions of this familiar figure, I attempt to alter the conventional mermaid form by imagining its top half as a fish's head and torso and its bottom half as the legs of a woman.[2] The project is readily realized: a figure answering to the description just given drifts before my mental gaze. But I notice that if I try to make this mermaid-like figure more determinate, I run into difficulties. I try, for example, to visualize exactly where the figure's legs begin to grow out from its fishlike torso. If I were *perceiving* such a creature in person or in pictorial form, I could specify a fairly precise area in which this outgrowth of legs occurs. But in the case of the imagined mermaid I can make no such specification. What I find upon examining the imaginative presentation is that there is an indeterminate region from which the mermaid's legs seem to extend outward but that, no matter how carefully I scan this region, I cannot determine its exact extent or indicate just where the mermaid's legs can be said to begin. In short, their point of origin reveals itself to be radically indeterminable.

Let us now contrast this situation with what happens in perceptual experience. What we perceive may also appear indeterminately and as vaguely located. Looking out of a window of the library in which I am presently writing, I see a statue of a woman shrouded in shadow.

1. The term "indeterminacy" will be used to designate the essential trait *per se*, while "indeterminateness" will signify the actual embodiment of this trait in a given imaginative presentation. "Indeterminability," a second aspect of indeterminacy, will refer to the difficulty we experience in attempting to make an imaginative presentation more determinate than it already is.

2. I shall continue to call this concoction a "mermaid," though perhaps it should be termed a "maidmer"!

I cannot now (it is dusk) say exactly where her right arm, which is curled inward toward the central mass of her body, begins. The point of origin of the perceived arm is initially as indeterminate as the point of origin of my imagined mermaid's legs. But the decisive difference between the two cases is that I know that I *can* determine the exact zone where the perceived arm starts. Tomorrow when it is brighter, or even tonight when a spotlight may be trained on the statue, I shall be able to see where the statue's right arm begins. Nor am I limited to direct seeing as a method of determination: I can also climb onto the statue in the dark and feel with my hands where it begins, or even consult a photograph of the same object.

In imagining, by contrast, such methods of disclosure are not available. There is no way in which I can determine the precise point or area where imagined objects begin or end, or exactly where they are located. These objects are strictly indeterminable in such respects and in others as well. Here we may concur with Sartre when he writes, "A hare which is vaguely perceived is in itself a determinate hare. But a hare which is the object of a vague image is an indeterminate hare."[3] A perceived object, then, remains determinate even though in certain circumstances it may be perceived as indefinite, while an imagined object is *inherently* indeterminate and can *never* be apprehended as perfectly definite. What we imagine not only presents itself as indeterminate at first glance; it also proves to be strictly indeterminable in subsequent efforts to make it more explicit in character or structure. As in the grasping of imaginative evidence, one's first apprehension is decisive; here too there are no second chances.

Thus far we have been referring for the most part to the essential indeterminacy of the object phase in general. Yet this phase is itself complex in structure, and we cannot assume that all of its parts exhibit the same kind or degree of indeterminacy. Consequently, we must consider how this trait appears in each of the basic components of the object phase.

Imagined Content

Imagined *objects* are indeterminate as a whole. Their vagueness, however, does not necessarily pertain equally to all of their parts. Some parts are more, some less, indeterminate than others. To cite again the imagined mermaid: when I repeatedly imagine such a figure, sometimes the leg region is given more determinately, and sometimes the head-and-torso region; but rarely are both regions given with equal

3. *Psychology of Imagination*, p. 19.

definiteness of detail. Moreover, my apprehending of an imagined object such as this has an inconstant, intermittent quality that is to be distinguished from the steadiness with which I may apprehend all of the presented features of a perceived object. Imaginative attention is typically cursory in character, flitting from one momentary point of interest to another. In its ephemerality, a given imagined object cannot sustain the imaginer's mental look indefinitely. Not only does it tend to fade rapidly from view, but even in the moment of apprehension it has a peculiarly uneven, undulating character.

Imagined *states of affairs* are also essentially indeterminate. Suppose that I begin once more with a mermaid of the type described above, but instead of imagining (i.e., "imaging") her as an isolated and unmoving object, I envision her as swimming under water in a murky sea, propelling herself by kicking her legs in froglike fashion. Gradually she rises toward the surface, emerges from the water, and seats herself on a protruding rock on which she dries herself in the sun. Here I have imagined a succession of different state of affairs, which together constitute a single sequence or episode. This episode is indeterminate both as a whole and in terms of the successive states of affairs that comprise it. If I attempt now to focus on these states of affairs, I soon realize that each one is quite elusive. One by one and in succession, they all disappeared into the evolving episode; none of them can be isolated and made determinate. The entire episode presents itself as a strange sequence of *tableaux vivants*—of motions suspended in midair and lacking in continuity and definite direction.

The imagined *world-frame* contributes to the indeterminacy of specific imagined content. The world-frame, it will be recalled, is the peculiar spatio-temporal setting in terms of which imagined objects and states of affairs appear. I say "in terms of which" and not "*in* which," for neither imaginal space nor imaginal time form a fixed field within which imaginative phenomena can be given determinate locations. Both of these frame factors lack the rigorously ordered structure and the all-inclusiveness of the spatial and temporal networks that serve as bases of location for perceptual phenomena.[4] As a consequence,

---

4. As Kant and Strawson have argued, any perceived object or event *must* be locatable in such totally encompassing networks. Cf. Kant, *Critique of Pure Reason*, B38-40, B46-48, and Strawson, *Individuals*, pp. 10-19. By transcendental arguments both philosophers attempt to show that there has to be a single, unified space and a single, unified time for all of perceptual experience. In imaginative experience, by contrast, there appears to be a different spatial and temporal system—or, more exactly, a different mini-system—for each successive imaginative presentation. No universal (or universalizable) system of space or of time is imputable to what we imagine.

the objects and states of affairs that go to make up specific imagined content lack definite positions, not being locatable within an encompassing and stable spatio-temporal grid. They present themselves instead within a decidedly indeterminate arena, a dimly defined region of pure appearance.

Imaginal Margin

The imaginal margin is the embodiment *par excellence* of indeterminacy in imaginative experience. This component of the imaginative presentation possesses very few, if any, designatable properties. There is no definite point at which we can say that the margin begins and imagined content ends. It has no determinable width or depth, and it does not terminate in any precise perimeter: it just trails off without appearing to end anywhere in particular. Furthermore, the margin is itself subject to considerable variation in form and function. In some instances it seems hardly to be present at all, as when the imaginer's attention is concentrated on an especially vivid imagined object or state of affairs. Careful consideration of imaginative experience reveals, however, that some trace of it is almost always present in the form of a pale, penumbral area into which specific imagined content and its world-frame imperceptibly fade.

Hence the imaginal margin is not a discrete or distinct zone of the imaginative presentation that rings around the content of imagining like a uniform belt or border. Even the word "margin," which has been used *faute de mieux* as a semitechnical term, is misleading insofar as it suggests a region located *alongside* or *behind* imagined content. In fact, the imaginal margin is an integral part of each imaginative presentation. We know that such presentations cannot be broken down into series of receding planes, each lying at a definite distance from the others. Precisely to the extent that the imaginative presentation is strictly frontal in character, it contains a single basic plane of presence, and the imaginal margin is *this plane itself as it trails off indefinitely.* It is the nondescript region in which the imaginative presentation becomes altogether indeterminate. This presentation, as we have just seen, is already infected with indeterminacy because of its specific content and world-frame, but it becomes still more thoroughly indeterminate in its outer reaches, that is, where it is no longer filled with content to which the imaginer attends. Lacking such content, it cannot be described in any precise fashion.

The imaginal margin is thus the most extensively and extremely indeterminate component of imaginative experience. When the imag-

iner attempts to make an imaginal margin more definite, he finds that
he is limited to imagining new content *in place of* the margin. And
yet this new content has in turn its *own* imaginal margin, and so on *ad
infinitum*. In each instance, the margin evades any attempt to make
it determinate.

The Image

The indeterminacy that characterizes the image or mode of presentation stands in striking contrast with that which was just encountered
in the imaginal margin. Instead of a pervasive and persisting indeterminate character, the image exhibits a highly variable indeterminacy
in accordance with the multiplicity of its forms. Let us confine ourselves to the three primary forms singled out in chapter two. First, in
clarity of presentation there can be considerable variation, ranging from
the murkily blurred to the relatively unambiguous. Yet a certain degree
of *un*clarity always attaches to the way in which the imaginative presentation is given to the imaginer, who is denied the sort of unclouded
clearness possible in perception. Second, we find a considerable variation in terms of *texture*, ranging from a sense of extreme coarse-
grainedness to polished smoothness. But in no case do we experience
the determinate textural character of the surfaces that are apprehended
by us in seeing, touching, and even hearing. The "surface" of the imaginative presentation is in this respect no surface at all. Its "feel" or texture, though variable, retains an inherent indistinctness no matter how
much we may try to remove it. Third, there are differences in the *directness* with which the imaginative presentation is given, varying from a
relatively straightforward givenness to diverse types of indirectness. In
no instance, however, do we encounter a directness comparable to that
found in many instances of simple perception: e.g., in examples of the
Moorean variety, such as "here is my hand before me now." In perceiving, we bodily confront, and are given directly, the object perceived. In
imagining, there is no such direct encounter, but only a characteristic
indefiniteness in the comparative directness with which imagined content is given. Although the imaginative presentation is frontal in character, the imaginer does not feel that he is genuinely *confronting* it; it
is not present to him with the same determinate and forceful directness
that is experienced in the case of perceptual objects.[5]

5. Nor even with a simulacrum of this directness: Ryle rightly denies that imagining is some sort of special 'seeing' in a private theater of the mind (*The Concept of
Mind*, pp. 253-55).

In sum, then, we have found indeterminateness and indetermin-ability—the two major ways in which indeterminacy exhibits itself in imaginative experience—to inhere in all three major components of the object phase. There is no part of this phase in which indeterminacy is not present in some form and to some degree. In this way it shows itself to be an essential trait of the entire intentional correlate of imagining. Further, by a rapid exercise of free variation, we can see to what extent it is an inalienable feature of this correlate: no matter how much we vary imaginative experience, it always possesses a residual indetermin-acy. Even if, for example, I imagine that I am in the process of *per-ceiving* something, what I manage to conjure up fails to possess the stolid determinateness of actually perceived objects; an instrinsic vague-ness continues to characterize the imaginatively "perceived" material. Indeed, if this vagueness were suddenly to vanish altogether from what I imagine, I would find myself no longer imagining but perceiving, remembering, or hallucinating—that is, focusing on material that is intrinsically determinate or in any case potentially determinable.

We should not, however, conclude that imagination's inherent in-determinacy automatically places it at a disadvantage vis-à-vis other mental acts. Such indeterminacy may even be a distinct advantage. Al-though the ingrained determinateness of perceptual experience gives rise to fully definite descriptions (as well as inductive inferences, which presuppose determinate phenomena), it is nevertheless *confin-ing* insofar as perceived phenomena cannot lose their inherent deter-minacy and still remain perceptual in status: perceiving ends by being constricted within its own determinateness. The indeterminacy of imaginative experience, in contrast, can be liberating to the precise ex-tent that it does not limit or restrict what we imagine. The presence of such indeterminacy, i.e., the very lack of sharply focused detail, means that what we imagine is essentially *open* in character. We shall find this openness confirmed and reinforced by the role that pure possibility plays in imaginative experience.[6]

---

6. The reader may ask questions at this point: Why do I continue to speak of *in*determinacy? Should I not, in keeping with preceding usage (e.g., "non-corrigibil-ity"), speak of *non*-determinacy? But non-determinacy would be something quite different from the characteristic to which I have been pointing. The unseen under-side of a perceived boulder that I cannot budge is non-determinate: neither strictly determinate nor strictly indeterminate. It does, however, remain determinable. But the imaginative presentation is intrinsically indeterminate in that it is not only not determinate but *cannot* become determinate under any conditions. Each time I try to make it determinate, I reach a point beyond which I cannot seem to go—a point which is, however, not itself definite or specifiable in advance—and thus I experience an inherent lack of determinability.

III

Pure possibility is one of the most critical, controversial, and complex essential traits of imagination. It is critical because it is the primary thetic character of the entire object phase; controversial because it is by no means obvious that possibility, particularly pure possibility, characterizes this phase in its entirety; and complex because the notion of possibility itself is not simple and demands a nuanced treatment.[7]

PRELIMINARY CONSIDERATIONS

By "thetic character" or "thetic quality" is meant the character or quality that consciousness posits in its intentional objects as an expression of its attitude toward the existential status of these objects. There are a number of such thetic characters, or posited properties, from which consciousness may choose; they are termed 'real', 'unreal', 'necessary', and 'possible'. Each of these terms can also be used to designate an object's actual *ontic* status, that is, its mode of existence considered independently of how it is regarded by the human subject. An object's ontic status refers to the way the object *is*—how it exists—regardless of the particular attitude that consciousness may assume toward it. As a metaphysical determination of the object, the ontic status does not as such figure into a phenomenological account. But in practice it is difficult to disentangle thetic from ontic attributes. Except when it takes up an expressly neutral stance, human consciousness tends to posit its objects *as* (i.e., as *genuinely*) real, unreal, possible, etc. If I posit a certain object as unreal, I tend to regard it as *being* unreal. This does not, however, prove that it *is* in fact unreal, and a distinction between thetic and ontic properties is always in principle possible.

To posit a thetic character or quality in something is to impute that character or quality *to* the thing. In perceiving, for example, I impute empirical reality to whatever I perceive; insofar as I am perceiving, I believe that what I perceive is empirically real. All intentional acts of mind—again with the exception of acts that are explicitly neutral—involve some such positing activity. This activity is an inherent "doxic"

7. The importance of pure possibility exceeds what can be compressed into the following pages. In recognition of this importance, I shall return to the relationship between imagining and pure possibility at the very end of this book, where pure possibility will be seen to be central to imagination's autonomous action. (See chapter nine, sections I-III.)

feature of every such act, and it occurs unless it is expressly checked or suspended.[8]

As an intentional act, imagining involves a specific thetic attitude (informing its act phase) which attributes a particular thetic quality or character to what is imagined (i.e., to its object phase). But to claim that imagining possesses its own positing or thetic activity is to run athwart the view that the ascription of thetic character to what is imagined is an act that is of a higher order than imagining itself. If such a view were correct, imagining could not bestow any such thetic character as possibility upon its own content. As Collingwood says, "The conceptions of past, future, the possible, the hypothetical are as meaningless for imagination as they are for feeling itself. They are conceptions which appear *only with a further development of thought.*"[9] In this interpretation the imputing of thetic character is seen as supervening upon a basic imaginative activity, which *per se* lacks any positing capacity. Yet such an interpretation, which invokes a higher-order act, overlooks the self-contained nature of imagination. If imagined objects do indeed display a specific thetic character, they must acquire this character through an activity indigenous to the act of imagining itself and not through some "further development of thought."

We shall term the thetic attitude of imagining "sheer supposal" or (alternatively) "self-entertainment" and the corresponding thetic character posited by this attitude "pure possibility." These two factors, sheer supposal and pure possibility, dovetail in each concrete experience of imagining. To imagine is to sup-pose something—an object, event, or state of affairs—as purely possible. Such entertaining of pure possibilities cannot be understood as an activity of negating what is empirically real, or even as being indifferent or neutral toward it.[10] For in sheer sup-

8. An example of such suspension of belief occurs, of course, in Husserl's notion of *epochē*. See his discussion in *Ideas*, secs. 31-32. The term "doxic" is also Husserl's. (Cf. *Ideas*, secs. 103-105.) It does not differ in meaning from "thetic" as we shall use this latter term. "Modal" is a third member of this series of near-synonyms, but it does not stress the belief-factor as much as the other two terms and its use here will be avoided.

9. *Principles of Art* (Oxford: Oxford University Press, 1938), p. 224. My italics.

10. These misinterpretations of imagination's thetic activity are found, respectively, in the following three authors: (1) For Sartre, the primary thetic attitude involved in imagining is that of de-realization—i.e., the attempt to nihilate and to transcend the perceptually real (Cf. *Psychology of Imagination*, pp. 233-46). (2) For Collingwood, "to imagine an object is not to commit oneself in thought to its unreality: it is to be wholly indifferent to its reality" (R. G. Collingwood, *Essays in the Philosophy of Art*, ed. A. Donagan [Bloomington: Indiana University Press, 1964], p. 54). (3) For Husserl, imagining is conceived as an application of the "neutrality-modification" to memory. (Cf. *Ideas*, secs. 109, 111, 112.) Each of these views errs by refusing to accord to imagination a thetic activity of its own.

posal I posit a thetic quality that can be described *in its own terms* and not merely in terms of some putatively more basic thetic character such as the real or the necessary. I assume a non-negating and non-neutral attitude, ascribing the distinctive and non-derivative thetic quality of pure possibility to whatever I imagine.

In making this claim, I am not denying that we can imagine real as well as unreal objects and state of affairs. I can certainly imagine a real person as in an imagined situation—say, my friend Dick as being on Jupiter when I know that he is in New York. And I can equally well imagine unreal things or events in real situations, e.g., a centaur entering my house at the present moment. But the ultimately confirmable reality of my friend and the manifest unreality of the centaur do not affect the specific thetic character that I attribute to them *insofar as I am imagining them.* When I imagine them, I posit them as purely possible, whatever their actual ontic status. Different as they may be ontically, they become companions in the realm of the imaginary. In this realm I do not take them to be either real or unreal, and this is so even if I know, independently of the experience itself of imagining, that they are one or the other. The poet who depicts in words a mythical monster no doubt knows that such a beast is unreal, or at least highly improbable, but in spite of this knowledge he regards it as a suitable imaginative possibility for the purposes of his poetry. Thus, knowledge of actual ontic status need not prevent the imputing of a *different* thetic character to what is imagined, and part of the "purity" of imaginative possibilities lies precisely in their independence of the mutually exclusive alternatives of reality and unreality.

PURE VS. OTHER TYPES OF POSSIBILITY

Expressed in the most general terms, a possibility is anything that *could* be. It is something which *can* appear or take place, but which at any given moment *need not* do so. It is thus to be distinguished from (a) a necessity, which *must* appear or occur at a given point and from (b) an actuality, which *does* appear or happen on a certain occasion, though it does so only contingently, not because it has to. Despite these differences, the three terms are not unrelated to each other. A necessity must be at all times possible: this is a precondition for its occurrence.

This activity is either reduced to denying and surpassing what is perceptually present (as in Sartre's theory) or confused with being noncommittal (as both Collingwood and Husserl maintain, and as Coleridge also holds in his notion of the "willing suspension of disbelief").

An actuality, by the very fact of its occurrence, is something that is possible at the time when it occurs.[11]

We cannot enter here into the exceedingly complex formal aspects of necessity and possibility, aspects that are explored in modal logic. Nor will we attempt to pronounce upon recondite metaphysical questions such as whether the realm of the possible exceeds that of the actual (e.g., by virtue of there being a vast reservoir of unrealized possibilities) or whether the possible always inheres in the actual. The task immediately before us is much more delimited: namely, to distinguish two basic types of possibility that must not be confused with each other.[12]

Hypothetical Possibility

In theories of imagination as a form of play and more recently in Ryle's interpretation of imagining in terms of make-believe, it has been implied that what we imagine has the status of a hypothetical possibility.[13] By "hypothetical possibility" I mean the sort of possibility that is viewed as a *means* to a preposited end or aim. Hence it is considered not for its own sake but for the sake of its role in the realization of a particular end-state. A hypothetically possible idea, entity, or event merits attention only insofar as it contributes to bringing about or illuminating a preestablished goal. Its own interest or value is accordingly a function of its role in relation to such a goal.[14]

11. Note that what is frequently called a "real possibility" is something embodying conditions that are *almost* sufficient to allow it to appear or occur; it is a possibility in the penultimate stage of becoming actual, that is, just before a particular event or circumstance precipitates it into actuality. On the notion of "real possibility" thus defined, see Nicolai Hartmann, *Möglichkeit und Wirklichkeit* (Berlin: de Gruyter, 1938), pp. 137ff., and the discussion of this book by J. N. Mohanty in *Phenomenology and Ontology* (The Hague: Nijhoff, 1970), pp. 129ff.

12. There is as well a third basic type of possibility that we might call "process possibility." By this is meant the sort of possibility that is *in the process of* becoming an actuality in view of an inherent *telos* that commands, as well as constricts, its ongoing course. Such possibility, which is most manifest in organic life and its evolution, is not a constituent feature of what we imagine. Even if a given imagined object happens to be the kind of thing which, outside the context of imagining, would be understood in terms of process possibility—e.g., a growing plant—*as imagined* it lacks an internal *nisus* toward actualization. Teleological dynamism is absent, and in its place there is only a sense of pseudo-development and, at best, pseudo-actualization—typically an uneven succession of more or less disjointed aspects or moments.

13. For Ryle's interpretation, see *The Concept of Mind*, pp. 258-72.

14. A hypothetical possibility is thus to be distinguished from a process possibility; in the case of the latter it is precisely its *own* actualization and not that of something else that matters. The sense of "hypothetical" I refer to here is found, for example, in the way that certain diagrams are used to illustrate abstract conceptual relations. Such figures represent what a given relation would look like *if* it were to

The thetic attitude that posits things as hypothetically possible regards objects and states of affairs *as if* they were actual or real. It is the factor of the as-if that distinguishes such an attitude from the thetic attitude found in perception or memory, in which objects and states of affairs are posited as being *in fact* actual or real. Now, an as-if thetic attitude of the sort just described is present in a wide range of human activities. To cite only three cases in point:

(1) *Hypothesizing* involves the projection of an idea or set of ideas as a preliminary and possible explanation of a given phenomenon. The hypothesis itself need not be formalized to the degree that it often is in the natural sciences, but whatever its precise form, it is projected as illuminating the origin, present appearance, or future course of the *explicandum*.

(2) *Pretending* of a playful sort involves the express exercise of an as-if thetic attitude, not in the interest of clarification or explanation but for the sake of the pleasure this very attitudinal posture brings with it. Thus, we pretend that certain things are the case—often knowing very well that they are not—because doing so is intrinsically pleasurable. Such pretending is basic both to children's play and to adult parody: in each, something is posited as if it were the case and yet with comparative indifference toward what really *is* the case.[15]

(3) In *anticipating* we regard a possible future entity or event as if it were about to appear or occur in the present. Anticipation is thus an instance of what Dewey somewhat misleadingly labeled "dramatic rehearsal in imagination."[16] We normally anticipate what form the future might take so as to be in a better position to deal with the projected object or situation if and when it does arise. Hence the primary aim is not to increase knowledge or pleasure but to induce more skillful or suitable action.

---

assume a visual form. We value such diagrams not for themselves but for the insight they afford into something that is precisely *not* diagrammatic in character. Nor is there any presumption that the diagram itself is in the process of *becoming* the relation it illustrates.

15. In children's play there is, in addition, the positing of a transitional state: a "play-space" neither strictly real nor strictly unreal. See the classical study of D. W. Winnicott, "Transitional Objects and Transitional Phenomena," *International Journal of Psychoanalysis* (1953), XXXIV, pp. 89-97.

16. *Human Nature and Conduct*, pp. 190-91. Dewey's description is misleading to the extent that it implies that anticipation must always be dramatic in nature.

In all three of these instances we have to do with a basic thetic stance in which possibilities are regarded as *intermediary* in status—as means toward improved knowledge, pleasure, or practical action. They are considered to be of instrumental, not of intrinsic, interest, and they are instrumental precisely as a means of coming to terms with the real (even if by expressly evading it, as in pretending). In the act of imagining proper, in contrast, there is no such concern with possibility as intermediary or instrumental, for what we imagine is not projected as a means toward an end that is established in the reality-oriented interests of knowledge, pleasure, or practical action. Indeed, in imagining, any reference to the real qua real (including even a highly hypothetical sense of the real) is excluded from the very beginning. Whatever may be the actual relationships between a given act of imagining and its attendant circumstances and whatever the subsequent uses or consequences of this act, the *experience itself* of imagining involves no such concrete relationships, uses, or consequences—not even as projected in an as-if form. In brief, we see or do nothing *through* or *with* an imaginative presentation, but 'see' or 'do' things *in* it and *on its terms* alone.

Pure Possibility

By "pure possibility" is meant a kind of possibility that is posited and contemplated *for its own sake* and not for the sake of anything external to, or more ultimate than, itself. It is the sort of possibility that is considered on the basis of its inherent interest, not on the basis of its actual or potential value in the realization of projects that transcend the act of imagining itself.[17] Consequently, pure possibility is the distinctive thetic character of what we imagine, and as such it serves to distinguish imaginative experience from other kinds of experience. The purely possible has no place, for example, in perception or memory, both of which posit the actual (i.e., the empirically real) as the primary thetic character of their respective contents: I perceive the tree outside my window as real, just as I remember it as having been real at some earlier point in time. No such anchoring in the actual characterizes imagined objects and states of affairs. In fact, it is precisely their *lack* of thetic actuality that renders their intrinsic sense of possibility "pure"— pure, that is, from entangling alliances with the actual.

What we imagine, then, is imagined as purely possible, as fully and yet only possible. To this we should add that it is not only experienced

17. Pure possibility should not be confused with *mere* possibility insofar as the latter connotes something that is barely, or just, possible—i.e., something that is only highly unlikely. With pure possibility the question of *likelihood* does not arise in the first place, since the issue of actualization is excluded from consideration.

as already purely possible but as *possibilizing* in the present, converting what is actual or necessary in other contexts into what *might be so* for the moment. Thus pure possibility refers not merely to what the imaginer imputes to the imagined. It also refers to an activity by which imagining presents as purely possible what is otherwise nonpossible or only hypothetically possible. For instance, when I imagine my cat Cinnamon gamboling in her usual frisky way, but now within an entirely imagined scene, I experience her movements as purely possible in thetic quality. Not only are these movements not experienced as actual, they are not even apprehended as pale replicas of actual movements. And this is so no matter how similar the imagined movements may be to empirically real movements that I have observed repeatedly in the past and that I can now recollect by a separate act of memory.[18]

Here we must take notice of a further aspect of pure possibility. If a given imaginative presentation is posited-and-contemplated as purely possible, it cannot be said to be something we *have* in the manner of an acquisition or possession. For what we can meaningfully be said to have must be fully *determinate* in character, and this holds true even within the realm of mind. As it is expressed in everyday usage, I "grasp" something in perception; I "recall" or "call up" objects or events in remembering them; and I may "fix" or "tie down" certain ideas in thinking them through. In each instance I experience myself as appropriating something which is quite determinate in existence or form and which offers itself as sufficiently substantial to be actively acquired by and then possessed ("held") in the mind.[19]

In imagining, there is no such appropriative relation to objects or states of affairs. The imaginer does not feel himself to be acquiring or coming to possess imagined content. He does, it is true, sense himself to be *apprehending* such content, but "apprehension" is here meant in a weakened and nonliteral sense of the term. Moreover, the imaginer is capable of concentrating on what he imagines so as to clarify its con-

18. On an empiricist theory of imagination, of course, whatever I imagine in a case such as this *must* represent a replication of past perceptions. Whatever the merits of this theory (and they are not very considerable in my view), its truth or falsity as a causal account does not affect the validity of my claims above. For I am only attempting to show that a given imagined object is *experienced as* purely possible by the imaginer himself, whatever its origins in previous experience.

19. The case of thinking is admittedly ambiguous. In thinking, we do sometimes merely contemplate ideas without any sense of appropriation and without positing the content of thought as existent. The affinity of such contemplative thinking with imagining is difficult to deny. Yet it also cannot be denied that some thinking is not contemplative in this sense but "fastens" possessively onto ideas. Thinking, says Aristotle, "is *active* when it *possesses* [its] object" (*Metaphysics*, XII, 1072b; his italics). In such thinking, we witness an appropriative element similar to that found in acts of perceiving and remembering.

tent. Yet such clarification does not constitute anything like an appropriation of this content as actual or determinate. The evanescence of
the imaginative presentation as a whole rules out any experience of what
Husserl called "an abiding possession."[20] This striking absence of ac-
quisitive and possessive factors is found before, during, and after the
act.of imagining itself. The imaginer does not *start* with anything that
is acquired as a legacy from other imaginative or nonimaginative acts;
he cannot be said to be in possession of anything determinate *during* a
particular imaginative experience; and he does not acquire anything in
this experience that can be reappropriated as such in *future* acts of
imagining.[21] As purely possible, what is imagined lacks the durable,
resistant quality that characterizes those experiential items which one
can be said to possess in some significant way. In fact, the purely possible collapses and vanishes in the face of all attempts to grasp it as
enduring or stable: any attempt at appropriation finds nothing definite
enough to hold on to.[22]

If the imagined qua purely possible is thus nothing that we can be
said to have by way of acquisition, what stance do we take toward it?
How do we relate to it if not by possessing it? The answer is that we
entertain a given imaginative presentation as purely possible. To entertain something in imagination means to posit it as purely possible regardless of its relation to what is actually the case at the time, or to
what was previously the case, or to what will be the case in the future.
Such an attitude is to be distinguished from supposition of a strictly
hypothetical sort (e.g., as when we 'suppose it to be true that'), since
the hypothetical factor brings with it a link to the actual through anticipation, make-believe, etc. The attitude in question is, rather, to be
conceived as *sheer supposition*: a supposing that is free from either
overt or covert connection with what is actual. Therefore, to posit
something as purely possible in imagination is to consider it as sheerly
supposable, that is, as worthy of our momentary attention on its own

20. *"Eine bleibende Habe."* See Husserl, *Cartesian Meditations,* p. 60.

21. This situation contrasts sharply with what is found in the case of conceptual
insights, which are subject to transmission (via written symbols), possession, reap-
propriation. On this point, see Husserl, *The Crisis of European Sciences and Transcendental Philosophy,* trans. David Carr (Evanston: Northwestern University Press,
1970), pp. 353-78.

22. For the imaginative presentation to lack such definiteness is for it also to lack
the ontic status of existence. Only what exists, or has existed, or will exist has sufficient "Secondness" (in Peirce's term) to be grasped in appropriative acts such as
perception or memory. Secondness is characterized by Peirce precisely in terms of its
"resistance" and is thus to be contrasted with Firstness, which is a sheer qualitative
immediacy lacking resistance. Cf. Charles S. Peirce, *Collected Papers,* eds. C. Hart-
shorne and Paul Weiss (Cambridge: Harvard University Press, 1931-58), 1.25,
1.527ff., 2.119, 3.63, 3.422-23, 5.66, and 5.194.

account. In this respect, imagining may be regarded as a special form of *self-entertainment* in which the imaginer amuses himself with what he conjures and contemplates by and for himself alone. To amuse oneself in this way is not necessarily to experience anything that is "amusing" in the sense of the comical or laughable. Instead, it is to enter into a *musing* state of mind in which everything that is imagined is a pure possibility and is enjoyed as such. *Imagining is entertaining oneself with what is purely possible.*

DESCRIPTION OF PURE POSSIBILITY IN THE OBJECT PHASE

Up to this point we have been speaking of pure possibility as the primary thetic character of the entire imaginative presentation—indeed, of the object phase in general. This simplifying view of the locus of pure possibility has been helpful as a basis for contrasting the distinctive thetic character of imaginative experience with other kinds of thetic character, most notably the hypothetically possible and the empirically real. Nevertheless, even if it is true that the purely possible pervades the object phase as a whole, we can no longer assume that it is present in each of the components of this phase in exactly the same way.

Imagined Content

If there will be a question as to the direct ingrediency of pure possibility in the other components of the object phase, there can be no such question with respect to imagined content, where the purely possible appears most conspicuously. When we imagine particular *objects* —persons, physical things, arrested actions, fictitious conglomerates, etc.—we imagine them not as if they were real or even in the process of becoming real but as things that merely might be. By "might be" is not meant that such things *might well be*, i.e., are likely to become real. Rather, they present themselves as sheer possibilities. Whether I imagine a hippogriff or the face of a friend, either object is something I suppose to be—and then only for the moment, as part of a transitory imaginative presentation. Since the mythical creature and my friend's face are posited as purely possible objects, they have no anchoring in a stable and situatable realm of being. Yet this lack of a firm foundation in factuality or in ideality does not mean that these objects may not be experienced as vividly present to my imagining mind, as capable of fulfilling quite diverse imaginative intentions, and as enormously variegated in form and structure. Their status as purely possible allows for, and even facilitates, such further dimensions of imaginative experience.

Imagined *states of affairs* are structurally complex, being composed of objects or events *and* their interrelations. Nonetheless, it is the state of affairs *as a whole* and not just parts of it that I experience as purely possible. For example, if I imagine that roses grow upside down on the moon, I posit the *entire* situation 'roses-growing-upside-down-on-the-moon' as occurring in a strictly might-be way. All distinguishable elements in this imagined state of affairs are entertained as fully *co*-possible within a single, self-enclosed unit. Where an imagined object or event *per se* is felt to be purely possible as a delimited and discrete atom of imaginative experience, an imagined state of affairs is experienced as purely possible in its essentially *relational* character. It is above all the way in which the elements of the state of affairs relate to each other—as the term "Sach-*verhalt*" implies—that is posited-and-contemplated as purely possible.

As for the *world-frame* of imagined objects and states of affairs, its thetic character is experienced as continuous with the thetic character of the specific content it subtends. For the imagined world-frame is only the immediate spatio-temporal arena in which imagined items of whatever sort appear as purely possible. It follows that the arena is itself experienced as a pure possibility. Imaginal time is a sheer might-be time without a basis in the calendar or the clock; it is a momentary temporal stretch that is no more actual in thetic character than what emerges in it. Similarly, imaginal space is a manifold of presentation that forms a purely possible setting for the appearance of specific *imaginata*. Indeed, if imaginal space and time had any thetic character other than pure possibility, they would be quite incapable of providing a world-frame for the purely possible things they serve to situate.

Imaginal Margin

We enter here upon considerably less certain terrain. Insofar as the imaginal margin is radically indeterminate, how can we attribute to it a particular thetic character such as pure possibility? But then we must ask ourselves: what *other* thetic character could it possess? We certainly do not posit the imaginal margin as empirically real—in contrast with our attitude toward a perceptual field's outer fringes. However vague these fringes may appear in a given case, they are still experienced as continuous with focally perceived objects and as possessing the same sort of empirical reality. It is equally evident that we do not posit the imaginal margin as necessary; it comes clothed in the same contingency as the rest of the presentation. Nor does the margin present itself as possible in a merely hypothetical sense, i.e., as the object of an as-if attitude. Therefore, if an identification of thetic character is rendered difficult by the imaginal margin's extreme indeterminacy, we are at least assured that this character cannot be subsumed under the real, the necessary, or the hypothetically possible.

There is another and more positive reason, however, for holding that the imaginal margin possesses the status of pure possibility. This margin is always the margin *of* a specific imagined content and its world-frame. As such, its thetic character must be compatible with that of the other parts of the imaginative presentation if this presentation is to be apprehended as a single coherent whole. To experience a distinct difference of thetic quality within one and the same presentation would be to undermine the felt unity of this presentation. Since imagined content and the world-frame present themselves as purely possible, their imaginal margin will also be experienced as purely possible, however dimly this margin presents itself to the imagining mind.

The Image

In the case of the image or mode of presentation, we are once again faced with a problematic situation. In what sense can a mode of *givenness* be said to be purely possible? Is not givenness always *already actual?* But in fact it is with the *mode* of givenness, not with givenness as such, that we are here concerned. And a mode by its very nature implies variation and hence the possible: a particular mode is always just one of several modes. Further, we need only note that imagined content is not presented in any ineluctable or unchanging manner; there is no sense that it *must* appear to us as it does on any given occasion. The specific degree of clarity with which it appears, for example, is subject to change at any point. Moreover, the imaginer remains free to modify the mode of givenness not only in terms of clarity but in terms of texture and degree of directness, and no doubt in other ways as well. Although imagined content is presented with a certain sense of finality in any given imaginative experience, such finality—the sense that the content is given in just *this* way and not some other—does not prevent us from experiencing a particular mode of presentation as only one among a number of possible ways in which a specific content *might* be given, where the "might" connotes what is purely possible in nature.

This is, then, a brief sketch of pure possibility as it is found in the main components of imagination's object phase. It is striking that only in the instance of imagined content is this thetic character present in a conspicuous and unequivocal fashion. But precisely insofar as such content (and especially the *specific* content) is that part of the total imaginative presentation on which the imaginer's primary attention is trained, the fact that it is posited as purely possible means that the imaginer tends to regard the *whole* intentional correlate of a given act of imagining as exhibiting pure possibility. Thus the specific content of an imaginative experience establishes, or at least predelineates, the thetic status of its entire object phase.

It remains only to add a few words concerning the relationship between indeterminacy and pure possibility. As was said at the outset, the two traits are *mutually facilitating*: each helps the other to appear. Consequently, their relationship is twofold in character.

(1) First of all, if something presents itself as indeterminate, its very lack of definiteness invites us to posit-and-contemplate it as purely possible. If it were to present itself as determinate, it would lead us to regard it as empirically real or as necessary, empirical reality being appropriate to the three-dimensional determinacy of perceived objects, and necessity to the conceptual determinacy of strictly defined terms or of formally valid inferences. We should also observe that if something *does* present itself in perception or memory as indeterminate, we are naturally tempted to impute to it an element of possibility. In our uncertainty we typically say, "That *might* be a tree over there" or "I think I remember what her face *might* have looked like." When we imagine, however, the basis for the attribution of possibility is significantly strengthened. Here possibility enters not as a function of conjecture or doubt but as an inherent aspect of the experience itself. In imagining, the indeterminacy of the object phase encourages—indeed, even requires—the projection of what we imagine as purely possible.

(2) The converse is also the case: the thetic quality of pure possibility brings with it a characteristic indeterminacy. If a pure possibility becomes overly determinate, it turns either into a hypothetical possibility—which is made determinate by its relation to a preposited end—or, at the limit, into an actuality or a necessity. In other words, if the structure of a certain pure possibility becomes too rigorously circumscribed—as when we speak of "the possibility that A met B at time t"—it risks losing its status as *purely* possible. Definiteness of detail involves a confinement and constriction that are inimical to the unconstrained and open character of pure possibility. Such possibility calls for an intrinsic indeterminacy of structure and content if it is to exfoliate

fully and freely. In imagining, the purely possible ranges so widely that any form of determinateness is experienced as an obstacle: hence our tendency to speak of "a *flight* of imagination," of "*freefloating* reverie," etc.[23] The purely possible fosters free mental movements—engendering unhindered "motions of the mind" in Wallace Stevens' phase[24]—within a milieu of indeterminacy. In this final way indeterminacy and pure possibility conjoin in imaginative experience and facilitate each other's appearance to consciousness.

We may conclude that these two traits are genuinely pervasive in imagination's object phase. Indeterminacy colors every component of this phase, though differently in each case, and pure possibility, despite its prominence in imagined content, is the exclusive thetic character of the phase as a whole. Each trait represents a basic way in which the act of imagining is related to its intentional correlate. Imagining is entertaining a given imaginative presentation as purely possible while at the same time experiencing it as inherently indeterminate.

23. It is worth noting that a number of metaphors used to describe imagining allude to the element of *air*, presumably because the ethereal realm symbolizes an area of minimal obstruction: imagining is thus "verticalizing," and the poet's pen "gives to *airy nothing* a local habitat and a name." On verticalizing, see Gaston Bachelard, *L'air et les songes* (Paris: Corti, 1943), esp. chapter five and conclusion. The Shakespeare quotation is from *A Midsummer-Night's Dream*, V, i, 7; my italics.

24. "Evening without Angels," *The Collected Poems of Wallace Stevens* (New York: Knopf, 1969), p. 137.

PART THREE

PHENOMENOLOGICAL COMPARISONS

CHAPTER SIX

Imagining and Perceiving: Continuities

So FAR IN THIS ESSAY imagination has been described in almost complete isolation from the rest of human mental activity. From time to time allusion has been made to other mental acts, particularly to perception. But no systematic attempt has been made to compare imagining with these other acts so as to bring out decisive differences as well as affinities and similarities. Carrying out such comparisons, however, is a crucial task in view of the pervasive tendency to subordinate imagination to putatively more fundamental acts—of which perception is often taken as the paradigm. The comparisons are also crucial because of the way in which imagining allies itself with a number of psychical activities, whether these are explicitly perceptual or not. In Baudelaire's words, imagination is "a mysterious faculty. It touches all the others, exciting and activating them. Sometimes it resembles them to the point of becoming confused with them, and yet it is always very much itself. . . ."[1] In order to avoid such confusion, and to show how imagining remains "very much itself," we must begin by comparing imagining with perceiving. In this way a basis will be provided for distinguishing imagining from other activities as well.

I

The relationship between perception and imagination has been interpreted in a bewildering variety of ways in Western philosophy. Within one and the same tradition of thought, the two acts have been regarded alternatively as modes of each other, contraries of each other, conjugate acts, different expressions of still another act—and, much more rarely, as equal but independent acts. Why is it that imagining and perceiving have been given such different and often conflicting

---

1. *Curiosités esthétiques* [*et*] *l'Art romantique*, p. 321.

treatments in Western philosophizing? We may isolate two explanatory factors of special significance.

To begin with, the very words that have been used to designate perceptual experience *per se* exhibit considerable ambiguity. Just as *aisthēsis* in ancient Greek stood for everything from sensation in the
strictest physiological sense to the diagrams used to illustrate mathe-
matical concepts, so the word "perception" in British philosophy of
the last few centuries has stood for anything from "sense-data" to
"ideas." Here we should observe that throughout the history of philosophy a dual thesis has been especially prominent: perception is
viewed both as the critical point at which the external world first im-
pinges upon the perceiver (thereby imparting sensory "data" to him)
and as the way in which these data are assimilated by the perceiver to
become the basis for subsequent cognitive activities. In other words, it
is at once the condition and source of cognition and the earliest stage
(or stages, since it may occur in several steps) in cognition. Hence it is
not surprising that what is called "perception" has acquired such an
amplitude of meaning that it has become an essentially ambiguous
term in everyday discourse.[2]

Given this ambiguity, it is also not surprising that there is a tendency to subsume other mental acts *under* perception as a generic term.
This subsumptive tendency helps to explain much of the obscurity that
beclouds former treatments of the relation between perception and
imagination. In particular it accounts for the temptation to regard
imagination as a mere mode of perception—i.e., as a direct extension of
sensory perception, or as a secondhand copy of such perception.[3] Since
the exact sense or scope of "perception" is rarely defined or determined,
it becomes all too predictable that its relation to imagination, presumed to be one of its own modes, will be difficult to delimit.

Second, and compounding the confusion, is the fact that imagination itself is an extremely elusive act. This elusiveness, which we have
encountered on a number of occasions and most dramatically in the
form of indeterminacy, means that imagining is exceedingly hard to

2. On the ambiguity of *aisthēsis*, see D. W. Hamlyn, *Sensation and Perception*
(London: Routledge & Kegan Paul, 1961), chapters 1-2 as well as Hamlyn's notes
to his translation of Aristotle's *De Anima*, esp. pp. 88, 99, and 112. On the ambiguity of the term "perception" in modern philosophy, see R. J. Hirst's article on
"Perception" in *The Encyclopedia of Philosophy*, ed. P. Edwards (New York: Macmillan, 1967), vols. 5-6, pp. 79ff.

3. Hume provides the classical view of the copy-relation: "Nor will this liberty of
the fancy appear strange, when we consider, that all our ideas are copy'd from our
impressions" (*Treatise of Human Nature*, p. 10). His broad use of "perception" to
include both impressions and ideas is also telling in the present context. (See ibid.,
p. 1.) For the view that imagination is nothing but "a determinate mode of perception," see Eugen Fink, *Studien zur Phänomenologie*, p. 75.

describe in its *own* terms, and thus that its relationship with other mental acts, and notably with perception, is correspondingly difficult to pinpoint. The fleetingness of imagining removes it from the ready reach of precise observation, making it remarkably resistant to analysis. As Hume says, "in the imagination the perception [i.e., the apprehension of what we are imagining] is faint and languid, and cannot without difficulty be preserv'd by the mind steady and uniform for any considerable time."[4] The result is that imagining, when not neglected altogether, tends to be regarded as an act that is only transitional, serving to link together other acts without possessing a separate status of its own.

In fact, there is an entire tradition of thought that considers imagination's sole function to be that of mediating between less evanescent acts. Since perception is almost invariably held to be one of the acts between which imagination mediates, the relationship between imagining and perceiving is rendered problematic from the very beginning. Can there be any significant relation between an act and a non-act (for so imagining is in effect regarded insofar as it is considered merely mediatory)? To be an intermediary is to be in effect optional, since *other* agencies can carry out the same mediations and since the ultimate aim of mediating is to arrive at a state in which the very need for mediation is no longer present. As merely *inter*mediary, imagination is but a passing phase on the way to a supposedly superior stage of mentation —whether this be sheer intellection or an enriched form of perception. A further consequence of viewing imagination as intermediary is an endless proliferation of accounts purporting to specify the exact relationship between imagination and perception. For there are many ways of being mediatory, ranging from simple conjunction to partial identification.[5]

Beyond the recurrent tendency to regard imagination as merely intermediary, there has been a striking diversity in earlier treatments of the relationship between imagining and perceiving. A close look at these treatments, though, reveals two distinct strands of analysis: one in which imagination and perception are seen as inherently discontinuous with each other, the other in which they are conceived as basically continuous. Of the two strands, the latter has been more central and influential in the history of Western philosophy. From Aristotle to Merleau-Ponty, philosophers adhering to this line of thought

4. *Treatise of Human Nature*, p. 9.

5. For a detailed critique of the conception of imagination as intermediate, see my essay "Imagination as Intermediate" in *Vers une esthétique sans entrave*, ed. G. Lascault (Paris: Union Générale d'Editions, 1975), pp. 93-113. The core of this critique is that the role of any given intermediary epistemological agency is tenuous, since its middle-range position implies its obsolescence and eventual transcendence.

have held that imagining and perceiving overlap or coincide in certain crucial ways, including extension of one act into the other, repetition of one by the other, resemblance between the two acts, combination of elements through an act of fusion, and in still other ways. A considerable portion of the various possible conceptions of the relation between perception and imagination can thereby be accommodated under the single heading of "continuity." At the same time, we can subsume under "discontinuity" several types of separateness that have been held to exist between the two acts: total independence, distinctness in kind, marked difference in degree, etc. Taken together, the two strands of analysis may be represented in the following quasi-historical and highly schematic manner:

Continuity   *Discontinuity*

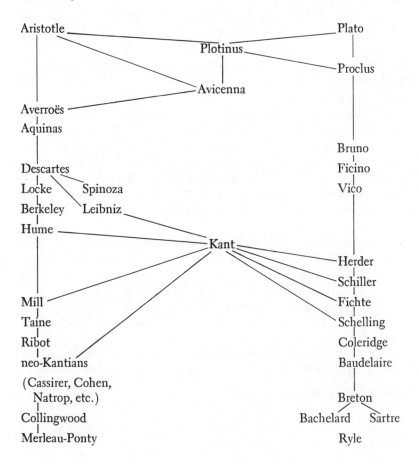

It is a curious and revealing fact that in this schematization there are three pivotal figures who represent a confluence of *both* lines of interpretation.

Plotinus

On the one hand, Plotinus espouses a quite orthodox view whereby imagination is situated precisely midway between sensation and intellect, being continuous with both: "the imaginative faculty . . . passes on information received by the senses to the discursive reason . . . and is somehow the bond between the upper and the lower soul."[6] On the other hand, Plotinus makes imagining into a distinct level of consciousness with its own criteria of insight and validity. In this latter capacity, it is held to be essential to intellection—and not merely in Aristotle's sense of providing a quasi-sensuous support for intellect.[7]

Avicenna

Imagination for Avicenna is inherently bivalent. As "representative," it is demonic and terrestrial in character, being wholly dependent on the report of the senses. In representative imagining, the sensible form "is preserved in the same state in which it was [first] seen . . . And there it subsists, although the visible object has disappeared."[8] As "active," however, imagination is not limited to what it receives from the senses. In sleep, for example, "we are freed from the preoccupations of the sensible faculties. The soul then aspires to the world of the Angels; and of that which is known to them—that which is still to come into being—the soul becomes conscious in part."[9] In this regard, the active imagination becomes "the organ of metamorphoses."[10]

Kant

For Kant, too, the imagination is an organ of metamorphoses.

---

6. H. J. Blumenthal, *Plotinus' Psychology* (The Hague: Nijhoff, 1971), p. 89.

7. On this aspect of Plotinus' view of imagination, see ibid., pp. 97ff.

8. Henri Corbin, *Avicenna and the Visionary Recital*, tr. W. Trask (New York: Pantheon, 1960), p. 349. Elsewhere the representative imagination is said to be "the treasury of forms" (ibid., pp. 301-302).

9. Corbin, pp. 310-11.

10. Ibid., p. 307n. Imaginative metamorphoses are achieved by inspecting "the treasury of forms [i.e., the content of representative imagination] and the treasury of significances [i.e., the content of memory]. Sometimes [active imagination] combines with one another significances of all kinds and figures of all kinds, and from this mixture produces something new. Sometimes it extracts a fragment from a single figure and a single significance. Sometimes it takes this figure and this significance as they are, and sometimes it combines figure and form with each other" (ibid., p. 350).

These metamorphoses are accomplished by a specifically "productive" imagination which in its spontaneity is to be distinguished from other mental acts: "insofar as imagination is spontaneity, I sometimes also entitle it the *productive* imagination."[11] As transcendental in status, the productive imagination is a necessary condition for all imagining— indeed, for perceptual experience as well. As empirical, it is "forma- tive" and is crucial in the creation of art. But Kant also recognized a *reproductive* imagination which operates by associating sensory con- tents given to it in intuition. It is in this latter regard that Kant's think- ing belongs to the strand of continuity, for reproductive imagination is entirely dependent on the material furnished to it through sensuous intuition. Hence Kant, like Plotinus and Avicenna before him, ends by holding that imagination is at once continuous and discontinuous with other acts of the mind.

I single out these three figures because their two-sided conceptions of imagination suggest that, however inimical to each other the two historical strands of analysis may appear to be, they are not entirely irreconcilable. Perhaps we are not forced to choose between a view of imagination as strictly discontinuous with other acts and one in which it is wholly continuous or merged with them. The dual allegiances of Plotinus, Avicenna, and Kant suggest the possibility that each view can justifiably be included in a broader position encompassing both lines of interpretation.

II

The following discussion will limit itself to brief descriptions of four fundamental ways in which imagination and perception show them- selves to be continuous with each other. These descriptions should suf- fice in view of the historical predominance of those interpretations from Aristotle onward which stress—and in my view overstress—the continuity between the two acts. Such interpretations have not, how- ever, been as explicit as they might have been and have tended to issue in generalities. Our task, accordingly, is to examine certain highly spe- cific forms of the continuity in question: forms which have been over- looked or obscured in previous treatments.

11. *Critique of Pure Reason*, B152, p. 165. His italics.

CONTINUITY OF CONTENT

It is important to distinguish between two very different sorts of claims concerning the respective contents of perception and imagination. In one case it is a matter of claiming that these two kinds of content are *sometimes* continuous with each other—i.e., that a description of the content of an act of perceiving *may* significantly overlap with a description of the content of an act of imagining. Such a claim is to be distinguished from the more ambitious claim of *necessary* continuity. In the latter case it is contended that imagined content not only may resemble perceived content but *must* resemble it. The basis for this claim is the epistemological thesis that what we imagine has no source other than perception itself. According to the necessitarian view, then, the content of imagining is ineluctably a repetition or recombination of what we have already perceived; hence a complete analysis would reveal a close correspondence between any given imagined content and the content of some previous perception or set of perceptions. Such a reductive view, which in its purest form is held by Hume,[12] cannot be refuted at this point, for the inherent independence of imagining from perceiving is establishable only after demonstrating the discontinuities between the two acts—discontinuities that will serve to undermine the epistemological thesis supporting the necessitarian claim. For the present we shall restrict ourselves to citing evidence for the first, more modest claim, which posits only a non-necessary continuity of content. Such evidence is abundant, since there is in fact a certain propensity to imagine the same kinds of thing that one perceives. Here a series of three internally related examples is in order:

(1) To start with, I *image* the room in which a meeting of the Philosophy Department is to take place later in the day. I visualize room 201 in a fair amount of detail, including the color of its walls, the sort of bookcases it has, its bay windows, the enormously long table around which members of the Department will seat themselves. Sunlight even streams into the imaged scene.

(2) I proceed to *imagine that* the projected meeting is taking place.

12. Cf. Hume's statement: "Neither the ideas of the memory nor imagination, neither the lively nor faint ideas can make their appearance in the mind, unless their correspondent impressions have gone before to prepare the way for them" (*Treatise of Human Nature*, p. 9). In the Humean view there must be a strict one-to-one correspondence between impressions and ideas: "All our simple ideas in their first appearance are deriv'd from simple impressions, which are correspondent to them, and which they exactly represent" (ibid., p. 4). Imagination is free only to change the "order and form" of the original impressions. (Cf. ibid., p. 9.)

Now my attentional focus is no longer on the room as such (which tends to become a mere backdrop) but on a certain state of affairs, a situation formed by the interaction of a small group of human beings. The people involved need not be presented in specific imagistic form, for I can just imagine *that-they-are-meeting* without their appearing to my mind as discrete presences.

(3) Finally, I *imagine how* the meeting proceeds—how it commences, develops, and finally comes to an end. Here the stress is on the dynamic development (instead of the mere happenstance) of the situation and thus on its temporal character. By my act of imagining, I am implicitly answering the question, how might such a meeting take place over time? What I come to imagine—e.g., such and such figures interacting, or such and such issues being discussed—shows me how the meeting I have in mind might proceed. And this can again happen in either a sensory or a nonsensory way.

Such cases of imagining call forth the following reflections. Undeniably there is a considerable continuity between what I have imagined in the above instances and what I would perceive were I to enter the actual room in question and witness (as I was in fact to do later that afternoon) a meeting of the Philosophy Department taking place there. This means that the *descriptions* I give of the content of these imaginative experiences will be strikingly similar to my descriptions of what I would perceive were I actually to be present at the imagined scene. Of course, descriptions of what I perceive can be made considerably more detailed and precise than descriptions of what I imagine. In perceptual descriptions I can say *just* how many chairs are arranged around the table, specify *precisely* the measurements of the bay window, and so on. Such precision cannot be achieved in describing the same scene as it is imagined.[13] Nonetheless, such a difference in the degree of detail that may be cited in the two sorts of description does not eliminate the possibility of significant similarity. Commenting on just such cases as we are discussing, Wittgenstein says, "the descriptions of what is seen and what is imagined are indeed of the same kind, and a description might be of the one just as much as of the other."[14]

Yet here we must ask two fundamental questions. What is the basis for such similarity of description, such continuity of content? And what are its limits? In the examples given above the criterion of descriptive continuity was met to the extent that what was imagined and what

13. Alain, says Sartre, "challenges any one to count the columns of the façade of the Pantheon *in an image.*" (*Psychology of Imagination*, p. 50, his italics; see also pp. 112-15.)

14. *Zettel*, sec. 637. I have substituted "imagined" for "imaged."

might have been (and, indeed, later was) perceived contained, if not precisely the same specific details, at least recognizably the same *sorts* of items. The room I imaged presented itself as having the same *kind* of color, shape, dimensions, and occupants as the room which I had perceived before and which I was to perceive again that same afternoon. Similarly, the meeting I imagined appeared as happening in the same *generic* way as its perceived counterpart was to take place later in the day, and this is so despite divergences in the detailed character of the two occurrences. Thus I can classify both happenings, the one perceived and the other imagined, as the same general kind of event, to which I may therefore apply the same descriptive phrase (e.g., 'meeting of the Philosophy Department in room 201'). It is on such a basis that one can justifiably claim a descriptive continuity between imagined and perceived contents.

That such "sortal" continuity occurs indicates, at the very least, that these contents are not always alien to one another. Hence we must reject the view that there can be no continuity *whatever* between what we imagine and what we perceive, as is implied in Sartre's contention that imagining and perceiving are "the two great irreducible attitudes of consciousness."[15] Such a strict bifurcation is unacceptable if it is meant as a universal description of the relationship between the two acts, whose contents may overlap in kind even if not in minute detail.

But it must be stressed that such overlapping remains *possible*, and not necessary, in character. It is mistaken to hold that "the mental image *must* be described in the language we use to describe the real object to which it refers."[16] Beyond the question as to whether a "mental image" can be said to "refer" to a real object in the first place, it is simply not true that we are forced to describe the content of this image in perceptual terms. Imagined content can defy such description, since we are capable of imagining things or events that have no place in the world of perception. In this lack of carry-over, we meet a first limitation upon the continuity of imagined and perceived contents.

A second limitation is found in the very notion of "kind" or "sort," a notion which has emerged as the basis of the continuity of imagined and perceived contents. To be continuous in kind is to overlap only at a generic level, a level at which minor differences of detail are no longer grounds for exclusion. It is to share not the same specific traits but the

15. *Psychology of Imagination*, p. 153. Sartre adds: "it follows that they exclude one another" (ibid.).

16. Robert Ehman, "Imagination, Dream, and the World of Perception," *Journal of Existentialism* (1965), V, p. 391; my italics. Ehman is on surer ground when he says that "the imagination appears to have the same *sort* of objects as perception" (ibid., p. 390; his italics), even though this is not true in every case.

same generic features, thus leaving considerable latitude as to precisely how these generic features are to be embodied in given instances of imagining or perceiving. This is not to deny that such embodiment may make a crucial difference in the felt qualities of the experiences in question. If it is pronounced enough, this difference may even obscure a basic or sortal similarity, with the result that the subject no longer realizes that what he is imagining and what he is perceiving are fundamentally the same type of thing. If I were to image room 201 in a sufficiently unusual way, I might no longer recognize it as the same sort of room that is used for Philosophy Department meetings; the phantasmagoric room might still contain the same kinds of things as before—the same sort of table, chairs, etc.—and yet in such a bizarre way as to obscure the fact that the newly imagined content is sortally continuous with what I can actually perceive of room 201. Only on analysis or reflection might the parallelism between the imagined and the perceived room emerge and then only at a quite abstract level. Therefore, although generic or sortal similarity of imagined and perceived contents is genuinely achievable, the very nonspecificity of such similarity is a limitation: on the one hand, the similarity is *only* generic; on the other, it may pass unnoticed when it is specified in certain particular ways.

CONTINUITY OF CONCEALED AND UNCONCEALED COMPONENTS

The fact that every act of perception is inherently partial and is never able to encompass *all* of the object it aims at gives rise to a second way in which perception and imagination are continuous with each other. At any given moment, some aspects of the perceived object will escape the perceiver's apprehension. This is most obviously true in the case of visual objects. When I look at the easy chair in my office while working at my desk, the backside of the chair and two of its legs are not present in my perceptual field. But the same partiality obtains in nonvisual perceiving as well. When I heard Rudolf Serkin playing the "Waldstein" last night, I took in the sound from a particular position in the first balcony. Had I been seated in another section of the concert hall, I would have heard the sounds differently—or, more exactly, I would have heard different aspects of the same sounds. Similarly, when I smell a certain perfume, it makes a difference whether I apprehend it at its source or on the periphery of the area through which it has spread. The intrinsic partialness or perspectivity of all these perceptual experiences is an expression of the fact that the perceiver is always anchored in some specific position in a particular spatio-temporal field. To be forced to perceive from a given standpoint and from no more than one such standpoint at a time is *ipso facto* to lack a complete or total grasp of what is perceived. The limitations of one's standpoint can, of course, be supplemented by various devices. Thus a system of mirrors can show me sides of perceived objects which I would not normally see at all. Yet even in this case my experience remains perspectival: I am still perceiving other sides *from* the front side, although these other sides are now made accessible to me by the mediation of mirrors. I still cannot see the object strictly aperspectivally.

In spite of the partialness of all perceiving, we nonetheless perceive objects as wholes and not merely as concatenations of components. It is *the easy chair* that I perceive and not only a series of its sides; or, more precisely, it is the easy chair itself which shows itself through the series of views that I take upon it and which is the true object of my perception. Similarly, I intend and hear the "Waldstein" itself—a discrete musical object—despite imperfections and variations in the way in which the sonata is apprehended. I am drawn toward and actually smell the particular perfume in question, not just an assemblage of semi-scents. But how can I perceive things in such a holistic manner when my perceivings are in each instance intrinsically incomplete?

Full-bodied perception occurs in these circumstances because I *intend more than is given*. I intend the object *totaliter* in each case and not only its momentarily proffered profiles. I aim at the total object, i.e., the perceived object insofar as it is a synthesis of given and nongiven components which do not exist in strict isolation from each other. As Aron Gurwitsch says:

> Every perceptual appearance contains a nucleus consisting of what is given in direct sense-experience. To this nucleus are attached references to what is not given in that privileged mode but nevertheless essentially pertains to, co-constitutes, and co-determines the perceptual appearance.[17]

Thus, when I perceive my easy chair, I intend it both in its givenness *and* in its nongivenness, and yet I do so without sharply distinguishing between the two sets of factors. Each set is co-constitutive of the perceived chair itself, and my perception of this chair is not annulled or even disrupted by the fact that what is given at the moment does not fulfill all of my explicit intentions. Indeed, I accept such unfulfillment

17. *The Field of Consciousness*, p. 237.

as an integral element of perceptual experience, which always involves a mixture of empty and fulfilled intentions.

What psychical agency is responsible for effecting a concordance between the given and the nongiven, the concealed and the unconcealed, the empty and the fulfilled, within perceptual experience? Is this concordance the work of imagination? It is tempting to believe so, especially in view of the fact that it is by imagining that we typically aim at what is *absent* from present perception: in Sartre's celebrated example, his friend Pierre is imagined as being in Berlin in his very absence from Paris, where he is not part of the present perceptual scene. Yet the temptation must be resisted. The unapprehended aspects of presently perceived objects are not absent from present perception in the same strict sense in which Pierre-in-Berlin is absent from view in Paris. If I am to render the strictly absent Pierre present to mind, I must make an express effort to summon up an imaginative presentation in which he figures.[18] But in the case of unapprehended aspects of a presently perceived object, no such explicit effort is required. For these aspects are already adumbrated—that is to say, *implicitly present*—as soon as I perceive the object in question, and the fact that they are not given directly or in detailed form, far from being a defect of perceiving to be overcome by imagining, is, on the contrary, one of perception's basic characteristics. Perceiving inescapably involves the experience of implicit presences; indeed, the felt coherence of perception derives in large measure from the perceiver's ready acceptance of a complex mixture of the implicitly and explicitly present. The nongiven is implied by the directly given, which tacitly refers to the presently concealed components of the perceived object, components that we *could* perceive were we in the proper position to do so.[19]

If imagination is not responsible for the peculiar coherence that exists between the given and nongiven aspects of a perceived object or event—since such coherence is part and parcel of perceptual experience itself—this does not mean that imagining is excluded altogether from collaboration with perceiving. Imaginative presentations may in fact

18. As Sartre says: "The characteristic of Pierre is not to be non-intuitive, as one would be tempted to believe, but to be 'intuitive-absent', given [as] absent to [perceptual] intuition" (*Psychology of Imagination*, p. 16).

19. Sartre again: "What is intended is never explicitly the invisible aspect of the thing. It is rather a certain visible aspect insofar as an invisible aspect corresponds to it; it is the upper face of the ashtray insofar as the very structure of an upper face implies the existence of an 'underneath' " (*Psychology of Imagination*, p. 155). It should be added that the nongiven in turn helps to determine the given; for it is only as harboring nongiven aspects that the given becomes a genuine perceptual given. On this point, see Gurwitsch, *The Field of Consciousness*, pp. 277-79.

serve to *supplement* perceptual presentations. Instead of emptily co-intending the unseen sides of a given visual object, I can actively imagine what these sides look like by summoning up a series of imaginative presentations. Such supplementation is not as rare as it might seem to be. It occurs frequently, for example, in the context of anticipation, especially when we are attempting to imagine how something presently unperceived will appear or occur in the future. In this particular context we are implicitly or explicitly asking ourselves such questions as: Will the unseen sides have the same texture as that of the sides we are now perceiving? What exact shapes will they have? What color? It is often by means of imagining in the specific form of imaging that we attempt to answer these questions in advance of actual acts of perception.

Nor is such supplemental imagining quite so arbitrary as it may appear at first glance. Although we are free to imagine the unapprehended sides of a given perceptual object in any form or order we choose, still we tend to imagine them in accordance with what previous perceptions of the object in question indicate or suggest. These perceptions help to make one's imaginings appropriate qua supplemental, for they embody and convey a tacit knowledge of the object as a whole, a knowledge on which the imaginer may draw in his attempts to clothe the nongiven in a specific imagistic form.[20] As a result, the imaginatively projected nongiven aspects of the object become quite continuous with its perceptually given aspects. In such cases perception provides a foundation for the imagination of what is not presently proffered in perception itself, and a cooperative partnership between perceiving and imagining is realized—a partnership in which these two acts achieve a continuity with each other that is of more consequence than the merely descriptive continuity of their respective contents.

Since such continuity is a familiar and even frequent phenomenon, it can hardly be regarded as an extraordinary feat of the human mind. In most instances it represents a natural and unforced extension of perceptual experience. Yet it must be emphasized that this extension is *imaginative* and not perceptual in character. A given perceptual experience is extended, but by means of *another* kind of act which differs intrinsically from perception proper. This supplemental act is one of imagination, even though its function can be designated as a form of

20. Note in this connection Sartre's use of the phrase "unformulated, prepredicative knowledge" (*Psychology of Imagination*, p. 154). The equivalent of such implicit knowing is also to be found in the writings of Mikel Dufrenne (cf. *The Notion of the A Priori*, trans. E. S. Casey [Evanston: Northwestern University Press, 1966], chapter six) and of Michael Polanyi (cf. *Personal Knowledge* [Chicago: University of Chicago Press, 1958], esp. part two).

"paraperception."[21] In its paraperceptual capacity, imagining is not only capable of linking up with preceding acts of perceiving: it carries on their work in a different modality. Qua paraperceptual, imagining is an act by which the inherent partialness of perceptual experience is momentarily suspended—though not, of course, overcome. Through such paraperceiving, perceived and imagined components become interwoven as conjoint elements of a perceptual object or event which we are striving to apprehend more fully than we could by perception alone.

CONTINUITY IN AESTHETIC EXPERIENCE

When in the presence of works of art, we sometimes experience a special continuity between perceiving and imagining that deserves brief mention at this point. In perceiving a given art work, we are not always so passive as the term "spectator" suggests. Not only may we actively identify ourselves with certain persons or situations represented in the work—as happens frequently in the theater—but we may also extend our aesthetic experience from its initial perceptual basis (from *aisthēsis* as strictly sensory) onto an imaginative plane. It is this latter process, the imaginative extension of perception, which interests us here. Such extension has been variously interpreted by aestheticians, e.g., as the spectator's imaginative "reconstruction" of the artist's original experience of imagining.[22] All that concerns us, though, is the fact that in this sort of aesthetic experience there is a continuation at the imaginative level of what began at the level of perception.

Let me cite an example from my recent experience: I am at the opera listening to Prokofieff's *War and Peace*. Although I am acutely aware of the perceived operatic spectacle, both auditory and visual, I find myself drifting into a state of mind that is qualitatively distinguishable from my perception of the sounds and sights before me and yet not a full-fledged fantasy. In this state I embroider in various ways on what I perceive: the Natasha that I see and hear on the stage becomes part of an invisible drama that carries on the actual stage production in imaginative terms. Unlike an irrelevant reverie, such imag-

21. Paraperception is to be contrasted with Merleau-Ponty's use of the term "teleperception": "Sartre [said] that the image of Pierre who is in Africa is only a 'manner of living' the very being of Pierre, his visible being, the only one there would be.—In reality this is something else than the free image: it is *a sort of perception, a teleperception*" (Maurice Merleau-Ponty, *The Visible and the Invisible*, trans. A. Lingis [Evanston: Northwestern University Press, 1968], p. 258; my italics).

22. Cf. R. G. Collingwood, *The Principles of Art*, pp. 139-44.

ining is not discontinuous with my initial and ongoing perceptions of the opera. The perceptual and imaginative components of the aesthetic experience shade into each other, and I cannot say exactly where one begins and the other ends. At any moment I can return from my imagining to the actual spectacle as it unfolds beneath my gaze and in my hearing. The transition from perception to imagination, as from imagination back to perception, occurs without any sense of abrupt break: the two activities become continuous with each other within a single self-enclosed aesthetic experience.

What is perhaps most noteworthy about such an experience is the way in which the imaginative extension of perception serves to enrich perception itself. We return to the work refreshed, and in such a way as even to *enhance* its perception. This enhancement occurs through the active animation of the work's perceptual qualities.[23] Such animation builds on prior imaginings: now that I have brought Natasha to life in imagination, the Natasha on the stage before me seems more vibrant and alive. The perceived personage gains in expressiveness by having passed through the alembic of my dramatizing imagination. In short, we witness here what R. K. Elliott has called "an imaginative extension and modification of what is actually seen."[24]

Yet, contrary to certain neo-idealist theories of art, aesthetic experience is not to be conceived as *wholly* imaginative in character.[25] Perception remains integral to this experience, even though it may be extended and transformed by acts of imagining. What had first been grasped as taking place *outside* the spectator's immediate sphere of consciousness can also occur *within* this sphere in the form of imaginative activity. But this transfer of locus is not abrupt, and the movement from external to internal—from perception to imagination—is often imperceptible. It is also easily reversible. At any given point the spectator who has been imagining in an aesthetically relevant manner can redirect his attention onto the perceived work. This is due to the fact that perception has not been wholly replaced or superseded by imagination. Perception continues throughout aesthetic experience as a *basso continuo* onto which the melody line of imagination may be subtly and nonirrevocably superimposed.

23. On the notion of animation, conceived as "concretization," see Ingarden, *The Literary Work of Art*, secs. 61-64. Ingarden, however, does not link concretization to imagination. (For his view of imagination, see ibid., sec. 34.)

24. "Aesthetic Theory and the Experience of Art" in *Aesthetics*, ed. Harold Osborne (Oxford University Press, 1972), p. 155. Elliott speaks of "imaginatively enhanced perception" on p. 157.

25. Cf. Collingwood, *The Principles of Art*, p. 148: the work of art is "an imaginative experience of total activity."

CONTINUITY OF SEEING-AS

A final continuity between perceiving and imagining is found in the phenomenon of seeing-as. To perceive something *as* such-and-such is to engage in a form of interpretative activity not found in ordinary passive perceiving. To see the classical duck-rabbit of Gestalt psychology *as* a duck or *as* a rabbit is not merely to register passively what is perceived. It is to grasp and to specify an initially ambiguous figure as one kind of thing rather than another.

Seeing-as is by no means a simple affair, and it occurs in at least two distinguishable forms. It is found, first of all, in the perception of strictly *double*-aspect figures such as the duck-rabbit, the white-and-black cross, and various line drawings of regular three-dimensional figures. These stock-in-trade examples are literally *ambi*-guous, allowing for only two alternative "readings." Imagining is only minimally active in the apprehension of such figures because of the strict binary choice they involve and because of the clearly demarcated clues that make this choice so evenly balanced. Here it is as if the essential work of interpretation has been predelineated by the perceived figure itself. The perceiver-interpreter does not so much imagine as *determine* which aspect he will see, and the range of this determination is delimited by the strictly either/or character of the perceived object: *either* a duck *or* a rabbit. It is true that a certain amount of imaginative activity may be helpful in envisioning an aspect that one has not yet managed to grasp. But once both aspects have been recognized, it becomes a routine matter of attending to whichever of the two aspects one wishes to apprehend at the moment.[26]

A second form of seeing-as occurs in the perception of *multiple*-aspect figures or objects. An inkblot in a Rorschach test, for instance, offers to its perceiver such a proliferation of possibilities that simple either/or interpretations are precluded.[27] A less complex example, cited by Wittgenstein, is that of a scalene triangle lying on its longest side:

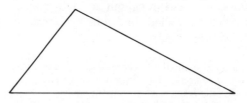

26. Even here, however, we may observe a special affinity between imagining and seeing-as: both are capable of being intended or willed by the human subject. Just as I can summon up imaginative presentations at will, so I can actively decide to see the rabbit rather than the duck once I have become acquainted with both

The triangle may be regarded as representing any number of things, and there is no way of predetermining precisely how many ways we may grasp it:

> This triangle can be seen as a triangular hole, as a solid, as a geometrical drawing; as standing on its base, as hanging from its apex; as a mountain, as a wedge, as an arrow or pointer, as an overturned object which is meant to stand on the shorter side of the right angle, as a half parallelogram, and as various other things.[28]

Now, it is precisely in view of the open-ended character of this list that imagining is called for in the interpretation of such a figure. The mere perception of a polyvalent object of this sort does not provide sufficient indication of the numerous interpretations to which it may give rise. In its projective capacity, imagination allows us to envision the multiple aspects of this kind of figure, enabling us to see it now as one thing, now as another, now as something still different. From the various possible specifications we can select those which most suit a particular occasion or purpose.

It cannot be claimed, however, that imagining is as active and efficacious as this in every instance of seeing-as. We have just seen that in the case of double-aspect figures imagining is normally of only marginal significance, being employed (if it is employed at all) as an aid in the initial recognition of a given aspect. It is primarily in the case of multiple-aspect figures that imagining assumes a more crucial role, allowing us to see a Rorschach figure as, say, a hydra-headed monster or an ordinary scalene triangle as an arrow or a wedge. In each of these latter cases we have to surpass seeing as such—seeing as a passive "state" of beholding—and to employ a more active mental process.[29] *This more active process is imaginative in nature*, for it is by imagining that we envisage the various ways in which a multivalent perceived figure may

---

aspects of the Gestalt figure. Observing that perceiving and imagining are both "subject to the will," Wittgenstein concludes that "the concept of [seeing] an aspect is akin to the concept of [forming] an image" (*Philosophical Investigations*, p. 213; cf. also *Zettel*, secs. 621-22, 627, 640-46).

27. As Roy Schafer observes, "Each Rorschach response spreads out to a greater or lesser extent along a continuum extending from reality-oriented perception at the one end, through directed and undirected daytime imagery, to autistic and dreamlike imagery at the other end" ("Content Analysis in the Rorschach Test," in *Psychoanalytic Psychiatry and Psychology*, eds. R. P. Knight and C. R. Friedman [New York: International Universities Press, 1970], p. 215).

28. *Philosophical Investigations*, p. 200.

29. On seeing as a "state" (*Zustand*), see Wittgenstein, *Philosophical Investigations*, p. 212.

be interpreted: the figure is *seen as* such-and-such because it is *imagined to be* such-and-such. It is at this point, i.e., when seeing-as involves imagining intrinsically, that perceiving and imagining become genuinely continuous with each other.

It is important to observe that previously examined continuities between perceiving and imagining have been strictly optional in character. The continuity of imagined and perceived contents is never more than possible, since what we imagine does not have to correspond descriptively to what we perceive. Likewise, in bringing about a continuity between concealed and unconcealed components of a perceived object, the use of imagination remains facultative; the object's already apprehended parts may allude to what is thus far unapprehended without our having to supplement former perceptions by special acts of imagining. Further, the imaginative enhancement of aesthetic perception is not anything that we are compelled to do, and it may be absent from the experience of the spectator who is wholly absorbed in the perceived work of art. Experiences of seeing-as, however, represent a different sort of situation. Here, and above all in cases of multiple-aspect figures, the role of imagination is no longer merely optional: it becomes essential or *necessary*. And insofar as imagining is required for the full realization of multiple-aspect seeing-as, we may conclude that the continuity between perception and imagination that is effected therein is the most crucial and consequential of the various continuities explored in this chapter.

The foregoing discussion of four types of continuity is aptly summed up by a statement from Wittgenstein's *Zettel*:

> There is of course a close tie-up of these language-games [i.e., of perceiving and imagining]; but a resemblance?—Bits of one resemble bits of the other, but the resembling bits are not homologous.[30]

If we were to substitute "continuity" for "resemblance," this statement would support the analysis that has been given in the preceding pages: perceiving and imagining are continuous with each other, but only in part and in certain non-homologous respects. We have discerned several varieties of such continuity, ranging from the fragile and optional to the deep-seated and required. Certain experiences allow a merely

30. Sec. 646. See also sec. 625.

occasional linking of imagination and perception; others actively solicit a more constant union of the two acts. Such variation is sufficient to exclude the presence of a single homologous structure within the perceptual-imaginal continuities in question.

Therefore, the mere fact that perceiving and imagining are capable of achieving continuity with each other in various ways does not prove that the two acts are inherently isomorphic in form or function. Contrary to Aristotle's dictum that imagination "must be like perception,"[31] they are never wholly assimilable to each other, however intimate their cooperation may become. Nor does such cooperation justify Kant's claim that "imagination is a necessary ingredient of perception itself."[32] Not even in multiple-aspect seeing-as can we say that imagination becomes *part* of perception; never an actual ingredient, it is at most an essential adjunct. Even in their closest conjunctions, imagining remains distinguishable from perceiving: continuity does not imply coincidence.

31. *De Anima*, 428b 14.
32. *Critique of Pure Reason*, A120 n.a., p. 144. The full statement is as follows: "Psychologists have hitherto failed to realize that imagination is a necessary ingredient of perception itself. This is due partly to the fact that that faculty has been limited to reproduction, partly to the belief that the senses not only supply impressions but also combine them so as to generate images of objects. For that purpose something more than the mere receptivity of impressions is undoubtedly required, namely, a function for the synthesis of them."

CHAPTER SEVEN

Imagining and Perceiving: Discontinuities

I

A RECOGNITION of the continuities that exist between perception and imagination must not bind us to their still more distinctive discontinuities. To single out these discontinuities is not to commit ourselves to the view—held by only a few heterodox figures like Blake, Novalis, Baudelaire, and Breton—that the two acts are so disparate as to lack *any* points of contact with each other. Rather, it is a matter of pointing to crucial differences between perceiving and imagining without denying what they also have in common. These differences express themselves in four fundamental forms: mode of approach, external horizon, internal horizon, and comparative certainty. Before we take up these types of discontinuity, however, we must discuss two preliminary matters: the mutual exclusion of perception and imagination and the apparent indistinguishability of these acts in certain experiences.

MUTUAL EXCLUSION

By the "mutual exclusion" of perceiving and imagining I mean that the performance of one act is incompatible with the simultaneous performance of the other act. The seemingly obvious character of such exclusion may obscure the fact that it covers two very different situations, only one of which involves mutual exclusion in a strict sense. On the one hand, we cannot simultaneously imagine and perceive *the same thing* in the same respect. As Wittgenstein bluntly puts it, "While I am looking at an object I cannot imagine it."[1] His claim is clearly true if it is interpreted within certain precise limits. It is undeniably the case that I cannot imagine *exactly* what I perceive while I am in the process

1. *Zettel*, sec. 621.

of perceiving it. If I am looking at a bookcase in my study, I cannot simultaneously imagine this bookcase as occupying just the same position within my field of apprehension; nor can the imagined bookcase be superimposed point by point upon the perceived bookcase so as to become one with it. We cannot have it both ways: *either* I perceive the actual bookcase before me *or* I imagine such a bookcase as appearing before me in the same position. To effect the latter while I am facing the actual bookcase, I must close my eyes, avert my gaze, or in some other way allow for the imagined bookcase to replace its perceived counterpart. Here we experience mutual exclusion in a rigorous sense.

On the other hand, I *can* imagine and perceive *different* things at the same time, or even the same thing viewed differently. To keep with the same example: while perceiving my bookcase, I can concurrently imagine a variety of *other* things as well, e.g., books that might fit into the perceived bookcase, other bookcases, or bookshelves in distant libraries; and I can also imagine the perceived bookcase in a different position, revealing other sides, etc. Usually when we imagine at the same time as we perceive, we tend to imagine objects that differ in kind—i.e., different *sorts* of things—from those that we are presently perceiving. In this way no direct competition between the two sets of objects occurs, for their type-differences allow them to coexist in consciousness without mutual interference. And in any case we must reject Sartre's claim that "insofar as I look at this table, I cannot form an image of Pierre; but if the unreal Pierre suddenly springs before me, the table which is under my eyes vanishes, leaves the scene."[2] This is not necessarily the case: we can imagine "with our eyes open" and frequently do so in everyday life. When this happens, and so long as their respective contents differ in some way, imagining and perceiving are not mutually exclusive.

APPARENT INDISTINGUISHABILITY: THE PERKY EXPERIMENT

But if perception and imagination can thus coexist within one and the same experience, how are they to retain distinguishable identities

---

2. *Psychology of Imagination*, pp. 153-54; "look at" (*regarde*) is in italics. It is perhaps noteworthy that here, as on several previous occasions, I have sided with Wittgenstein rather than with Sartre. This has not been done in an effort to be perversely nonphenomenological in my choice of supporting evidence—or merely to prove myself to be "open-minded." Rather, I am pointing to certain inadequacies in Sartre's account in the interest of providing a more satisfactory phenomenology of imagination than Sartre himself provides. In this critical assessment of Sartre, Wittgenstein shows himself to be a useful ally.

as different mental acts? Will they not sometimes intermingle so deeply as to realize what Sartre calls "a hybrid state which is neither completely perception nor wholly imagination and which deserves description on its own account"?[3] Sartre himself cites the example of 'seeing' a face in a flame before which one is seated.[4] Such a case is admittedly difficult to classify. When I seem to see a face in the flame, I do not want to say about this experience that the face is literally *in* the flame, contained there as if it were a separate perceptual object. Yet I also resist the idea that I am merely projecting an imaginary object onto the flame as an indifferent material substratum. Somehow the flame itself invites or solicits me to 'see' a face in it—a face which seems to be at once perceptual and imaginative in character. A phenomenon such as this suggests not only that imagination and perception do not exclude each other but that they may become co-constitutive of an experience in which they are no longer distinguishable from one another. And if this is so, how can we continue to claim that imagining and perceiving are eidetically distinct, that is, different in kind and not merely in degree?

A more telling test case of the apparent indistinguishability of imagining and perceiving is the "Perky experiment" of 1910.[5] In this experiment the psychologist C. W. Perky seated subjects before an initially blank screen and asked them to imagine a simple object, e.g., a single piece of fruit. Unknown to the subjects, a dim outline of the object mentioned was then projected onto the screen. Almost invariably, the subjects took the dimly projected object to be an imagined object. If requested to say what they had *imagined*, the subjects would describe the image *seen* on the screen (the "screen image," as we shall call it). Assuming that this experiment was accurately reported, it seems to present us with a convincing case in which what is imagined and what is perceived become indistinguishable—and to an extent that might appear to warrant Perky's conclusion that perceiving and imagining differ from each other only in degree.[6]

3. *Psychology of Imagination*, p. 37.
4. Cf. ibid., p. 25: "There are intermediary types [of acts] which present us with syntheses of external [i.e., perceptual] and of psychical [i.e., imaginative] elements, as when one sees a face in the flame or in the arabesques of a tapestry. . . ."
5. "An Experimental Study of Imagination" in *American Journal of Psychology* (1910), vol. 23, 422-52.
6. This conclusion is seconded in later discussions of the Perky experiment. Cf. Julian Hochberg, *Perception* (Englewood Cliffs: Prentice-Hall, 1964), p. 33; also, R. W. Pickford in C. M. Wyburn, R. W. Pickford, and R. J. Hirst, *Human Senses and Perception* (Toronto: University of Toronto Press, 1964), pp. 223-24. What is now generally referred to as the "Perky effect" has been reconfirmed in recent experiments. See esp. S. J. Segal, "Assimilation of a Stimulus in the Construction of

It is not sufficient to object to the Perky experiment by simply denying its significance, as Sartre does:

> [Perky's] experiment would be meaningful only if the image were a real
> perception. But [an image] gives itself *as an image,* and thus any com-
> parison between it and a perception in terms of intensity is impossible.
> It is difficult to know who is the more confused: the experimenter who
> poses such questions or the subject who answers docilely.[7]

It is pointless to claim in this context that an image always gives itself
as an image, for it is this very claim that the Perky experiment puts into
question. The experiment must be criticized on a different ground,
namely, that it fails to prove conclusively the existence of the alleged
indistinguishability between perception and imagination. Consider the
options that the experiment presents to a subject who is seated in
Perky's laboratory. On the one hand, if this subject is *not* imagining at
the moment the screen image appears, he will simply and straightforwardly *perceive* this mechanically projected image and will not be confusing the latter with a mental image (for there is no such image to
confuse it with). On the other hand, if he *is* imagining when the screen
image is projected, one of two possibilities will obtain: either he will
thereupon cease imagining and devote his attention to the screen image
(once more a straightforward instance of perceiving) or he will continue imagining. And if the subject continues to imagine, one of two
things will happen: either he will notice the difference between what
he is imagining and what he is perceiving on the screen or he will ignore
what he perceives and attend to the imagined object alone. At no
point, then, will the subject fail to differentiate, or confuse between,
what is imagined and what is perceived. He will either actually distinguish between the two or not need to make such a distinction in the
first place. (He will not need to make the distinction in those circumstances where he is either simply imagining or simply perceiving; with
only a single act and its content present, there is no motive for distinguishing this act-*cum*-content from some other act-*cum*-content.)

The reason for this lack of confusion is not difficult to discover. We
know that it is not possible to imagine and perceive exactly the same
thing at the same time and in the same respect. If this is indeed the
case, then there cannot be a failure to distinguish between imagining
and perceiving the same object, for a given object as imagined can

---

an Image: the Perky Effect Revisited" in *The Function and Nature of Imagery,*
ed. P. W. Sheehan (New York: Academic Press, 1972), pp. 203-30.
  7. *Psychology of Imagination,* pp. 68-69; his italics.

never completely coincide with the same object as perceived. Thus the subjects in Perky's laboratory cannot have been doing what Perky took them to be doing: failing to discriminate between a perceived and an imagined object. The only way such confusion could arise would be if the subjects did not know to begin with that there is a difference between perceiving and imagining. Yet this is clearly not the situation in Perky's experiment. The adults who were tested were, like all normal adults, able to distinguish between the two acts in ordinary circumstances. Hence they were fully cognizant that perceiving and imagining are different acts.[8]

Of course, to know that there is such a difference does not mean that one might not be misled under special circumstances to misinterpret the nature or status of what one experiences on that occasion. Indeed, the Perky experiment purports to be a case in point. The experiment was devised so cleverly that, although the subjects were in fact perceiving a screen image, they took this artificially projected image to be their own mental image. Yet such a mistake could arise only if they were *not* imagining at the time—or (a remote possibility) not realizing that they were imagining. In other words, the mistake, if it does occur, shows only that one is capable, in certain carefully contrived conditions, of *mis*taking what one perceives. In an ordinary case of perceptual illusion, there is a confusion between one perceptual object and another, e.g., a distant tree and a man. In the Perky experiment, a particular perceptual object (the screen image) is erroneously taken to be an imagined object. This is not an error of confusion but of mischaracterization: what is perceived is wrongly held to be imagined. But the possibility of such a misattribution does not prove that what we perceive and what we imagine have become indistinguishable or, still more presumptuously, that they differ only in degree.

The same inconclusiveness infects the example cited by Sartre: 'seeing' a face in a flame. In this instance there is not even the possibility of the special sort of error that arises in the Perky experiment. When I pick out a face in the fire, I am not misled into believing that an actual face is present before me. I know that the face I 'see' is only *suggested* by the fire. But I also know that I am not merely imagining it as when

8. There is perhaps only one instance in which a knowledge of this difference is systematically lacking: in children who are capable of eidetic imagery. Because of its vivacity, this imagery may be taken by children to be identical with genuinely perceived content. But adults do not so take it, no matter how vivid the imagery is. On the question of eidetic imagery, see E. R. Jaensch's classic study, *Eidetic Imagery* (London: Kegan Paul, 1930). Cf. also the studies on eidetic imagery contained in the Fall 1969 issue of *Scientific American*.

I imaginatively project a face onto the blank surface of a wall. Rather, my imagination (if it is active at all here) takes its cue from perception: it is the fire as perceived that is the primary factor in the experience. And I am quite aware of the difference between this perceptual base and whatever might transcend it as a result of concerted or spontaneous imaginative activity. Thus, what is perceived and what is imagined remain inherently distinguishable, even if I do not always distinguish them explicitly at the moment of their interaction. We see once again that the imagined and the perceived may enter into a close partnership without thereby dissolving into each other. Their differences are more than differences of degree; they are also, and more crucially, differences of kind.

II

With the foregoing clarifications in mind, let us consider four primary ways in which perceiving and imagining are discontinuous with each other and thus genuinely different in kind.

MODE OF APPROACH

A first significant way in which perception and imagination differ distinctly is found in their respective modes of approach. By "mode of approach" is meant the manner in which increased proximity to something is achieved. Approaching something involves at least three interrelated factors: movement through space, intermediate objects, and the approached object as such (where "object" is taken generically to include events and states of affairs as well as objects in the narrow sense of material entities).

Traversing Space

In approaching perceived phenomena, I must move in a continuous, point-by-point manner through a given stretch of space that lies between my present position and the location of the approached object. To take an example from everyday existence: after parking my car in the university parking lot, I have to walk a finite and measurable distance in order to reach my office in Strathcona Hall. This distance is not always the same, varying as a function of the route I take. But insofar as I have chosen a given route and stick to it, I must traverse every inch of it in getting to my office. No part of the route may be omitted if I am to reach such a destination: I cannot leap over the space of this route any more than I can leap over my own shadow. (Or than I can leap over the time it takes me to get to my destination: time too must be traversed in a continuous and complete manner. But we shall restrict consideration here to space.)

When I approach things in imagination, I am not bound by the same necessity of traversing given stretches of space in a continuous manner. By merely wishing or thinking that I am at my destination, I can represent myself as already being there. Thus, I can imagine myself emerging from my car and in the very next second entering Strathcona Hall, having eliminated the spatial interval between my car and the building. Far from being extraordinary, to imagine in this leapfrog manner is quite common. Imagined movement is for the most part discontinuous, proceeding from one place to another without any need to cover a certain prescribed distance. Indeed, lacking a constant spatial setting, the imaginative presentation not only allows for but encourages discontinuous traversals within its shifting boundaries.

Intermediate Objects

When we approach something in the perceptual world, we typically encounter entities or events along our chosen route. If I walk toward Strathcona Hall, things situated between myself and this building are themselves approached, passed by, and left behind: the pavement I walk on, people I meet, other buildings. As I move past these intermediate phenomena, they seem to glide toward the outer edges of my perceptual field in a quasi-automatic fashion, fading away in a gradual and almost self-dissolving manner, until they take up a position behind me and out of sight.

The role of intermediate objects in experiences of imagined approach is much more minimal. If such objects appear at all, they lack the stability that would allow them to be bypassed in the continuous manner just described. Instead, they appear so intermittently and disconnectedly that it is difficult to say that I move *by* or *beyond* them toward my destination. And even if I do succeed in imagining that I have passed them by, there is no sense of their remaining behind me as enduring presences now vanished from view. Indeed, we would not normally say that such imagined objects *fade from view* at all. Rather, they characteristically evaporate as abruptly as they have appeared in the first place, and yet without situating themselves *somewhere else* where they could be reapprehended at a later point. Once what I imagine has disappeared from what Merleau-Ponty calls "the inward traces of vision,"[9] it must be *re*-imagined—which is to say, recreated as a whole.

The Approached Object

When we consider, finally, *what* it is that we approach in perception and imagination, significant differences once more arise. In approaching a perceived object such as Strathcona Hall, I note that it looms progressively larger as I draw closer to it. It occupies increasingly more of my perceptual field until in the end it dominates that field and perhaps even becomes its exclusive occupant. By the time I reach the entrance, I confront the building itself in its monolithic and commanding character. It towers up in my perceived world as a primary determinant of further action on my part. Either I shall enter the building or I shall turn away from it; whichever I do, my action must take the building into account: I cannot ignore its insistent presence.

If I now imagine myself approaching such a building, it is immediately evident that as an *imaginatum* it plays no comparably commanding role. Even if an imagined Strathcona Hall suddenly looms up in my consciousness, it does not dominate this consciousness or determine its subsequent actions. I can always banish the imagined building in the next instant, putting it out of mind or at least eliminating it from my mind's central concerns. There is thus a shift from a situation in which *what I perceive* is determinative to one in which the *act of imagining* is directive. Moreover, I notice that the imagined building does not increase gradually in size as I approach it mentally; nor does it take up a continually larger portion of my imaginative presentation. Rather, the way in which its size changes is characteristically inconstant and non-incremental, and may alter in an arbitrary manner, e.g., by suddenly *decreasing*. While the perceived building as approached amasses itself before my eyes at a steady rate—only the "constancy effect" keeps this growth from seeming monstrous—its imagined counterpart lacks any such regular aggrandizement.[10]

EXTERNAL HORIZON

A perceived object always appears within a particular perceptual field and is related, implicitly or explicitly, to the other members of this

9. "Eye and Mind," trans. C. Dallery in *The Primacy of Perception*, ed. James Edie (Evanston: Northwestern University Press, 1964), p. 165.

10. On the constancy effect, see J. Hochberg, *Perception*, pp. 50-55, and R. J. Hirst, *The Problems of Perception* (London: Allen and Unwin, 1959), pp. 255-77.

field. The field, along with its occupants, constitutes an object's "external horizon."[11] The horizon is external insofar as the field and the field-occupants *surround* the object and are distinctively *other* than this object—exterior to, and set apart from, it. Borrowing terms from Gestalt psychology, we may speak of the external horizon as providing the "context" of a given "thematic" object. Whenever I attend to or thematize a perceived object, this object reveals itself to be in the midst of a setting of con-textually given objects. This setting and the objects appearing within it make up the thematic object's external horizon.

To revert to our previous example: both in approaching and in reaching Strathcona Hall, I am aware of the two factors that constitute its external horizon. On the one hand, the building itself is perceived as stationed in a fixed field which consists not merely of my path of approach but of an entire setting. Beginning with the patch of ground on which Strathcona Hall is built, this setting stretches out in all directions. It includes the places in which the immediately surrounding buildings are located, the contiguous areas on the far (and presently not visible) sides of these buildings, still more distant parts of the city—and so on *ad indefinitum*. On the other hand, Strathcona Hall itself is seen as standing in certain definite relations with objects around or near it—objects that are co-given as discrete but integral elements in the total perceptual scene. Thus, the Becton Engineering and Applied Science Center presents itself as situated on the near side of Strathcona as I approach the latter from the rear, flanking it on the north and west, approximately fifty yards distant from it, and so on. Becton, together with other buildings and objects surrounding Strathcona, constitutes a coherent set of entities and attendant relations, "a plurality of simultaneously co-affecting substrates."[12]

Let us examine in more detail these two basic components of the external horizon.

A. The Perceptual Field

The external horizon encompasses a field, a spatial expanse within which specific objects, events, and states of affairs are located. This per-

---

11. Cf. Husserl's early description of the phenomenon of the external horizon: "Every perception has its perceptual background. The thing which is grasped in perception has an *environment* of things which co-appear perceptually . . ." (*Ideas*, sec. 113; his italics). The term "external horizon" (and its cognate "internal horizon") appears much later in Husserl's writing, e.g., in *Experience and Judgment*, sec. 33.

12. *Experience and Judgment*, p. 149.

ceptual field *underlies* or subtends all of the discriminable items that populate it, providing for these items a continuous and stable spatial foundation. In this capacity it fulfills three critical roles in perceptual experience:

(1) It furnishes a *background* for what we perceive thematically. As a background, the perceptual field makes it possible for particular perceived objects to stand out as discrete, since it introduces an element of contrast into the perceptual situation: a sense of greater or lesser depth which allows for increased specificity of thematic content.

(2) The perceptual field allows for *location* in space. Specific perceived items require an underlying medium within which to be located. Such items can be securely situated only within a relatively perduring framework such as is furnished by the perceptual field. This framework is the basis for the various co-ordinate systems, whether commonsensical or scientific, by means of which precise spatial locations are determined.

(3) Finally, the perceptual field is the basis for *transfer* in space. By "transfer" is meant both motion as such and change of place. Both of these modes of transfer presuppose a persisting field within which, and within which alone, they can occur. The factor of transferability helps to establish the independence of thematized items from the rest of the field, i.e., their ability to move through this field as distinct from it and its unthematized occupants.

In addition to its functions as an underlying factor, the perceptual field also serves to *open up* and to *open out* the immediate boundaries of perceptual presence. It gives to these boundaries the sense that they could be pushed back indefinitely without ever reaching a last limit. Thus, any apparent limit of a given perceptual field—e.g., the wall beside which I walk—is only a provisional demarcation, for the perceptual field always extends beyond the bounded area or sector within which I presently find myself as a perceiver. Consequently, there is always more to a given perceptual field than can be discovered in a single act of perception—or perhaps even in an infinite series of such acts. Much as in the bustling, capacious scenes depicted in many of Brueghel's paintings, there is a sense of endlessness combined with an extraordinary diversity of content.

Imaginative experience contains no exact equivalent of the perceptual field. Its world-frame of space and time most closely corresponds to this field in terms of function and structure. But the world-frame cannot, as we have already remarked in chapter two, be considered a *field* in any strict sense. It exists only as a transitory frame for imagined content and does not extend beyond the delimited boundaries of this content in an ever expanding manner. Instead of opening up or out, imaginal space characteristically acts to enclose, to *close in upon*. Moreover, it is itself enclosed by the imaginal margin, into which its outer edges shade off. (The imaginal margin's basic indefiniteness is such that we cannot consider it as a field either; nothing can move or be located within such radical vagueness.)

Not only does the world-frame fail to open up the imaginative presentation in which it inheres, it also cannot be said to underlie imagined content as an undergirding and stabilizing element. Nor does it precede or outlast a given imaginative presentation. It is strictly concurrent and coincidental with the particular presentation it serves to situate, and thus provides no lasting foundation for what we imagine. As a result, the imagined world-frame cannot fulfill any of the three primary roles that the perceptual field plays within perceptual experience. (1) The world-frame does not furnish a background for imagined content. This lack of background accords with the insistently frontal character of the imaginative presentation, which decrees that imagined content does not recede in depth except in a quite superficial fashion. The imaginative presentation contains no *Hintergrund* into which this content can sink or against which it can stand out: the background is swallowed up by the foreground, which dominates the spatiality of all that we imagine. (2) The world-frame does not allow for any genuine locations in imagined space. To be sure, what we imagine is momentarily "localized." But to be localized—i.e., to appear in a certain indeterminate area of a given imaginative presentation—is not the same as to be located at an objectively specifiable point within a fixed framework. Instead of locations there are only transitory *locales*, which do not last from one imaginative presentation to another. Of course, an express effort may be made to perpetuate these locales, as when a novelist continues to constitute a certain imaginary landscape. But this landscape cannot be said to endure *between* episodes; its continuing existence is only presumptive and depends upon the novelist's repeated positings. (3) There is, finally, no basis within the world-frame for what we have called "transfer." In the absence of an underlying and persisting substratum, we cannot speak of transferring items—of changing positions through specific movements. Transferability in any strict sense is thus excluded. At the most, we can talk of "shifts" within the world-frame. But such shifting consists of desultory pseudo-motions, not of movements from one determinate position to another.

B. *Surrounding With-Objects*

"With-objects" (*Mitobjekten* in Husserl's term) constitute the second basic component of the external horizon. They are those environing entities which surround a thematically perceived object and enter into various relationships with it. With-objects are never entirely absent from perceptual experience. As Husserl says, "Everything given in [perceptual] experience . . . has an endless, open *external horizon of co-given objects.*"[13] These co-given with-objects are genuine perceptual objects in their own right; they are "real objects (with properties, relations, etc.) *in* the world . . . existing within the one spatial-temporal horizon."[14] This being the case, every relationship between such objects and a given thematic object will be determinate or at least determinable.[15] Thus, as I stride toward Strathcona Hall, I find myself moving toward a thematic object whose external horizon includes several surrounding buildings, the people I encounter, and still other miscellaneous things which are spread before and around me. *I too* am a constituent member of this external horizon, being related to all other members in a number of determinate ways. Within such a situation we may discern three different kinds of with-object:

(1) *With-objects adjacent to the thematic object.* Those objects which immediately surround the thematic object are almost as determinate as the latter. They may become still more determinate by a simple shift of attention on the part of the perceiver. Because of their proximity to the thematic object, they tend to form with it a cluster of closely interrelated items which stand out from the background constituted by nonadjacent with-objects. Various relations at close quarters structure this cluster of objects and give it an identity of its own. As such, it forms the focal region of a given perceptual field.

(2) *With-objects not adjacent to the thematic object.* These are of two types. (a) First, there are all of those objects which are noncontiguous with the thematic object, yet which still form part of what one is presently perceiving. What we earlier termed "intermediate objects" belong here: they are those currently perceived with-objects I must pass by in order to reach a destination. (b) Second, there are those noncontiguous objects which are *not* presently perceived but whose presence is indicated by some or all of those objects that one does currently apprehend. Thus, a row of houses partly cut off from view is nonetheless presumed to continue beyond the point at which it becomes occluded.

---

13. *Experience and Judgment,* p. 33; Husserl's italics.
14. Ibid. I have slightly altered the translation here.
15. "Everything is either here or there, and its place [*Ort*] is determinable" (Husserl, ibid., p. 34; cf. also Gurwitsch, *The Field of Consciousness,* p. 405). The point is that whenever I perceive, I am assured that every discriminable item in the perceptual field possesses certain definite relations—above all, spatio-temporal relations—with every other discriminable item in this same field.

The nonvisible houses are implied by those that are present to vision; and yet the row as a whole may be nonadjacent to the focal point of my attention.

(3) *Remote with-objects*. Beyond adjacent and nonadjacent with-objects, there are still other with-objects that are only remotely related to a given perceptual scene. Not only are such objects not perceived within this scene, they are not even indicated or expressly alluded to by anything that one is presently perceiving. Nevertheless, they are *implicit* in the particular perceptual experience one is having. Taken in their totality, remote with-objects constitute everything that is perceivable and yet is not the object of present or imminent perception.[16] Such with-objects together form what Merleau-Ponty calls the "horizon of all horizons."[17] *This* horizon encloses the perceived world as a whole and includes all that we can ever perceive; as such, it is always a latent or tacit dimension of any given perceptual experience.[18]

It might seem that imaginative experience includes genuine with-objects. Can we not imagine a given object as standing in definite relations with co-posited objects, all within the same presentation? When I imagine, say, a certain tree as situated in an imaginary backyard, such a tree may very well present itself as growing in a given area of the imagined backyard, behind a certain part of an imagined house, at a certain unspecified distance from other imagined trees, etc. Nevertheless, although all of this is certainly possible, I find that I cannot determine the *precise* form and extent of the various relations between the thematized tree and its neighboring objects. In what exact part of the imagined backyard is the imagined tree found? How far is it from the imagined house? How distant from other imagined trees? There are no unambiguous answers to these questions, all of which would be answerable in precise terms if I were to *perceive* the same scene. The fundamental difficulty, as demonstrated in chapter five, is that a particular

16. I say "imminent" so as to cover the case of nonadjacent with-objects that lie in a nearby perceptual field. Remote with-objects are not only nonadjacent in this sense; they are so distant from the present perceptual scene and its immediate borders that they are not subject to perception in any immediately foreseeable context.

17. The full citation is as follows: "The natural world is the horizon of all horizons, the style of all styles, guaranteeing for my experiences a given and non-willed unity beneath all of the ruptures of my personal and historical life" (*Phenomenology of Perception*, p. 381). As I am using it, the phrase "horizon of all horizons" is not restricted to the natural world but may refer to any totality of perceivable objects, natural or man-made.

18. If the perceived world is, in Husserl's definition, "the sum of all the objects of possible sensory experience" (*Ideas*, sec. 1), then it is composed for the most part of remote with-objects, i.e., of objects we *might* perceive but which, in present circumstances, are not readily accessible to perception.

imaginative presentation cannot be made more determinate than it first presents itself as being, and as it first presents itself it is intrinsically indeterminate.

Every attempt at exact determination of what I imagine is stymied by the character of imagining itself. I cannot, for example, vary my position as imaginer-observer in order to scrutinize more closely a given object and its relations with other objects. For as soon as a new viewpoint is assumed, I have to do with a new imagined content: *to imagine something differently is to imagine something different.* Nor can I vary the positions of the imagined objects themselves so as to elucidate the relations in which they stand to each other. For once I imagine these objects as possessing different positions vis-à-vis one another, I am confronted not only with a new set of relations but also with a new set of objects.

If imagined objects do not possess determinate or determinable relations among themselves, they cannot be said to exist *with* one another in any significant sense. Only when I am *describing* an imaginative experience am I tempted to speak of imagined objects as being "with" one another; and even then I am using the term in an attenuated sense, as when I say that I imagine a tree "along with" a house, other trees, a dog, etc. These latter objects do not strictly coexist with the thematic tree. There is no sufficiently stable setting for imagined objects to become genuinely co-present with each other. Lacking such a setting, these objects are set adrift and are not *with* or *beside* one another as determinate entities sharing the same plane of presence.

It follows that imaginative experience cannot contain with-objects of any of the three sorts found in perception. (1) A thematic imagined object and the objects surrounding it cannot be said to be truly adjacent to one another. Adjacency implies contiguity of position and the possibility of making contact in space. Yet both contiguity and contact are ruled out because of the inability of imaginal space to provide definite locations. (2) Outlying unthematic imagined objects are not genuine with-objects. They are related to the thematic object of a given presentation only adventitiously and not as noncontiguous but still co-present objects within the same field. Nor can we imagine unthematic objects that reside *behind* or *beyond* the presentation, since the total content of an imaginative presentation is given in the presentation itself and is not to be found, not even by implication, somewhere else. (3) A further consequence of this imprisonment within the presentation is that imaginative experience cannot contain any remote with-objects either. What we imagine does not present itself as encircled by an indefinite number of nongiven and nonindicated objects. Hence, there is no sense of entering an environing *world* when we imagine—only a momentary world-frame. The world-frame encloses the specific content of a given imaginative presentation, but it does so without adumbrating anything more comprehensive. In place of a single all-encompassing world—where "world" means minimally "a linked whole, in which each object has its determinate place and entertains [determinate] relations with other objects"[19]—there is only a fugitive and perpetually disintegrating mini-world. Fieldless, what we imagine has no external horizon; worldless, it possesses no horizon of horizons.

INTERNAL HORIZON

A perceived object reveals itself through a series of partial appearances. Only some of these appearances—never their totality—can be directly perceived on a given occasion. Although the other appearances are unapprehended at the moment, they are nonetheless predelineated by what we have so far grasped, and they are accordingly potentially discoverable (or rediscoverable) features of what we perceive. Together with the presently apprehended aspects or sides of the perceived object, they constitute the "internal horizon" of this object, its delimiting boundary. In contrast with the external horizon, the internal horizon is a structure of the perceived object taken in isolation from its surroundings.[20]

The internal horizon of what we perceive is characterized by an inherent indefiniteness of detailed character, which is not to be confused with the radical indeterminacy of the imaginal margin. The latter, as we know, is a featureless limbo that is almost wholly indefinite in nature. The internal horizon, in contrast, is determinate as to *type*. It gives itself as the internally delimiting horizon of a particular *kind* of object: as the horizon of a house and not of a horse, of a table instead of a tree. Any subsequent specification of the horizon takes place *within* the boundaries of the object-type that has been established from the very beginning by the object's presented appearances. Hence the

19. Sartre, *Psychology of Imagination*, p. 169. Sartre speaks of "this great law of imagination: *the imaginary has no world*" (ibid., p. 217; his italics). He does concede, however, that there is "a worldlike atmosphere" (ibid., p. 175) which permeates what we imagine.

20. Note Husserl's description of the internal horizon: "this real [i.e., perceived] thing itself is more than that which at any given time attains (and has already attained) actual cognizance. It is provided with a sense which continuously confers on it its 'internal horizon'; the side that is seen is a side only insofar as it has sides which are not seen, which are anticipated and as such determine the sense" (*Experience and Judgment*, p. 35; cf. also pp. 32-33).

internal horizon combines indefiniteness of detail with determinacy of type.[21]

To return once again to our former example: drawing close to the rear entrance of Strathcona Hall, I perceive the entire back side of the building as well as a delimited portion of its northern side. Although this is all that I presently perceive, I assume that what I am now only partially perceiving possesses other exterior sides and an inside. I presume this is so even though these components of the building's internal horizon are not within the purview of my current perceiving. Instead, they exist as strictly potential contents of perception—as what I might well see were I to station myself in positions different from the one I now assume. At the moment all that I can meaningfully say concerning such unseen aspects is that they will in all likelihood continue to exemplify the same generic type-structure that characterizes those sides of the building which I perceive in the present or have perceived in the past. The formula for this type-structure would be 'massive-stone-building-with-tower', and I fully expect the contents of future perceptions of Strathcona Hall to fall within the scope of this formula.

But the internal horizon is predelineated on a more specific level as well. By perceptual adumbration, I am led to surmise that the sort of stone covering the back and north walls of the building will be found on the unseen sides as well, that the fenestration will be similar in character, that the various stories will be evident from the outside in roughly the same way, etc. Any or even all of these prefigurations can, of course, prove to be inaccurate as I come to view the other sides. The front of the building might, for example, be constructed with a different kind of surface stone and display another type of window. Yet even if such reversals of expectation occur, I am not likely to be mistaken in my basic belief that I will be perceiving other aspects of a certain *sort* of perceptual object—in this case, 'massive-stone-building-with-tower'. The object's type-structure will almost certainly persist even when the particularities of its total form fail to bear out what was prefigured at an earlier point. The contingent character of the predelineation of detail is compensated for by the continuity of the type-structure. The latter allows the building to be perceived as the *same* building throughout many possible variations in its presented appearance. Thus it circumscribes and draws together the various components

21. Gurwitsch has brought out this dual aspect of the internal horizon in the following way: "However indeterminate and vague the perceptual inner horizon may be in a given case, it is always delineated and specified along certain lines. Any indefiniteness affecting the inner horizon is bounded by, and contained within, lines of delineation and specification concerning typical and generic pattern and style" (*The Field of Consciousness*, p. 242).

of the internal horizon, making this horizon an intrinsic feature of the perceived object as a whole.

Is the internal horizon as thus described equally inherent in what we *imagine*? Here we must distinguish between two sorts of cases.

First of all, what we imagine is sometimes so extraordinary or fantastic that it cannot be considered as the sort of thing we would ever be likely to perceive. For example, in imagining what beings from other planets might look like, I can conjure up a surrealistic creature that will probably never be encountered by humans. In such a case it may be quite difficult to describe to others what I have before my mind's eye. Even if I do convey its general contour to others, there is no certainty that it has anything answering to an internal horizon; indeed, its fantastic character may be such as to put into question the essentiality of this very feature. Moreover, if an imagined object is sufficiently unusual—i.e., to point where I cannot even identify it as to kind —then it makes no sense to speak of its unapprehended aspects: having such aspects, even *seeming* to have such aspects, is a function of belonging to an identifiable type-structure. To lack this structure is to lack the basis for possessing an internal horizon.

A second sort of case concerns the imagining of nonfantastic, quasi-perceptual objects—where by "quasi-perceptual" is meant the kind of objects that would be perceivable were they empirically real. For example, I might imagine what the state capitol building in Albany, New York, looks like, although I have never seen this building or a photograph of it. The description of what I imagine in this instance might very well resemble a description of someone's perception of the building itself in Albany. Yet whether the imagined building closely resembles the perceived building or not, in this case I am very tempted to say that the imagined object possesses something like an internal horizon. What I now visualize presents itself as the sort of object that would, *were it actually to be perceived,* have other outer sides and an interior. Precisely as quasi-perceptual, it appears as the kind of thing that would in other circumstances possess an internal horizon, and it also seems to possess a determinate type-structure. Nevertheless, the imagined capitol remains only *quasi-*, not actually, perceivable. Its seeming to have an internal horizon is solely a function of such purely hypothetical perceivability. In fact—i.e., in my actual imaginative experience—such a quasi-perceptual object possesses no internal horizon; insofar as it is imagined, it has no aspects other than those immediately presented to my imagining mind, despite its apparent specificity of type.[22] And to lack unapprehended aspects is *ipso facto* to be without an internal horizon.

What the absence of an internal horizon means in practice is that in imagining either a fantastic or a quasi-perceptual object I am free to imagine almost anything whatever as what *might* be the object's 'other sides' and 'hidden aspects'.[23] No longer am I bound by the requirement that such sides and aspects exemplify a certain kind or type that has been established by what has been previously apprehended. At each moment I am able to imagine an aspect or side that belongs to an essentially *different* kind of object. What would be exceptional and even dismaying in perception—e.g., to find that the other side of Strathcona Hall consists of a waterfall—is easily enactable in imagination. The imaginer, as Gurwitsch says, is "entirely free to imagine any of [many] possibilities as realized, and to replace any possibility by any other."[24] *The basis of this freedom is precisely the lack of an internal horizon,* that is, the absence of any strict predelineation of unapprehended aspects by means of a particular type-structure.

The converse holds as well: the *presence* of an internal horizon precludes the very freedom to which Gurwitsch refers. Thus, while it is true that I can alter the order in which I perceive the now unseen sides of Strathcona Hall, I am not free to perceive anything whatsoever as a side of this building. In perceiving a given object I am guided by various probabilities as to what I will experience in coming to know it better. Will the front of Strathcona Hall exhibit the same architectural style as its back side? Does its front entrance have the same kind of door as its rear entrance? Will the front side be visually impressive? In each case my answer will have to be expressed in terms of relative likelihood: the front side of the building will *very likely* exhibit the same style as its back but *could well* be more visually impressive, and the front door will *almost certainly* be different in form from the back door.

No such situation obtains in imagining, since no element of the imaginative presentation can be used as a basis for projecting the likelihood of subsequent appearances of a given imagined object. Insofar as

22. I say "apparent specificity" because it cannot be presumed that an imagined object, however perspicuously presented, ever possesses a determinate identity of type. Does an imagined ostrich belong to the same distinct class of phenomena as a perceived ostrich? There is no unequivocal answer to this question.

23. I put these two terms in single quotes to indicate that in fact imagined objects do not *have* other sides or hidden aspects: we project the latter into a vacuum of content. Thus the "might" underlined in this same sentence refers to a situation characterized by pure possibility and not by probability.

24. *The Field of Consciousness*, p. 246.

this object is given at all, it is given *totaliter*. Nothing of it remains over, and thus nothing can be *pre*figured by what has already been given. Lacking genuine density and depth, the imagined object also lacks an internal horizon by which aspects or sides not presently apprehended could be adumbrated in advance. And if there is no genuine adumbration in advance, then we cannot say that certain things are more likely to appear or to be apprehended than others. In place of probabilities, there are open possibilities—possibilities that cannot be predesignated either as to generic type or as to exact structure.

CERTAINTY AND THE POSSIBILITY OF ERROR

Perception represents an area of human experience in which philosophers have traditionally sought certainty. Nevertheless, from Platonic *pistis* to Hegelian sense certainty, from the Kantian manifold of sensibility to Russellian sensibilia, certainly has not been forthcoming. Plato was forced to transcend *pistis* because of its inherent contradictions, Hegel realized that sensory experience requires recourse to universals for its barest description, Kant found that the only intrinsic order in sensibility is due to space and time and that the certainty of knowledge demands a move to the plane of understanding, and the contradictions in Russell's notion of sensibilia have been effectively exposed.[25] The unfulfilled quest for certainty at the level of sensory perception is perhaps best epitomized in the notion of sense data. These were posited by Moore, Broad, Price, and other twentieth-century epistemologists as the immediate objects of perceptual or sensory awareness,[26] and thus as something of which we can be completely certain. And yet the principal argument for the existence of sense data —the "argument from illusion" as it is revealingly called— is based precisely on the presumption of the possibility of perceptual *error*. It is just because we are inescapably subject to such error, i.e., to perceptual illusion, that sense data were posited in the first place. For if in illusory

25. Cf. H. H. Price, *Perception* (London: Methuen, 1973), pp. 41-43, as a critique of Russell's early belief in unsensed sense-data.

26. The reader will note that I am not distinguishing in any significant way between "sensation" and "perception" or between "sensory experience" and "perceptual experience." Such distinctions are not necessarily invalid, but they are not called for in the present context. On sensing vs. perceiving, see Erwin Straus, *The Primary World of Senses*, trans. J. Needleman (Glencoe: Free Press, 1963), esp. pp. 316-31.

experience we are not perceiving the full-blooded object itself, then (so the argument goes) in its absence we must still be perceiving *something*—a something that is christened a "sense datum." The sense datum itself is conceived as the most directly graspable constituent of a perceived object. Although it is assumed that we apprehend sense data themselves with complete certainty, we are not to count on any such certainty in our judgments concerning the nature of the actual perceptual objects they help to compose. In this way an element of certainty is claimed, but only in regard to a single level of perception—a level that seems to have been posited primarily for the purpose of salvaging an at least minimal sense of certainty.

Without discussing further the merits of the argument from illusion,[27] we need only note that its very existence is an admission that *complete* certainty, i.e., certainty at *all* levels, cannot be attained in perceptual experience. Such certainty is not achievable even in the most concerted and comprehensive efforts to explore a particular perceived object. Hence the paradox of perception: even if capable of being indubitable in one respect (e.g., on the supposition of sense data), perception is never indubitable in *every* respect. When we perceive, partial certainty is the most that can be hoped for. Yet partial certainty means *un*certainty: to be certain in relation to part of an object is nevertheless to be uncertain in relation to the whole object.

Four factors may be identified as the major sources of the uncertainty inhering in all perceptual experience:

(1) *Contingent character of perceptual anticipations.* Ever since Kant it has been explicitly recognized by philosophers that anticipations form part of perception.[28] Whenever we perceive, we anticipate to some extent the subsequent course of perceptual experience—above all, those aspects of it which seem to be on the verge of being revealed. However much we anticipate in perception, though, we are always in basically the same predicament: our expectations are subject to disappointment. Nothing guarantees that the further course of perceptual experience, in the short *or* in the long run, will bear out our anticipations. Even if these anticipations are based upon considerable previous experience of the object or event in question, they cannot

27. For a devastating critique of sense-data and of the argument from illusion, see John Austin, *Sense and Sensibilia* (Oxford: Oxford University Press, 1962), chs. 2-4.

28. Cf. Kant, "Anticipations of Perception," in *Critique of Pure Reason*, pp. 201-208. Kant himself, however, interprets anticipation in a different manner from the strictly descriptive sense on which I rely in what follows.

achieve complete certainty concerning its future appearances. At any moment (a moment which is not itself predictable), they may be contradicted and shown to be baseless.[29]

(2) *Lack of certainty due to milieu.* An example first: I observe the bright glow on the weather vane of Timothy Dwight College changing from a brilliant, almost flaming gold to an indistinct, barely visible sheen. Since it is late in the afternoon, I assume that the decreasing brilliance of the copper weather vane is due to the waning incandescence of the sun, and I judge accordingly that the sun's setting is the cause of the diminishing glow. On closer inspection of the situation, however, I recognize that this preliminary judgment is mistaken. The weather vane reveals itself to be one that circulates around a central axis, changing position in accordance with the direction of the wind. I suddenly realize that when I was observing it initially, the weather vane was in fact oscillating from a position in which it caught the sun's rays directly—thereby producing the brilliant glow—to one in which it failed to catch these rays to any significant degree. What I had taken to be the exclusive effect of the sun's setting was really due to interaction between the weather vane, the sun, and the wind. Hence it is a relatively complex surrounding situation that here accounts for the variations in what I perceive. This surrounding situation or *milieu* is the most important element of the weather vane's external horizon. Since every perceived object or event has its own external horizon, the basis for possible perceptual illusion is continually present. And if this is the case—if the effect of the perceptual *milieu* can be as deceptive as this—then I cannot claim complete certainty as to whether what I am perceiving in any given case *is* as it appears to be.

(3) *Lack of certainty due to the perceived object or event itself.* Standing in the garden of a country estate in England, I see situated on a distant hill what appears to be a small castle. Curious as to how I might visit this castle, I ask the gardner for directions. I am surprised and mildly disappointed when he tells me that the distant building is no castle at all, but only a facade built to look like a

---

29. To be contradicted is not, of course, the same thing as to be under an illusion in any strict sense. The difference is that in the case of perceptual illusion I *judge*, implicitly or explicitly, that a certain perceptual situation is present before me—that, for example, a certain clump of trees in the distance is a herd of cattle. I *take* the presented object to be one thing or one kind of thing even though it is in fact another thing or kind of thing. Hence the concept of *mis-taking* is basic to perceptual illusion: I mistake something for something else. In ordinary anticipation, in contrast, I do not explicitly judge as to the existence, identity, or character of what I anticipate. Rather, I presume—i.e., implicitly assume in advance—this existence, identity, or character. And it is this nonjudgmental *pre*-sumption which is subject to contradiction in the future course of experience.

castle from the particular vantage point of the estate's garden. What I took to be a genuine castle thus turns out to be an eighteenth-century "folly," a sham construction. Such a case of mistaken identity represents only one instance in an entire series of situations in which incomplete perception of an object's unseen sides misleads the perceiver into false claims. At the same time, it exemplifies a fact about *all* perceptions, illusory or not. This is that no single perception can claim certainty concerning the exact nature of the internal horizon of a given perceived object, for the character of its unperceived parts must, like the unseen sides of the sham castle, remain conjectural until we actually perceive them.

(4) *Change and permanence in perception.* The uncertainty of perception is such that we cannot even be altogether certain that what we perceived with a high degree of certainty a few moments before has remained exactly as we perceived it. Although perceived objects may exhibit considerable permanency—particularly in comparison with imagined entities—they are nonetheless capable of changing in character or structure at almost any point. There is a whole spectrum of possibilities here: from a barely perceptible change (e.g., a slight modification of hue or timbre) to a conversion so radical that the very identity of the perceived item is altered (e.g., water changed into ice). Yet the sheer diversity of possible transformations does not affect the basic point that in view of the possibility of *any* such changes, radical or minimal, perception will always be less than fully certain in its claims. If perceived objects are the kinds of things that *can* change over time, then I shall never be entirely certain in a given case that some change, however miniscule, has not intervened between the moment of my original perception and the moment at which I formulate a judgment as to what I have perceived. Consequently, I cannot claim certainty for this judgment.

In each of these four ways perception is an experience whose exact course and content are never entirely certain. The uneliminable uncertainty of perceptual experience stands in stark contrast with the unqualified certainty that characterizes imaginative experience. I can be perfectly confident that everything I imagine is just as it appears to me. This means that in imagining there is no prospect—indeed, no possibility—of being in error as to the character of what I imagine. Nor can mistaken judgments occur when there is no such thing as misapprehension in the first place. In short, although I can misperceive, *I cannot misimagine.*

How does this extraordinary situation come about? What is it about imagining that rids it of any basis for misapprehension and mistake? To answer in the briefest terms: imagined objects and events are *not such as can be doubted*. In other words, they lack those very four features that are responsible for the dubitability of what we perceive:

(1) In imagining, there is no such thing as disappointment of anticipations. In every instance and within the limits discussed in chapter three, there is a successful matching of the given with the meant. What the imaginer aims at in anticipation arises before him by his own efforts. If I try to anticipate in imagination how Strathcona Hall will look when viewed from the top of a neighboring building, I bring forth a visualization (insofar as I am capable of visualizing at all) that answers satisfactorily to the view in question. The visualized scene may not embody this view in as sensuously rich a manner as would an actual view; yet, however indistinct it may be in comparison with a perceived scene, it unfailingly fulfills my project of imaginative anticipation. Contrary to what occurs in perception, where I must always be prepared for the disappointment of my anticipations, in imagining I can be certain that they will be borne out.

(2) Such certainty is further reinforced by the absence of a genuine *milieu* within the imaginative presentation. If no such factor is present, then its potentially distorting effects will be eliminated. When, for example, I now imagine a situation similar to that involving the weather vane described above, I discover that in doing so I am not subject to anything comparable to the illusion that befell my original perceptual experience. For either I already know the reason for the alteration in the weather vane's glow—in which case I simply imagine the weather vane as circulating in the wind in such a way as to bring about the change in glow—or, lacking such knowledge, I imagine the setting sun as the efficient cause. In spite of the fact that the latter state of affairs incorrectly represents the actual perceptual situation, *as imagined* it is neither correct nor incorrect. In imagining such a circumstance I am free from error or mistake because the imaginative presentation cannot distort whatever it is that I apprehend within it.

(3) The same lack of distortion or deception is found when we turn to specific imagined objects themselves. Nothing we can imagine thematically is capable of containing concealed aspects of itself. Whatever we imagine presents *all* of itself, leaving no remnant of unpresented content. If I imagine what the interior of a given building looks like, the resulting presentation possesses no more content than it can directly proffer to me in the moment of apprehension. Nothing

lurks hidden within the imagined interior as part of a still-to-be-appre-
hended internal horizon. The absence of such a horizon abolishes the
uncertainty that its possession entails. How can I doubt the accuracy
of an undistorted apprehension of something of which there is *nothing more* to apprehend?

(4) Change, as Kant argued, implies permanence: only something
that continues to exist from one point in time to another can be said
to *change* during the interval.[30] The specific content of imagining
cannot be said to change in this strict sense, for it does not endure
from one imaginative presentation to the next. Nor does it alter as
such even within a single presentation, since the latter is itself non-
enduring. We are thus assured that what we take ourselves to be
imagining does not change in character either while we are imagining
it or afterward. Each successive imaginative presentation is final in
form, identity, and existence, and our certainty as to its content is
accordingly incontrovertible.

From these observations it becomes clear that imagining and perceiving differ decisively in regard to the issue of certainty and the possibility of error. None of the four fundamental sources of perceptual
error (and hence of a corresponding uncertainty) is found in imaginative experience. Not being capable of error, this experience is an
experience about which we can justifiably claim to be fully certain at
any given moment. While the possibility of error can never be removed from perceiving, it *never even arises* in imagining, which is not
subject to anything comparable to perceptual illusion. The basic
reason for this lies in the identity of appearing and being within the
imaginative presentation: whatever appears there appears without dissimulation and in total transparency.

III

It is a basic, seemingly even obvious, truth about perception that
it is always less than complete in character. What could be more evident than Gurwitsch's claim that "every single perception is one-
sided and incomplete"?[31] And yet, innocent and uncontroversial as
this assertion may be in itself, it has crucial consequences for a comparison of perception and imagination. It points to a quite generic

30. "In all change of appearances substance is permanent" (*Critique of Pure
Reason*, A 182 B 224, p. 212; cf. the entire First Analogy, pp. 212-17).
31. *The Field of Consciousness*, p. 279.

trait of perceiving that serves to distinguish it all along the line from imagining: its *incompleteness*. Being generic, this trait encompasses and elucidates the particular discrepancies between the two acts that have been the primary focus of this chapter. What forms does such incompleteness take, and with what does it contrast in imaginative experience?

In every major respect perceiving reveals itself to be incomplete in nature. This is so whether we consider it noetically or noematically, that is, whether we regard it as act or as content. As *act*, perception shows itself to be irremediably partial. No matter how directly or fully we confront a given perceptual object or event and no matter how optimal the conditions of perceiving at the time, no single perception can take in all of its aspects. There is always more to be seen, as well as more ways in which to see what has already been seen. I may be able to perceive all six sides of a transparent glass cube at once, but I cannot, in any finite period of time, assume all of the various positions from which this cube may be seen. Even when viewings from other positions are not explicitly called for, they remain possible and, once assumed, will reveal new aspects of the object in question. To exhaust this object, such viewings would have to be infinite in number: there is always at least *one more* possible perception than is contained in any finite series of perceivings. Consequently, a truly complete perception of a given object or event represents a regulative idea that exceeds what any human perceiver can actually attain.[32]

What of the *content* of perception? Can perceptual phenomena be presented all at once? Clearly not. There is no such thing as a single complete presentation of a perceived object or event. However detailed a given perceptual presentation may be, it never manifests *every* aspect of the object or event it proffers. In practice this means that what we perceive cannot be fully described by any list of particular structural or qualitative elements, for such a list does not include all of the manifold ways in which these elements may be perceived—and here the possibilities are endless. There is a certain structure or quality as-seen-*from* a, b, etc.; as-seen-*at* time x, y, etc.; as-seen-*in* sunlight, artificial light, etc.; as-seen-*by* myself, yourself, others, etc. And

32. As Gurwitsch says, "the process of perception and [of] the perceptual determination of a material thing is an infinite process" (ibid., p. 215; in italics in text). For Kant, ideas employed regulatively direct "the understanding towards a certain goal upon which the routes marked out by all its rules converge, as upon their point of intersection. This point . . . lies quite outside the bounds of possible experience" (*Critique of Pure Reason*, A 644 B 672, p. 533).

so on indefinitely. No single description—no finite series of descriptions—can convey all of the manifold modes in which the perceived object or event may appear. 'Complete content' is thus just as much a regulative idea as is the infinite series of acts required to apprehend such content in its totality; in either case, completeness is no more than an asymptotic limit. Therefore, in both of its primary intentional phases, as act and as content, perception reveals itself to be both incomplete and incompletable.

In striking contrast to the intrinsic incompleteness of perception stands the correspondingly intrinsic *completeness* of imagination. This completeness characterizes both the act and the content of imagining.

Each *act* of imagining is complete inasmuch as it does not call for supplementation by further acts. It is strictly self-contained in the sense discussed in chapter four. Even if a given act forms part of a coherent sequence of acts, it never calls for—much less *requires*—specific predecessors or successors within such a sequence. Each separate imaginative act is thus complete in itself. In this respect imaginative experience resembles the experience of works of art as forming closed wholes. Just as a fully satisfying aesthetic experience needs no continuation or supplementation, so each act of imagining suffices by itself as a single self-cohesive unit.[33]

The *content* of imagining is similarly complete. Every imaginative presentation comes in plenary form. Nothing is left out or left behind. Nothing is not yet given. Nor is anything indicated as *about* to be given or as *likely* to be given. All *is* given—all that can be given by imaginative means. The entire content is there to be savored, and nothing is hidden from view; everything lies lucidly before the imaginer's psychical gaze. This means that each imaginative presentation is a complete monadic whole. As Collingwood says, "everything which imagination presents to itself is something complete in itself."[34] Even the indeterminacy of the imaginal margin contributes to this completeness, since it does not (in contrast with occluded regions in perception) suggest that there is more to the presentation than meets the mental eye. Only so much meets this eye as is there, and in imagining there *is* only what appears in each unrepeatable presentation.

33. On the question of closure in aesthetic experience, see Barbara H. Smith, *Poetic Closure* (Chicago: University of Chicago Press, 1968). For further discussion, see my article, "Imagination and Repetition in Literature: A Reassessment" in *Yale French Studies* (Spring 1976).

34. *Principles of Art*, pp. 252-53.

The relationship between imagining and perceiving may be summed up by stating that, vis-à-vis perception, *imagination is phenomenologically self-sufficient but epistemologically non-self-sufficient*. By "phenomenologically self-sufficient" I mean that, *as experienced* (and hence apart from questions of causes and conditions), imagining exhibits itself as nonderivative from perception. No matter what the exact course of experience has been up to a given moment, we always remain free to imagine things that are descriptively discontinuous with the subject matter of preceding perceptions. Moreover, although imagination does form alliances with perception—e.g., in the hybrid instances discussed in chapter six—a felt difference between imaginal and perceptual components remains. However closely allied imagining and perceiving may become in particular cases, our analysis has shown that, as described phenomenologically, the two acts are much more deeply discontinuous than continuous. This finding supports the common tendency to separate perceiving and imagining sharply in practical and linguistic contexts: "I was only imagining," we say, implying precisely that we were *not perceiving* at the time.

But when the relationship between perceiving and imagining is considered from an epistemological viewpoint, the picture changes, for it cannot be denied that imagination presupposes perception. I cannot imagine unless I am at the same time capable of perceiving. The point is not that in order to imagine a given object or event I must have formerly perceived *that very* object or event: to hold this would be to succumb to what Sartre calls "the illusion of immanence," the belief that what I imagine is nothing but the inward elaboration of previous perceptions.[35] Rather, the point is that *I must be a being who perceives if I am also to be a being who imagines*. In this regard (and in this regard alone), perception is a condition of imagination, just as it is in the same respect a condition of every other mental act: to be-in-the-world is necessarily to be a perceiving being.

Nevertheless, far from confining or constraining imagination, perception in its epistemological role serves precisely to *make imagining possible*—possible as one form of mentation among others—while not predetermining its specific course. Although it is epistemologically posterior to perception,[36] imagining is not beholden to perceiving for its

35. *Psychology of Imagination*, pp. 5-6, 69-70, 108-109, 113.
36. Whether it can be claimed that perceiving arises first in a strictly chronological or developmental sense is another matter. Impressive support for such temporal priority is to be found in Piaget's observations on the specific stages of cognitive growth in the child. The sensory-motor period, that of perception proper, precedes all the others and is thus, in the beginning, independent of them. Only later does

particular content on any given occasion; it is still less derivative with regard to its own intentional structures and eidetic traits. From a descriptive or phenomenological perspective, that is, at the level of conscious experience, imagination possesses peculiarities that render it unreducible to perception or to such offshoots of perception as memory or hallucination.[37] Imagination's uniquely self-completing, self-enclosing, and self-transparent character has no counterpart—not even a forerunner—in perceptual experience proper. Consequently, even if imagining relies on perceiving regarded as a premise of all human experience, it remains master in its own house, displaying an autonomous action that is without parallel in perception.

---

a mutual dependence of modes of experience occur: perceptual and symbolic powers come to support each other. See Jean Piaget, *The Construction of Reality in the Child* (New York: Basic Books, 1954).

37. For a confrontation between imagining and these "postperceptual" acts, see my essay "Comparative Phenomenology of Mental Activity: Memory, Hallucination, and Fantasy Contrasted with Imagination," in *Research in Phenomenology*, VI (1976).

PART FOUR

THE AUTONOMY OF IMAGINING

CHAPTER EIGHT

The Nature of Imaginative Autonomy

A. WHAT IMAGINATIVE AUTONOMY IS NOT

A Proof of Imagination's Superior Position Among Mental Acts

To ESTABLISH that imagining is unreducible to perceiving as well as independent of it is not to prove its superiority over this or any other act. We must not confuse unreducibility and independence on the one hand with supremacy on the other. Imagining is independent and unreducible not as a potentate of the psyche but in its sheer idiosyncrasy, that is, in its inherent disparateness from other acts. Imagining does not command the mind from a position of unchallenged power. In fact, it does not command at all—which is not to say that it acquiesces either!

Consequently, to impute psychic hegemony to imagination, as so many Romantics attempted to do, is to fail to be faithful to the phenomenon; it is to substitute delirium for .description. Thus we are forced to reject Baudelaire's imperialistic claim: "All the faculties of the human soul must be subordinated to imagination, which puts them all into its service."[1] But to deny Baudelaire's contention—which underlies his celebrated treatment of imagination as "the Queen of the faculties"—is not only to renounce a specific claim for the preeminence of imagination vis-à-vis other mental acts. It is also, and more importantly, to reject the general notion of a hierarchy of faculties.

The hierarchical model, which has dominated Western theories of mind, is particularly inappropriate as a schema for a descriptive phi-

---

1. *Curiosités esthétiques* [et] *L'Art romantique*, p. 329. This passage is from the essay of 1859 entitled "La Reine des facultés." The phrase "Queen of the faculties" is itself borrowed from Edgar Allan Poe. Note that Wordsworth had declared still earlier that "the Imagination is conscious of [its] indestructible dominion" (1815 Preface to *Lyrical Ballads*).

losophy or psychology of mind because of its presumption that some single faculty or act is superior to all others and rules over them unremittingly. By a further twist this uppermost member of mind becomes the only, or at least the most, autonomous form of mentation. If pure thought is given the place of honor—as it is by Plato, Aristotle, and assorted rationalists—then it is regarded as the autonomous act *par excellence*; such is the significance of Aristotle's notion of active intellect and of all subsequent attempts to demonstrate the supremacy of rational thinking. If imagination is accorded the highest position, as in Romantic literary practice and philosophical theory, the presumption is that *it* is the only truly autonomous act of mind. But rationalists and Romantics cannot *both* be correct in their claims, and it is very likely that both groups are wrong. For other mental acts are also autonomous, though in different fashions, and no single act is privileged in this regard.

Imagination's autonomy, in short, does not entitle it to a position of predominance. This autonomy is indeed distinctive, but to be distinctive is not *eo ipso* to be preeminent. To say this is only to underline a more general point: a recognition of the multiplicity of the mental—a multiplicity that is borne out precisely by the existence of eidetic differences between various kinds of mental acts—must replace a vertical view of mind if we are to avoid the harmful consequences of thinking in exclusively hierarchical terms. It is only within the mind's multiplex structure that imagination's autonomy has its place—a place which, however singular it may be, is not rankable as topmost, *or* as bottommost, *or* as middlemost. As Aristotle said, even the intellect is "a form *of forms*,"[2] that is, a basis for plural possibilities of cognition. What is called for is a nonhierarchical model of mentation in which the constrictiveness of scalariform thinking is no longer operative. It is by means of such a nonscalar model that the teeming pluralism of psychical phenomena can best be acknowledged and accommodated—and that imaginative autonomy can be given its just due.

Self-Legislation in the Kantian Sense

If imagination is not the Queen of the faculties, it is also not their sovereign lawmaker. Imaginative autonomy is not the autonomy of law, even of self-prescribed law. It is in precisely this respect that the autonomy of imagination is to be distinguished from the autonomy of reason. The latter finds its classical formulation in Rousseau's dictum that autonomy ("freedom" in his term) is "obedience to a law which one

2. *De Anima*, 432a 1-2. My italics.

has prescribed to oneself."[3] It was Kant, however, who explored most thoroughly the implications of Rousseau's dictum, and we shall take his conception of autonomy as paradigmatic for our purposes.

In Kant's stern view, autonomy is always and only the autonomy of reason—and, moreover, of pure *practical* reason. Pure theoretical reason is not, strictly speaking, autonomous. It is spontaneous (i.e., in Kant's special sense of self-initiating), and in the guise of understanding it functions in a legislative capacity. Yet pure theoretical reason is dependent upon sensibility for its specific content. Moreover, its legislative powers are not *self*-prescriptive but determinative solely of nature and of the phenomenal self. Pure practical reason alone is capable of genuine self-legislation; it lays down laws that are prescriptive for the noumenal self, the radically free and wholly self-determining person. These laws are moral in tenor and are formulated by the action of rational will as categorical imperatives. For Kant, then, there is an intrinsic link between autonomy, pure practical reason qua rational will, and the prescription of moral laws: "autonomy of the [rational] will is the property the will has of being a law to itself (independently of every property belonging to the objects of volition)."[4]

Imagining is not autonomous in any such sense as this. It is true that we have spoken of imagining as "self-delimiting" (in chapter four) and that we have also (in chapter three) stressed its considerable capacity to control its own activity. Nevertheless, it would be mistaken to attribute to imagination anything remotely comparable to what Kant calls the "sovereign authority" of practical reason conceived as "the supreme maker of law."[5] The crucial point of difference resides in the fact that the autonomy exhibited in imagining is not *legislative* in any meaningful sense, moral or otherwise. Not only is imagination not the supreme maker of moral law, *it proposes no laws at all* for itself or for any other psychical agency. By the same token, we cannot speak of imagining as "self-legislative" either. Its basic activities do not include the propounding-and-prescribing of formal rules to be followed by itself in the future, and there is no binding, much less self-binding, character to its enactments. Just as we are only rarely coerced to imagine in the

3. *Social Contract*, Bk. I, ch. 8.
4. *Groundwork of the Metaphysics of Morals*, trans. H. J. Paton (New York: Harper, 1964), p. 108. Rational will (*Wille*) contrasts with the "elective will" (*Willkür*), which decides between competing maxims or subjective expressions of the moral law. The elective will always acts from a specific "incentive" stemming from empirical motives or desire—hence it is *heteronomous* in comparison with the rational will. Cf. *Groundwork of the Metaphysics of Morals*, ch. two; and Lewis White Beck, *A Commentary on Kant's Critique of Practical Reason* (Chicago: University of Chicago Press, 1963), pp. 194-203.
5. *Groundwork of the Metaphysics of Morals*, p. 109.

first place, so we are almost never obliged to proceed in accordance with what we have already imagined.[6] Hence imaginative autonomy, not being rule-bound or rule-binding, must not be confused with the self-legislative autonomy of pure practical reason. To determine its own course is well within imagining's normal powers, but to determine this course in rigid adherence to a prescribed, even a self-prescribed, rule of reason is not part of its proper province.[7]

Secondary Autonomy in the Ego-Psychological Sense

Contemporary psychoanalysts, and especially those who call themselves "ego psychologists," distinguish between two forms of autonomy exercised by the ego understood as the seat of conscious thought and action. The ego's *primary autonomy* is founded upon certain innate functions—e.g., perception, memory, and motility—which serve to meet the demands of instinct and of the external environment. Such functions antedate conflict between ego, id, and environment, and they are so basic to normal ego activity that we are scarcely aware of them in their everyday operation. The *secondary autonomy* of the ego is built up from functions that result originally from the ego's efforts to cope with conflict but that have since formed a "conflict-free ego sphere."[8] These functions include defense mechanisms (e.g., intellectualization, denial, flight) insofar as they are no longer directly motivated by con-

---

6. This is not to deny, of course, that we are able to imagine what following a certain law—including a Kantian categorical imperative—*might be like*: 'How would I appear if I were to act in accordance with the third formulation of the categorical imperative?' Here I might envision myself as a righteous member of the Kingdom of Ends, performing certain altruistic acts such as ministering to the sick without recompense. But no matter how elaborate or ingenious my imagined scene of the Kingdom of Ends becomes, my act of imagining itself cannot be said to be legislative or prescriptive *of* this Kingdom. At most, it helps to illustrate a rational conception whose formulation and acknowledgment are independent of its dramatization by imagination. The conception itself remains a product of pure practical reason.

7. It should be noticed that Kant's conception of the autonomy of practical reason reinstates a hierarchy of faculties in which practical reason is made "supreme" precisely by virtue of its autonomy. The rational will is conceived as ruling over the domain of elective will, inclination, incentive, and desire. Thus a rigid, two-tier hierarchy of empirical/rational is ingredient in the Kantian notion of rational autonomy. Imaginative autonomy, as was suggested in the preceding section, requires no such hierarchical stratification into inferior/superior levels.

8. The key terms "conflict-free ego sphere," "primary autonomy," and "secondary autonomy" all derive from the pioneering work of Heinz Hartmann. See especially Hartmann's *Ego Psychology and the Problem of Adaptation*, trans. D. Rapaport (New York: International Universities Press, 1961), chs. 1, 8, 9. Cf. also David Rapaport's excellent discussion of these terms in "The Autonomy of the Ego" and "The Theory of Ego Autonomy: A Generalization," both in *The Collected Papers of David Rapaport*, ed. M. M. Gill (New York: Basic Books, 1967).

flict situations but have instead become largely self-motivating and "synthetic." Secondary autonomy is also exhibited by such disparate phenomena as values, ideals, specific cognitive organizations and ego interests, and superego influences.

If imagining is to be granted autonomy within the framework of ego-psychological theory, it is clear that its autonomy will be secondary and not primary in nature. Ego psychologists subsume imagining under conscious fantasy, and since the latter is capable of secondary autonomy alone, any autonomy enjoyed by imagining qua fantasy will be *a fortiori* of the secondary sort. In other words, it is just insofar as it is claimed that fantasy may be genuinely synthetic in function that imagining, considered as a form of fantasy, comes to be located in the conflict-free ego sphere, where secondary autonomy is the only permissible autonomy.

Here we must ask: does the notion of secondary autonomy in the ego-psychological view offer a satisfactory *descriptive* model for the characteristic autonomy of imagination?[9] The answer can only be that it does not. To say that a specific mental act such as imagining possesses secondary autonomy is to claim that this act is autonomous in the merely negative senses that it does *not* arise directly from conflict as a motive force and that it is capable of motivating and maintaining itself only by means of a neutralized, *non*libidinal, *non*aggressive energy.[10] Even if this two-part claim could be scientifically confirmed, it does not provide an adequate account of how the autonomy of imagining is actually experienced by the imaginer himself. The assessment is that of a third person, an observer or theorist who is discounting the conscious character of his own imaginative experience. To be sure, a first-person imaginer might well agree that when imagining he is in fact conflict-free and using de-instinctualized energy. But he cannot pretend that what he has thus agreed to represents a description of the *felt* quality of imagining: this quality is left untouched and unexplicated.

Further, the very notion that autonomy (primary *or* secondary) is rooted in the ego gives rise to a host of special problems. For one thing, to posit an ego in the psychoanalytical meaning of the term is to co-

9. In raising this question, I must stress that I am not seeking to criticize the notion of secondary autonomy as it figures in a general developmental psychology such as psychoanalysis proposes. From the epigenetic, explanatory perspective of this psychology, it may be extremely valuable—and it is at least economical—to conceive of imagining as a form of secondary autonomy.

10. On the notion of neutralized energy, see Hartmann, Kris, and Loewenstein, "Notes on the Theory of Aggression" in *The Psychoanalytic Study of the Child* (1949), III/IV. "Neutralization" is a negative concept to the extent that it implies *de*-instinctualization. But it is true that once de-instinctualization has occurred, autonomous ego processes can draw on neutralized energy as their *own* resource.

posit a whole hierarchy of psychical agencies—id, ego, super-ego—and thus to succumb to the verticalizing tendency whose deleterious effects have already been alluded to above.[11] For another, it is unnecessarily restrictive to locate a protean function such as imagining in a single sphere of the mind. Freud himself claimed that "defense too [is] multi-locular," and came to see that the ego has unconscious as well as conscious dimensions.[12] If Freud's own observations are to be followed in this regard, it is surely mistaken to confine imagining, the most multi-locular of mental acts, within one particular psychical region. Moreover, to situate imaginative activity in the ego sphere alone is perforce to stress one aspect of imaginative autonomy—that stemming from controlledness—at the expense of others. For the ego's primary form of action is control; all of its activities are procedures for controlling its internal and external environment.[13] Yet autonomous imagining does not require the presence of any such centrally controlling agency and is perfectly capable of proceeding without the directive power of a supervising ego. More strongly put: in becoming autonomous, imagining also becomes egoless—ceases to need an ego. And if this is so, we must reject any theory of imaginative autonomy in which the ego plays the central role.

Creativity in the Romantic View

Each of the previous misconstruings of imaginative autonomy has involved a different error. To say that this autonomy proves the superiority of imagination over other mental acts is an error of *overestimation*. To claim that the autonomy of imagining consists in self-

11. It does not help to posit a *horizontal* hierarchy instead of a strictly vertical one. Freud presents the former in the famous "picket fence" model of chapter seven, section B, of *The Interpretation of Dreams*; but he cannot eliminate evaluative overtones from this ingenious construction: the ego (here simply called 'Cs.') is still trapped between more powerful instinctual and environmental forces. Latter-day psychoanalysts have more explicitly owned up to hierarchical tendencies in their thinking. Cf. Rapaport, *Collected Papers*, pp. 372-75, 434-36, and 703-705; and Schafer, *Aspects of Internalization*, pp. 188-90 and esp. p. 210: "it is necessary to envisage a number of these libidinal and aggressive organizations within the ego, juxtaposed to each other and arranged hierarchically."

12. The quotation is from Draft N of the correspondence with Fliess and is found in *Standard Edition*, I, p. 256. For an account of the unconscious dimensions of the ego, see *The Ego and the Id* (*Standard Edition*, XIX), secs. II and III, and esp. p. 27: "Not only what is lowest but also what is highest in the ego can be unconscious."

13. Even "regression in the service of the ego," a notion of Kris's that is designed to explain artistic creativity, is a subtle strategy of control. As Kris writes: "[My] general assumption is that under certain conditions the ego *regulates regression*, and that the integrative functions of the ego include voluntary and temporary withdrawal of cathexis from one area or another [so as] *to regain improved control*" (Ernst Kris, *Psychoanalytic Explorations in Art* [New York: Schocken, 1964], p. 321; my italics).

legislation is to commit an error of *misapplication* whereby the sort of autonomy that rightly belongs to one mental faculty (in this case pure practical reason) is misapplied to imagination. To assert that imaginative autonomy is an instance of the secondary autonomy of the ego is a mistake of *mislocation*: imagining is not constricted to the conflict-free ego sphere, and its autonomy is not adequately describable as a form of ego-controlled action. In the case of creativity in the Romantic view, we encounter a fourth type of error, that of *overconnection*. Here the mistake is to single out a certain link between imagining and another phenomenon (i.e., being creative) and to assume that this connection is intrinsic and not merely contingent.

That there is an intimate tie between imagination and creativity is an ancient theme that can be traced back at least as far as Plato, for whom the lyric poet is a person who is capable of being seized by a "divine frenzy."[14] Mere image-making, conceived disparagingly by Plato as an imitation of imitations, becomes creative when transmogrified into an ecstatic state in which one is momentarily "out of his senses."[15] The mimetic model, which nonetheless dominated Plato's conception of art, was finally abandoned only by the Neoplatonists. Thinkers from Plotinus to Ficino developed and refined the notion of an afflatus stemming from divine and mystical sources and literally "inspiring" artists and philosophers to creative activity. By the time of the Italian Renaissance, imagination had become the primary vehicle of human creativity, being "entrusted with autonomous creative powers of its own."[16] The persisting though often subterranean influence of Neoplatonism was a critical factor in the rise of the Romantic movement, as we can see most graphically in Blake, Coleridge, and Shelley.[17] For these figures, as for others clustered around them, "imagination" became a watchword denoting the source of all human creativity. In its

14. This frenzy is conceived by Plato as a form of madness: "But he who, having no touch of the Muses' madness in his soul, comes to the door and thinks that he will get into the temple by the help of skill alone—he, I say, and his poetry are not admitted; the sane man disappears and is nowhere when he enters into rivalry with the madman" (*Phaedrus*, 245).

15. *Ion*, 534.

16. Milton C. Nahm, *The Artist as Creator* (Baltimore: Johns Hopkins Press, 1956), p. 9. Nahm also observes that from the Renaissance onward "imagination is used by writers to rid the philosophy of art of vestiges of mimetic theory" (ibid.).

17. For an excellent account of the influence of Neoplatonism on English Romanticism, see Kathleen Raine's Introduction to *Thomas Taylor, the Platonist* (Princeton: Princeton University Press, 1969), esp. pp. 3-12, 29-39. Raine demonstrates the crucial role of Neoplatonism in modern poetry as well, particularly in the work of Yeats. Her general claim is that Neoplatonic thinking is not only historically influential upon, but *essential to*, great poetry: "The Platonic philosophy is the necessary basis of all imaginative art" (ibid., p. 6).

world-creating and visionary role, such creativity mirrors that of God; more modestly conceived, it enlivens nature and converts the merely mechanical into the profound and the purposeful.

More than any other single figure, it was Kant who prepared the way for the expansive claims of the Romantics. He did so by stressing two core traits of human imagining: "Insofar as imagination is *spontaneity*, I sometimes also entitle it the *productive* imagination."[18] By "spontaneity" Kant means initiated by the human agent himself, rather than proceeding from externally located forces of nature—forces that rule over what Coleridge called the "cold inanimate world."[19] By "productive" Kant refers to a form of activity which cannot be reduced to the mere reproduction and recombination of prior experiences. As was noted briefly in chapter six, Kant draws a firm line of demarcation between a productive and a reproductive imagination. While the latter operates by *associating* fragments of previous experiences with one another, productive imagination works by *synthesizing* discrete spatio-temporal manifolds into genuinely new organic wholes. Now, it is a short but fateful step from Kant's conception of a higher order of imagining, which is both spontaneous and productive, to the full-blown Romantic thesis that imagination is essentially creative—that it is the basis of all significant human creation: "what the imagination seizes as Beauty must be Truth."[20] While Kant himself demurred at this point, specifically denying the creative character of productive imagination,[21] an entire generation of German and British poets and philosophers took the plunge: imagination was no longer to be confused with "fancy" or the mere association of "fixities and definites" (in Coleridge's phrase) but was to be affirmed as human creative activity *par excellence*.[22]

The Romantic effort to link imagination with creativity in an indissoluble union is still a living legacy. It became a credo which for over a century has dominated the theory and practice of painting, poetry, music, and sculpture in the West. It has enlisted such diverse disciples

18. *Critique of Pure Reason*, B152, p. 165; my italics.
19. "Dejection: An Ode." It should be pointed out that the Kantian notion of self-initiated action is not necessarily in conflict with the Neoplatonic view of inspiration. In the latter, poetic inspiration arises not from the world of nature but from an encompassing World Soul that is continuous with one's personal soul. Because of the continuity between the individual soul and the World Soul, spontaneous or self-initiated action may be said to have a divine source. To assert such compatibility between Kantian epistemology and Neoplatonic metaphysics is not, of course, to claim that Kant himself would endorse the philosophical premises of the latter.
20. John Keats, Letter to Benjamin Bailey, Nov. 22, 1817.
21. "Productive imagination is not, however, creative" (*Anthropology from a Pragmatic Point of View*, sec. 28; p. 47 in Foucault's translation).

among poets as Baudelaire and Rilke, Hopkins and Stevens, and such strange bedfellows in philosophy as Bachelard, Collingwood, and Sartre. Sartre, who in *Nausea* parodies Romanticism in its Proustian form, nevertheless continues to espouse the central Romantic belief in imagination's essentially creative nature: "[imaginative] consciousness *appears to itself as being creative,* though without positing this creativity as an object."[23]

Precisely in view of the pervasive influence of the Romantic exaltation of imagination's creative powers, we must pose a series of critical questions: What in fact does the Romantic credo proclaim concerning the relationship between creativity and imagination? Does this relationship really obtain? If it does not, what is the actual relationship between creative and imaginative activity?

According to the Romantic credo—and as predelineated in part by its Neoplatonic precursors—all authentic imagining (as opposed to the spurious imagining of mere fancy) is creative: to imagine authentically is to *be* creative, whether or not this creativity is embodied in a work of art or any other tangible product. At the limit—a limit most closely approached in the aesthetic doctrines of Croce and Collingwood, who bring the Romantic doctrine of imagination to its logical conclusion— one need not concern oneself with the concrete expressions of creative imagination. Such expressions are merely a matter of "technique," of "externalization," and are of secondary importance compared with the activity of pure imagination, which alone is truly expressive.[24] On such a view imagining is in and by itself creative in character; in Kantian terminology it is spontaneously productive on its own account and has no need of external support. But conversely, and equally a part of the Romantic position, any significant display of creativity must involve imagination; indeed, any such display *is* imagination in action. Thus, according to Coleridge, one cannot be creative as a poet without drawing on the "shaping spirit of Imagination."[25] Creativity is not so much

22. Coleridge, *Biographia Literaria,* p. 167. For an account of the varying and competing uses of the terms "fancy" and "imagination," see R. L. Brett, *Fancy and Imagination* (London: Methuen, 1969) as well as chapter 18 of W. K. Wimsatt, Jr., and Cleanth Brooks, *Literary Criticism: A Short History* (New York: Knopf, 1957).

23. *Psychology of Imagination,* p. 17; my italics.

24. Cf. Benedetto Croce, *Aesthetic,* trans. D. Ainslie (New York: Noonday Press, 1956), chs. 1 and 2; and R. G. Collingwood, *Principles of Art,* esp. chs. 2 and 7. Notice that Collingwood goes on to identify imaginative activity with creation in art: "The actual making of the tune is therefore . . . called the making of an imaginary tune. This is a case of creation . . . Hence the making of a tune is an instance of imaginative creation" (ibid., p. 134). Yet Collingwood never tells us in what precise sense imagining *is* creating.

25. "Dejection: An Ode."

a matter of being "imaginative" (in the honorific sense of ingenious, bold, daring, etc.) as of exercising one's innate powers of imagining. Hence we may state the dual assumption underlying the Romantic credo: *to imagine authentically is to be creative; to be genuinely creative is to imagine.*

The elegant simplicity of this reciprocal formula should not blind us to its problematic aspects.[26] The assertions contained in its two clauses are highly questionable. First of all, it is simply not the case that all authentic imagining is creative. Much *bona fide* imagining is banal and repetitive, manifesting an impoverished and threadbare character. Nor can we claim, invoking Kantian criteria, that all authentic imagining is spontaneous—spontaneity, as we know, is an optional and not a forced feature of imagining—or that it is always synthetic in a strong, "productive" sense: not every instance of imagining brings forth a new synthesis of previously experienced elements. Sometimes there is no synthesis at all within the imaginative presentation but only the simple appearance of a single element, as in imagining 'the head of Cerebus'. And even when imagining does present us with a synthetic product, the synthesis is not necessarily of factors that were apprehended in advance of the imaginative experience itself: I can imagine a chimera all of whose parts are as chimerical as the whole they together constitute. Therefore, contrary to what many Romantics (tacitly adopting Kant's criteria) assumed, much imagining is quite unspontaneous and unproductive.

But it is just as false to claim that to be genuinely creative one must imagine. Examples abound of cases of creativity into which imagining does not enter in any crucial way. When Poincaré arrived at a creative solution to a problem in higher mathematics as he stepped onto an omnibus, no specific acts of imagining had preceded the moment of discovery. By his own account he had first reflected on the problem for a considerable period—a period of intense intellectual concentration—and then had put the problem "out of mind."[27] Even if one were able to

26. Linguistic usage reinforces the tie between creativity and imagination by practically equating "imaginative person" with "creative person" and "she has imagination" with "she is creative." Such verbal links, whose historical roots lie in the Romantic conception of the human being, should not be taken as a license for indulging in descriptive confusion: despite the near-equivalency of these locutions, the activities of imagining and creating remain descriptively distinct from each other.

27. Poincaré's account is reprinted in Brewster Ghiselin, ed., *The Creative Process* (New York: Mentor, 1955), pp. 33-42. I introduce an example from the experience of a working scientist not to show that creativity has the same form in science as in art but only to suggest that the link between imagination and creativity is as problematic in scientific as in other kinds of human endeavor.

show that Poincaré's unconscious mind had continued to work toward a solution, this would not entail that Poincaré was *imagining* during the critical period of intellectual gestation. And even if one were to dispute the accuracy or authenticity of Poincaré's account, there is no way of decisively demonstrating that imagining was an essential constituent of creativity in such a case.[28] Indeed, in many instances it is quite difficult to determine whether imagining was present in any significant form. Take Paul Valéry's famous description of the genesis of *Le Cimetière marin*:

> As for the *Cimetière marin*, [my] intention [of creating a poem] was at first no more than a rhythmic figure, empty, or filled with meaningless syllables, which obsessed me for some time ... [Thus] the *Cimetière marin* was *conceived*.[29]

The ambiguity of Valéry's final word, *"conceived,"* reflects the ambiguity of his original creative act. Was this act one of intellectual conception, as he implies when he adds: "I discover my work little by little, beginning with *pure conditions of form* ..."?[30] Or was it one of conception in imagination, as the term "rhythmic *figure*" implies? We cannot say which analysis is more correct; *both* interpretations appear to fit Valéry's account. But if so, we cannot claim with any well-grounded confidence that imagining is an indispensable concomitant, much less an uneliminable component, of creativity.

We may generalize the foregoing critique in the following fashion. Instead of being related to each other in an intrinsic and interdependent manner, imagination and creativity stand in a non-necessary relation to one another. By this is meant that imagining may, but need not, be ingredient in a given creative effort, and that imagining itself may, but also may not, be creative on a given occasion. The two activities, in other words, can support each other in specific situations—and no doubt frequently do so in the case of innovative artists and scientists—but they can also take place in isolation from each other. I can, and often do, imagine in a manner that is utterly insipid and uninspired, i.e., in such a way that I could not accurately apply to it the descriptive adjectives "creative," "original," "synthetic," "novel." Similarly, I

28. Note that this is a more general claim than that of Galton, for whom imagining (specifically, visualizing) is not necessary to scientific creativity, and is perhaps even detrimental to it: "an overready perception of sharp mental pictures is antagonistic to the acquirement of habits of highly generalized and abstract thought" (*Inquiries into Human Faculty*, p. 60).

29. *The Art of Poetry*, trans. D. Folliot (New York: Pantheon, 1958), p. 148; Valéry's italics.

30. Ibid., p. 149. My italics.

can, and sometimes do, act creatively (and precisely in the Kantian-Romantic meaning of spontaneously, productively, etc.) without imagining in any significant way. The conclusion can only be: *there is no inherent or necessary connection between imagining and being creative; they are only contingently connected.*

If this conclusion is correct, then it follows that the autonomy of imagining cannot consist in creativity. Whatever the ultimate meaning of imaginative autonomy may be, it does not include creativity in the Romantic sense as an *essential* aspect of its enactment. Thus it is only obfuscating to speak of imagination's "creative autonomous powers" as if creativity and imaginative autonomy were interchangeable with each other. The dissociability of imaginative activity from creativity means that the autonomy of which I am capable in imagining is not necessarily creative in character. Nor is it the case that by means of such autonomy I shall necessarily *become* creative: imagining gives no guarantee or strict promise of creativity, even though it may sometimes be involved in the full accomplishment of certain creative acts. Just because I am an adept imaginer proves nothing of definitive significance with regard to my creative capacities in art, science, philosophy, or whatever. And conversely: just because I am or have been creative in various ways demonstrates nothing definite with regard to my actual imaginative powers.[31] Whether occurring simultaneously or separated over time, imagining and being creative do not exhibit any elective affinity for each other, that is, an affinity such that one activity could be taken as an infallible sign of the presence of the other. Therefore, the autonomy that I realize in imagining is not to be confused with the autonomy that I may attain in being creative: the two kinds of autonomy, though capable of overlapping, are by no means identical with one another.

B. WHAT THE AUTONOMY OF IMAGINING IS

In the preceding section we have explored various ways in which imaginative autonomy may be misconstrued: as implying imagination's superiority over other mental acts, as signifying self-legislation in the Kantian sense, as equivalent to secondary autonomy in ego-

---

31. This assertion is supported by the observation that great painters have not always been skilled imaginers. Many have been; but many, by their own testimony, have not. Among the latter is apparently Leonardo da Vinci, who testified that "the imagination cannot visualize such beauty as is seen by the eye" (*Trattato della Pittura*, sec. 15).

psychological theory, and as entailing creativity in an effusive Romantic interpretation. Now that we have some idea of how *not* to conceive of the autonomy of imagining, we must attempt to discern what in fact this autonomy consists in—its main manifestations and most crucial characteristics.

This task is rendered especially difficult by the fact that the autonomy of imagining is a *thin* autonomy. By "thin autonomy" is meant an autonomous mode of functioning that is essentially disconnected from the robust world of *praxis*—from the "life-world" in Husserl's telling term.[32] This functioning involves a characteristic *indifference* to the concrete concerns and particular projects of the life-world. The imaginer displays such an indifference inasmuch as he does not seek to change either the given structure of his life-world or his apprehension of that structure. To assert this is not, of course, to deny that imagining can form part of some larger scheme to alter or transform historical or natural givens. Yet insofar as the act of imagining is isolatable from the primary intentions and goals of such a scheme, we find that it does not seek to make an impact outside its own immediate orbit. It aims only at completing itself qua act and not at anything more ultimate or more efficacious within the world of perception and action.

Imagining, in short, is not an expression of that pervasive "care" (*Sorge*) that Heidegger claims is the fundamental and encompassing dimension of our being-in-the-world. As imaginers, we do not indulge in either of the two basic forms of activity care may assume: "concern" (*Besorgen*) for nonhuman "categorial" features of experience and "solicitude" (*Fürsorge*) for other human beings. Indifference, on Heidegger's analysis, represents a defiicient mode of solicitude.[33] Yet it should be remarked that indifference *toward others* is not the only significant kind of indifference of which human beings are capable. There is a specifically philosophical indifference, e.g., as advocated by Stoicism, toward the tumults of human experience. And there is, in addition, the special indifference with which we are here concerned: *imaginative indifference*, where it is not only a question of being indifferent to others or to the vicissitudes of experience as such. It is also, and still more basically, a matter of being unconcerned with the kinds of commitment other mental acts entail—especially the thetic commitment to present or past reality that is inseparable from acts of perceiving, remembering, and hallucinating. When we imagine, as

32. On the notion of life-world, see Husserl, *The Crisis of European Sciences and Transcendental Phenomenology*, esp. secs. 33-34.
33. On concern, solicitude, and indifference, see Heidegger, *Being and Time*, sections 12, 26, 41, 42, and esp. p. 158.

when we perform the phenomenological reduction, we "bracket" or "suspend" any such commitment, showing our indifference to the real. Precisely in this way *we render our act of imagining non-efficacious*. For any mental act to be genuinely efficacious— i.e., to have a direct and demonstrable effect in the life-world—it must become engaged by taking on a commitment of the sort just described. To refuse such engagement is to refuse to participate in what Heidegger calls "the worldhood of the world," that is, in that network of ramified significances which structures the life-world as a domain of concern and solicitude. In imagining, it is not so much a matter of withdrawing from mundane obligations and tasks as of *decommissioning* these obligations and tasks themselves—removing them from the sphere of our ongoing mental activity. We put the demanding engagements of the life-world out of play so as to move mentally in a less encumbered manner.

This is not to deny that we can also imagine, and may even do so frequently, *while* engaged in life-world activities. Yet precisely by suspending belief in the reality of what is imagined, we achieve a state of disengagement. This is seen most clearly in extended acts of imagining: to imagine in the relatively prolonged fashion illustrated in the three examples given in chapter one, I found it essential to disengage myself from concrete and particular demands of my immediate environment. In contrast with such full imaginative experiences, more transient instances may come and go while we perform tasks in the life-world; in themselves, however, they remain no less disengaged than full-blown acts of imagining: they are merely more momentary caesuras in the pace of existence. As such, they are not incompatible with the simultaneous enactment of routine and undemanding life-world projects which the imaginer treats with indifference even as he carries them out.

"Thin autonomy" refers, then, to the disengaged state into which we enter when we imagine. In such a state we are autonomous, but not in any of the "thick" senses we examined earlier. In each of the latter there is an element of commitment—as is found in the very notions of a prescriptive hierarchical model of mind, the obligatory nature of moral law, the ego's control over id and environment, or the concrete creative work required in art and science. Imagining proper lacks all of these specific forms of engagement—of what Merleau-Ponty calls "interinvolvement" with the natural and historical world of spatial beings, temporal becomings, and interpersonal complexities. The world of imagining is a thin world, a mini-world whose ephemerality precludes any engaged activity comparable to that required in the life-world. There is no place *within* such a realm to be engaged and nothing *with which* to be engaged, for in imagining we do not encounter the fully individuated entities and events that form the focus of ego control, ethical conduct, and creative endeavor. Instead of becoming involved with such entities and events, we find ourselves disinvolved. In short, the *épaisseur* of an engaged autonomy is replaced by the thinness of a disengaged autonomy.

Recognizing the thin character of imaginative autonomy vis-à-vis other denser types of autonomy may help us to understand why the autonomous action of imagining has so often been questioned—or simply bypassed—by previous investigators. It is as if they had asked themselves the following skeptical question: How can an experience so tenuous, so fragile and fleeting as imagining be autonomous? Overlooked in this question is the possibility that imagining's very tenuousness may provide a clue to its mode of autonomy. Perhaps imagining is autonomous *in its very insubstantiality*. Perhaps, in other words, the autonomy of imagining is to be found in the enactment and exemplification of its own gossamerlike thinness. To realize autonomy in imagining may be to realize *next to nothing*, that is, nothing concrete, concernful, or consolidated.

But what then *is* imaginative autonomy? The answer to this question may be encapsulated in the following two statements:

1. The autonomy of imagining consists in its strict independence from other mental acts, from its surroundings, and from all pressing human concerns.

2. The autonomy of imagining consists in the freedom of mind of which imagination is uniquely capable.

In the remainder of this chapter I shall expand upon each of these assertions by delineating in detail two fundamental notions that have surfaced only intermittently in the course of this essay: *independence* and *freedom of mind*.

Autonomy as Independence

A first basic form of imaginative autonomy is found in its essentially independent character. Such independence is not only a matter of the descriptive differences between imagining and other acts. Important as these differences are, we must also recognize four other ways in which imagination manifests its independent status.

CAUSAL INDEPENDENCE

It can hardly be denied that certain acts serve as *conditions* for the occurrence of imagination. Perception in particular presents itself as a conditioning act. As was affirmed at the end of the last chapter, if we were not already perceivers, we could not be imaginers. We may add that to be able to imagine is not only to be *capable* of perception—it is *in fact* to have perceived before. For if we were endowed with a given perceptual capacity we had never actually utilized, we would find ourselves unable to imagine in the corresponding sensory modality. To visualize, for instance, is both to be capable of seeing and to have exercised this capacity on former occasions.[34]

But such a general truth about necessary conditions of imagining should be carefully distinguished from the mistaken claim that any and every imaginative experience must be directly preceded by a particular act of perception that serves as its immediate cause. Of course, sometimes such causal precedence is indeed the case: my perception of Ann crossing the street just now may give rise directly and unambiguously to my imagining of Ann *déshabillée*. But this need not happen. In many other instances there is neither an immediate temporal priority of perceiving to imagining nor a specifiable causal connection between the two acts. Such temporal-causal independence[35] is present both in spontaneous and in controlled imagining. A human face that suddenly appears before my visual imagination may be just as independent of its preceding perceptual context as a face I conjure up deliberately.

What is of critical importance, then, is that we not confuse *condition* with *cause*. Perception is certainly a condition of imagination because imaginers are necessarily also perceivers. Indeed, as human, we *must* be perceivers, whatever else we are capable of. Human imaginers all have bodies; and the body is, in Merleau-Ponty's words, "the subject qua perceiver."[36] To be human is to be incarnate, and to be incarnate is to perceive, to be in various forms of sensory contact with the immediate environment by means of our own body. If imagining is also one of our capacities, then it, like every other capacity, is dependent on the prior existence and exercise of perceptual powers. These powers accord-

---

34. A corollary of this particular point is that congenital blindness must bring with it a lack of ability to visualize. This effect has been confirmed in a number of studies. (See, for example, C. W. Kimmins, "Special Features of the Teaching of the Blind," *Teachers of the Blind*, LXI [1923]; H. R. Blank, "The Dreams of the Blind," *Psychoanalytic Quarterly*, XXVII [1958].)

35. By this term I refer to cases in which both temporal precedence and causal efficacy are absent. To point to such cases is not to deny that the two factors are dissociable in fact and in principle. A given act may be causally relevant to and yet temporally distant from another act; or it may be temporally proximate and causally irrelevant to that act.

36. *Phenomenology of Perception*, p. 206: "Perceiving as we do with our body, the body is a natural self and, as it were, the subject *qua* perceiver." (I have slightly modified the translation.)

ingly represent a condition of possibility for imagination. But to be a condition of possibility is not perforce to be a specific cause. By "specific cause" I mean either an initiating cause in a chain of efficient causes (i.e., a "first cause") or the precipitating factor that triggers the appearance or existence of some object or event with which it is temporally and/or spatially contiguous. Perception may, but *does not necessarily*, act as a specific cause of imagination. Yet it remains a general condition of imagination, a *sine qua non* for its enactment.[37]

CONTEXT-INDEPENDENCE

A given act of imagining may not only be independent of various temporally precedent and causally efficacious factors in its immediate environs. At the limit, it may also be independent of *all* surrounding entities and events, whether or not they have causal potency over or temporal priority to the imaginative act itself. Thus, the imaginer can disengage himself not just from those elements of his environment that might directly influence his imagining—i.e., the focally perceived items that obtrude themselves on his awareness—but also from those things that form the general context of his imaginative experience. When I imagine as I gaze from my window onto the surrounding city, my act of imagining need not be a mere expression of, or reaction to, the urban scene before me. Although the panorama *may* affect the course of my imagining—e.g., by insinuating itself in various ways into what I imagine—it does not have to do so. It need not even figure as a dim backdrop, as a *setting* for my imaginative experience. For no matter what the particular makeup or nature of such a circumambient context may be, my imagining can soar beyond it, disregarding it both as a whole and in regard to any of its details.[38] Such radical context-independence is peculiar to imagining: no other mental act displays a

37. Can we say the same of memory? Perhaps, but only in a considerably weaker sense. Memory functions as a condition of imagination only in the sense that, were it not present in the imaginer *at all*, much of what one imagines would not have the minimal consistency required for any human experience to be labeled "*an* experience." Memory necessarily provides not the details of imagined content but a ready stock of material on which we can draw in making an otherwise chaotic imaginative presentation more coherent. But this is not to say that imagination always builds on, or has to imitate, memory.

38. In fact, recent experimental studies have shown that imagining with one's eyes open is accompanied by a marked reduction in focused perception of the immediate environment. See J. S. Antrobus, J. S. Antrobus, and J. L. Singer, "Eye Movements Accompanying Daydreaming," *Journal of Abnormal and Social Psychology* (1964), pp. 244-52; and E. Klinger, K. C. Gregoire, and S. G. Barta, "Physiological Correlates of Mental Activity," *Psychophysiology* (1973), pp. 471-77.

comparable capacity to be so oblivious to its surroundings, so indifferent to the *milieu* of its occurrence.

CONTENT-INDEPENDENCE

The specific content of a given act of imagining need not replicate or even resemble the specific content of any other experience, past or future, imaginative or nonimaginative. When we describe what we imagine in a particular case, our description is not inherently interchangeable with the description of, say, what we have once perceived or remembered—or will someday perceive or remember. In brief, the structure and character of imagined content are intrinsically independent of the structure and character of other kinds of content.

But in claiming this, we cannot refuse to recognize two further facets of the situation. First, to assert content-independence is not to deny the possibility that the specific content of an act of imagining *may*, now or in the future, quite closely resemble the specific content of other, quite different experiences. What I imagine may someday coincide in character with what I perceive, remember, or even hallucinate. By the same token, what I have once perceived, remembered, or hallucinated may coincide with what I am now imagining or may someday imagine. And what I imagine now or have once imagined may resemble what I shall imagine at a later point. Nevertheless, despite all of these possibilities of descriptive overlap—of "continuity of content" —it is not the case that imagined content *has* to be a replica of, or even isomorphic with, the content of any other act or experience.[39] However infrequently a case of complete content-independence or zero overlap may occur, it remains an essential possibility whenever I imagine.

Second, to affirm content-independence is not to deny that what we imagine may still be *perceivable in principle*. Even if a given item of imagined content is so bizarre that it is highly improbable that it will ever become a candidate for perception, we cannot rule out the dual possibility that: (1) the nature of the perceptual world will change in such a way as to present to us an actually perceivable specimen of the item in question; or (2) the nature of human perceptual capacities will alter so as to allow us to perceive what is presently unperceivable. There is, then, a *theoretical* perceivability—and hence rememberability—of whatever it is that we imagine. Yet to admit this is by no means to un-

---

39. By "replica" is meant an exact copy that resembles its original not only in structure or shape but in color, number of dimensions, etc. An "isomorphic" copy is similar only in formal structure and proportion and is typically a diagram or schema of the original. Cf. Plato's similar distinction between *eidolon* and *eikon* in *The Sophist*, 235a-236c.

dercut the content-independence of imagining. The qualifying terms "theoretical" and "in principle" invoked here do not constrict imagination or its powers in any significant manner; for these terms gain meaning in the present context only by referring to fundamental (and quite unlikely) changes in the perceptual world or in our perceptual apparatus. Therefore, the theoretical perceivability of imagined content does not make this content derivative from what we perceive, and the content-independence of imagining remains an intrinsic feature of imaginative experience.

USE-INDEPENDENCE

A few pages ago, I referred to "the strict independence [of imagining] from other mental acts, from its surroundings, and from all *pressing human concerns.*" Up to this point we have dealt exclusively with the independence of imagining from its surroundings (i.e., its context) and from other acts (i.e., in terms of causation and content). But imagination is equally independent with regard to its application or use in the affairs of daily life, in art, or in science. In all of these ongoing human activities there is an indisputable tendency to appropriate the fruits of imagining as a source of inspiration or insight. The artist may imagine in order to discover new motifs for his work; the scientist conjures up imagined situations by means of "thought-experiments" as an aid to his research; and almost everyone uses the projective powers of imagining in anticipating dreaded or wished-for situations.

Despite such a wealth of possible uses, however, the act of *imagining itself* is not predestined to utilization of any particular kind. Even if we admit that the "dramatic rehearsal in imagination" of which Dewey speaks is a central ingredient in human affairs,[40] this still does not mean that it is imagining's ineluctable fate or abiding purpose *to be put to use* in certain determinate ways. To be us*able* or use*ful* is one thing, and it can hardly be denied that imagining may be of considerable practical value in day-to-day living, in vocational pursuits, and even in extending and refining perception or memory. (As we have seen, imagination may combine with perception to make possible a composite experience such as seeing-as. The same is true of memory,

40. Cf. John Dewey, *Human Nature and Conduct*, pp. 190-91. Dewey also remarks that "imagination is primarily dramatic, rather than lyric, whether it takes the form of the play enacted on the stage, of the told story, or silent soliloquy" (*Experience and Nature* [New York: Norton, 1929], p. 89). As employed by the individual, the dramatizing power of imagination allows for a more vivid anticipation of some projected use. Nevertheless, such dramatization is not necessarily linked to any concrete application, and it would be mistaken to suppose that it is always a prelude to concerted action.

which is sometimes revived *by means of* imagination.) But to be use-*bound* is quite another matter. An activity that is use-bound is one that exists or appears only insofar as it is actually being used. Hammering, for example, is an activity which cannot be divorced from specific aims of construction and production; it exists only as use-bound.[41] Imagining, in contrast, is not tied to any constant utilitarian aims. It is capable of occurring outside the province of any particular use, and thus as independent of application to given tasks of any kind. This essential use-independence of imagining—its "purposiveness without a purpose," to adapt a phrase from Kant—means that it resists efforts to link it intrinsically and invariably with any of the special uses to which it may on occasion and for various reasons be put.[42]

Autonomy as Freedom of Mind

"Freedom of mind" refers to the facility with which we are able, within the mind alone and by means of the mind alone, to carry out a particular project which the psyche has proposed to itself.[43] In such autonomous activity it is above all a question of the freedom with which the mind can maneuver in its own self-delimited and yet infinitely variable sphere. Thus it is a matter of the free movement of mentation, of the peculiar "pleasures of merely circulating"[44] within the psyche. As such, freedom of mind is not merely a freedom with respect to causal determination—nor is it to be equated with the special intellectual freedom that may result from a knowledge of such determination.[45] The freedom enjoyed and exhibited in imagining is not limited

41. See Heidegger's analysis of hammering in terms of its "ready-to-hand" (*zuhanden*) character in *Being and Time*, pp. 98-99. It can be seen that the present discussion is continuous with previous remarks concerning the disengagement of imagining from the world of concern and solicitude—the world, precisely, of use or what Heidegger calls "serviceability" (*Dienlichkeit*). (Cf. ibid., pp. 109-110.)

42. It should be evident from what has just been said that the earlier discussion of creativity in section A represents a case (albeit a particularly striking and important case) of what I am here calling imagination's "use-independence." To be creative *in* or *by* imagining is to *make use* of imaginative powers—to apply or bind them in this particular way. For further discussion of what may be termed in general "bound imagining," see my article "The Image/Sign Relation in Husserl and Freud," *The Review of Metaphysics*, XXX (Dec. 1976).

43. I do not distinguish in any decisive way between mind and psyche, mental and psychical. Although I am aware of efforts to make just such a distinction, e.g., by Jung and Jungians, the notion of mind on which I am drawing is capacious enough to include most of what the term "psyche" conveys to Western readers. If there is any significant difference implicit in my discussion, it is that mind is the *enacting* or active element in psyche—where psyche itself is the *region* of activity in which the movements of mind occur.

44. The title of a poem in *The Collected Poems of Wallace Stevens*, pp. 149-50.

45. This latter freedom is basic to Spinoza's philosophy of mind, in which the issue of freedom is inextricably intertwined with the question of causality. On this

to freedom *from* a nexus of causal influences or *from* specific obstacles (external or self-imposed). The freedom at issue here differs from such strictly negative freedom in being a positive freedom *to* realize imaginative plans and projects of one's own choosing—in short, to act autonomously, where "autonomy" implies more than lack of hindrance. Freedom of mind may presuppose an absence of specific impediments, but it cannot be reduced to unimpeded activity *per se*.[46]

Although such freedom has not yet been focused on in this book, it was adumbrated by a reference early in the Introduction to two salient characteristics of imagining: its ease of access and the almost sure success with which it is executed in a given instance. Both of these characteristics evince imagination's unique manner of manifesting freedom of mind. The first characteristic was already obvious to Aristotle, who said (in a statement we have quoted before) that imagining "is up to us when we wish."[47] Whatever it is that we seek in imagination's endless repertory of shifting scenes lies ready at hand and can be brought into being at our merest whim. Such facility bespeaks a freedom that is as effortless as it is continually available.

The second characteristic, the self-assured success of imaginative projects, requires more comment at this point. This characteristic arises from the fact that there is seldom any significant discrepancy between an imaginative project and its realization; with but few exceptions, intention and fulfillment coincide. In chapter three we observed that controlled imagining cannot fail provided it remains within certain predetermined logical and ontological limits (and provided, too, that the imaginer's own empirical powers are equal to the task). What such inbuilt, self-guaranteeing success implies in the present context is that the freedom of mind evidenced in imagining is not only a freedom that is enacted with facility but a freedom that rarely falls short of full realization. For controlled imagining is not a matter of merely random movements; its freedom is not reducible to aleatory activity. Even though a given case of intended imagining may be un-

---

point see Stuart Hampshire's essay "Freedom of Mind" in *Freedom of Mind and Other Essays* (Princeton: Princeton University Press, 1971).

46. Hobbes effects this reduction in holding that freedom means solely "free from being hindered by opposition" (*Leviathan*, Part I, ch. 5). I do not wish to argue that *all* significant forms of freedom can be reduced to two, i.e., negative and positive in the senses just used. Nevertheless, these two forms do correspond to the most important kinds of freedom implicated in imaginative experience. (For an enlightened discussion of negative and positive freedom in a social context, see Isaiah Berlin, *Two Concepts of Liberty* [Oxford: Oxford University Press, 1958] esp. pp. 6-19. For a full survey of types of freedom, see M. J. Adler, ed., *The Idea of Freedom*, 2 vols. [New York: Doubleday, 1958-61].)

47. *De Anima*, 427b 16.

dertaken in a spirit of caprice, its realization is far from capricious. This realization, i.e., the imaginative presentation itself, is the embodiment or expression of whatever it was that we desired to imagine in the first place. In the congruence between intention and fulfillment that is thereby effected, we witness a basic feature of imagination's freedom of mind: its success-proneness, its tendency to achieve precisely what it sets out to achieve.

What then of spontaneous imagining? Does its existence invalidate freedom of mind insofar as we can no longer speak of fulfilling preexisting intentions? Leaving aside the possibility that unconscious or preconscious intentions may constantly be present,[48] we need only remark that the fact of spontaneous imagining, far from invalidating freedom of mind, represents an extension of it. Or, to be more exact, imagination's spontaneity introduces another dimension of its freedom of mind, for such freedom is not just a freedom to realize what we intend but presents to us what we have not expressly intended at all. What is brought forth in controlled imagining represents the satisfaction of certain explicit intentions, yet *just this and no more*. With spontaneous imagining, in contrast, what appears or occurs in imaginative form differs from what we had expected—if we were expecting anything specific to begin with. Spontaneous imagining is imagining *in surfeit*, and the new dimension of freedom that it introduces is found in its capacity to surprise us by a sudden and unanticipated onset of content. We are surprised precisely because so much of imagining is *un*eventful and *un*surprising, being circumscribed within the confines of controlledness. But whenever an imaginative presentation flashes before us in an absence of express intention or expectation, we become aware of an unusual sense of mental freedom, one which occurs in disregard of explicit wishes and motives. Freedom of mind in this sense is an autogenous freedom of psychical appearings which arise separately from conscious intentions and in disconnection with them.[49] If con-

48. In the classical psychoanalytic claim, of course, *any* imaginative presentation has to answer to *some* intention, conscious or not. It is only a matter of proper (and sometimes prolonged) investigation to discover the exact intention or motive in a given case. It should be noted that this claim is not necessarily incompatible with a phenomenological account of imagination. The existence of unconscious intentions does not undercut or undermine conscious intentions; it only serves to ground such intentions and to make them intelligible in a context broader than that provided by consciousness itself.

49. To be disconnected is not, of course, to be *in conflict*. Conflict entails obstruction: e.g., I want to imagine an elephant and I imagine a mouse in its place. Here the appearance of the mouse conflicts with and obstructs the appearance of the elephant. In spontaneous imagining there is no project *to be* obstructed: the imaginative presentation appears unsolicited, irrespective of previous psychical projects and thus in no way conflicting with them.

trolled imagining shows mind in a moment of self-incurred but slender success, spontaneous imagining manifests mind in a flurry of *excess:* of freedom beyond the freedom realized by design.

Further reflection shows that, in addition to spontaneity and controlledness, each of the remaining eidetic traits of imagining examined in part two displays a different facet of imaginative freedom of mind. *Self-containedness* exhibits the way in which imagining tends to isolate itself within a discrete sector of the psyche so as to exercise an uninhibited maneuverability—and thereby to be uninfluenced by other acts of mind and untempted by invitations to collude with them. In *self-evidence* we observe a similar tendency toward a self-enclosed state, but one characterized by the transparency of the imaginative act-*cum*-presentation, which offers itself unresistingly to the imaginer's consciousness. This consciousness, wholly certain of its own non-corrigible intuitions, shows a new aspect of the mind's freedom, i.e., the ability to proceed unencumbered by doubt as to its own course and content.

The *indeterminacy* of the imaginative presentation introduces still another parameter of psychical freedom, one that results from its not being constrained by a strictly determinate content. What I perceive or remember is ballasted with determinacies that serve to structure the subsequent course of my experiencing. No such preordination of content occurs in imagining, whose very vagueness leaves it free to establish and continually to reestablish its own itinerary. *Pure possibility*, finally, is the thetic expression of imaginative freedom of mind. Even if the purely possible is subject to certain formal and practical limits, these ultimate boundaries are not nearly so constrictive as those imposed upon whatever is empirically real. Pure possibility enables the mind's free movement to traverse a terrain considerably more vast than the region occupied by perceived and remembered things alone. Moreover, this latter region may itself be viewed *sub specie possibilitatis.* As Husserl says, "in the realm of [imagination's] arbitrary freedom, we can lift all actuality to a plane of pure possibility."[50] There is no end to the number or type of forays we may make via imagination into this realm: in the domain of the purely possible, everything becomes possible. And each journey into such a domain is potentially endless, since a given series of pure possibilities has no fixed terminus. Here freedom is the freedom of never having to come to a preestablished or peremptory end.

It should be evident by now that imaginative freedom of mind is by no means a simple, monovalent phenomenon. Its diverse facets and

50. *Experience and Judgment*, p. 352.

plural expressions demonstrate its manifold character. Just as we should in all strictness speak of imagination's various "autonomies," so we should also refer to its *freedoms*—or at least to its several senses of freedom. If for the sake of simplicity we continue to speak of the "autonomy" of imagination and of its "freedom" of mind, each of these singular terms should henceforth be understood to include as essential constituents a number of aspects, forms, and modes.

The variousness with which imagining shows itself to be a free act exemplifies the multiplicity of the mental. In the present context such multiplicity assumes the specific form of *variability*, that is, the mind's freedom to vary itself indefinitely and without end. It is significant that variability is a feature of imagining that Husserl singled out for incorporation into his mature conception of phenomenological method, a point we shall explore further in the next chapter. And yet the value of imagination in this regard cannot be restricted to its role in the intuition of eidetic structures. *Imagining is variational by its very nature*, and not only as employed in a particular method. To imagine is not only to project variations *of* the eidetically self-identical; it is also to vary or differ *from* the spatio-temporally determinate and the historically actual. Further, it is to vary *in* its own content: the evanescing of this content is a form of self-variation, of variation among its own self-chosen themes. If it is easy to summon up an imaginative presentation to begin with, it is correspondingly difficult to maintain before the mind precisely the *same* presentation with the *same* specific content clothed in a constant and unvarying form. An imagining consciousness is attuned and attached to variety, and its span of attention is characteristically brief because of its fondness for the fleeting. When Hobbes wrote of the "Celerity of Imagining,"[51] he spoke with phenomenological precision. Even if attempts at protracted imagining are made, the results tend to vanish swiftly, and they do so in accordance with the imaginer's own penchant for viewing a continually changing psychical show.

Variation means multiplicity; being a variation upon something else, a given variation always implies *other* variations, actual or possible. Consequently, a mental act whose basic operations continually engender variety will be free in the special sense of giving rise to multiple options, directions, and routes. To be free in this fashion is to realize freedom of mind to the fullest. For the human mind thrives on variation, even as it seeks unification; and imagining, more than any other mental act, proceeds by proliferation: it is the primary way in

51. *Leviathan*, pt. I, ch. 8.

which the mind diversifies itself and its contents. Mind is free—is indeed most free—in imagining.

Independence and freedom of mind are, therefore, the two fundamental forms assumed by imaginative autonomy. In the first case, the autonomy consists in not being directly determined by factors prior to, contiguous with, or surrounding a given imaginative experience, and in not being constrained by the way this experience may be used for some extra-imaginative purpose. In the second case, it is a question of autonomous action proper—of imagination's proclivity for free movement and for endless variation. Both forms of autonomy, the one predominantly negative and the other predominantly positive, are valid and required. Imagining would be less than fully autonomous if only one of the two basic forms were operative. To be essentially independent alone is not sufficient for the achievement of autonomy; by itself, and without the taking of specific action, independence might mean mere isolation. By the same token, to attempt to exercise freedom of mind without achieving adequate independence would be an exercise in futility, for the mind would then find itself ensnared by a number of severely delimiting determinacies.

There is, accordingly, an important internal relationship between the two forms of imaginative autonomy. This relationship is reciprocal and may be expressed in two final propositions.

1. *Independence is a prerequisite for freedom of mind.* There must be independence in the four specific senses discussed earlier if freedom of mind is to be meaningfully enacted. Only in the absence of interfering factors of causation, context, content, and use can the mind find itself in a position to pursue its imaginative projects as it wishes—or to allow imagining to arise spontaneously. Without such independence, variation in imagination becomes either a mere repetition of what has already been experienced or a vain attempt to cancel or transcend all of one's previous experience. Either way, freedom of mind is not attained, and the imaginer remains bound to the real—whether by repeating or by denying it—instead of gaining access to the open domain of the purely possible.

2. *Freedom of mind, though based on independence, has an activity of its own.* To achieve essential independence in imagining represents a Pyrrhic victory if specific action does not ensue, i.e., what we have just called "autonomous action proper." This action is found in freedom of mind—in the free maneuverability by which the mind can

range unopposed over a broad spectrum of possible variations. The imaginer is free to entertain such variations *ad libitum*, to arrange them in more or less complex groupings, and to rearrange or undo these groupings themselves. Whatever course imagining takes, however, the imaginer is entering into an action which is at once affirmative and nonconcrete: affirmative, insofar as he is undertaking an action that is specifically imaginative and is not only disentangling himself from other types of action (as he must do in establishing independence); nonconcrete, inasmuch as the resultant psychical action takes place entirely on the plane of imagination and does not form part of ongoing practical projects pursued within the life-world. Such action is properly autonomous: self-generating, self-regulating, and self-sustaining within the province of mind.

CHAPTER NINE

The Significance of Imaginative Autonomy

THERE IS A FINAL LINE of inquiry to which we must turn our attention. Even if it is agreed that a descriptive account of imagining reveals this act to be autonomous in the ways indicated in the last chapter, the reader may still feel tempted to ask, what is the significance of such autonomy? What is its actual place in human experience? I shall attempt to answer these questions by focusing on three disparate domains: art, psychology, and philosophy. To show the importance of autonomous imagining in these domains is not, of course, to demonstrate the significance of imaginative autonomy in human affairs at large. But it is to point to three quite specific areas in which this significance manifests itself, and it is also to suggest what it might mean in other areas as well. What will emerge most clearly in the pages to follow is that wherever imagining appears as autonomous *it matters*: it makes a difference, though sometimes a subtle difference, to those human endeavors upon which it bestows its protean power.

I

There have been two dominant Western conceptions of the essential function of art: representation and expression. (1) According to theories centered around the idea of *representation*, a work of art is representational in the sense that it *re*-presents isomorphically in its own medium some preexistent entity or event that serves as its model. The represented entity or event need not be material or historical in nature; it can equally well be affective or ideational, as occurs when a painter attempts to represent a certain attitude or state of mind. Furthermore, several different sorts of things may be represented at once: Hogarth's etchings often represent at one and the same time a parodied event and a given mood (e.g., ribaldry) associated with that event. But in every case, no matter how complex, it is presumed that the structure of the art work is isomorphic with the structure of what is represented therein. Apart from the special difficulties arising from the demand for isomorphism,[1] the gravest consequence of the representationalist view of art is that imaginative activity on the part of the artist and the spectator alike is radically curtailed. On this view the free movements of imagining are subject to suspicion. They are seen as meddlesome distractions from two primary tasks: for the artist, transmuting the form of what is represented into a form immanent in his chosen artistic medium; for the spectator, apprehending the immanent form as integral to the completed work. It is not so surprising, then, that theories of art as representation, from Plato onward, have denigrated and even denied the place of imagination in art. When isomorphic representation is the paradigm, the suppression of the significance of imagining is only to be expected.

(2) What is not expected, and is less often admitted, is that theories of art as *expression* also leave little room for imagination. For these theories, the proper function of a work of art is to express a given content—or, more exactly, to make this content (which may be quite unexpressive independently of the work itself) truly *expressive*. Expressive of what? Above all, of emotions—but also of ideas, memories, beliefs, and other contents of human experience.[2] These contents need not (in contrast with represented objects or events) preexist the creation of the work of art, but they must be capable of expression in a variety of different works and perhaps even in different artistic media. Mozart's music often expresses a certain characteristic joyfulness that we are tempted to label specifically "Mozartean." And yet Mozart himself expressed the same emotional quality in differing ways in various musical works, and other composers are capable of re-expressing an equivalent joyfulness—even to the point that we may misidentify their compositions as Mozart's own. Over a series of different instances the

1. For a discussion of these difficulties, see E. H. Gombrich, *Art and Illusion* (New York: Pantheon, 1961), part I, "The Limits of Likeness." Gombrich holds that the artist "cannot transcribe what he sees; he can only translate it into the terms of his medium" (p. 36); even "the correct portrait, like the useful map, is an end product on a long road . . . it is not a faithful record of a visual experience" (p. 90).

2. Tolstoi provides a classical statement of the theory of art as expression: "To evoke in oneself a feeling one has once experienced, and having evoked it in oneself, then, by means of movements, lines, colors, sounds, or forms expressed in words, so to transmit that feeling that others may experience the same feeling—this is the activity of art" (*Tolstoi on Art*, trans. and ed. Alymer Maude [Oxford: Oxford University Press, 1924], p. 173). For a more detailed critique of the expression theory of art, see my "Expression and Communication in Art," *Journal of Aesthetics and Art Criticism*, XXX (1971), pp. 197-207.

music remains expressive of a certain analyzable and nameable affective state, a state whose specific embodiment is subject to considerable variation.[3]

This situation obtains whenever art is held to be expressive; though specifiably expressive in one particular manner at one moment, the same expressiveness may appear as well on different occasions and in different guises. And this is so whether what is expressed is an intention or volition of the artist, an unusual experience he has had, a special state of mind he posits and idealizes, or even a purely symbolic content. Now, it is precisely such an expressivist view that eliminates or at least minimizes the role of imagining in the making and appreciating of art. If the aim of art is to be maximally expressive of some particular quality or form of experience, then imagining in its indifference to the actual will appear as unimportant in the attainment of this aim. At best, imagining might be seen as one means among others of attaining full expressiveness—e.g., through its ability to envisage competing candidates for an optimally expressive form. At worst, it will be regarded as a species of self-indulgence on the part of the artist or spectator—as mere *self-expression*—and thus as an obstacle to the attainment of art's proper *telos*. Either way, whether it is considered as mere means or as sheer deviation, imagining is made marginal.[4]

In representationalist and expressivist theories of art, then, we find imagining demoted or discredited in advance. Consequently, it is almost predictable that an aesthetician like Mikel Dufrenne, who combines elements of both theories in his comprehensive *Phenomenology of Aesthetic Experience*, ends by questioning the significance of imagination in art. The aesthetic object, writes Dufrenne, "takes us back to innocence by repressing emotions and imagination"; and "the genuine work of art spares us the expense of an exuberant imagination."[5] These stern judgments themselves come into question, however, when we recognize imagining to be an act that is autonomous in its basic action. For we then realize that it may have a role in art that is overlooked by both of the leading theories just considered. This role is one of *possibilizing*.

3. We are discussing here what Dufrenne calls the "affective *a priori*" and Ingarden "metaphysical qualities." See Mikel Dufrenne, *The Phenomenology of Aesthetic Experience*, trans., E. S. Casey et al. (Evanston: Northwestern University Press, 1973), chs. 16 and 17; and Ingarden, *The Literary Work of Art*, ch. 10.

4. Collingwood is a notable exception, since he makes both expression and imagination indispensable in his theory of art: "By creating for ourselves an *imaginary* experience or activity, we *express* our emotions; and this is what we call art" (*Principles of Art*, p. 151; my italics).

5. Dufrenne, *The Phenomenology of Aesthetic Experience*, pp. 340 and 366.

The function of possibilizing cannot be reduced to the projection of alternative means to a preconstituted end, an end determined by the demands of representation or expression. To utilize imagination in this workaday way is to reduce pure possibility to hypothetical possibility—autonomy to serviceability—and thus to undermine the essential thetic character of imagining. But possibilizing does not mean randomizing either. Pure chance and pure possibility are inherently distinguishable from each other; or rather, we should say that chance events form a subset of purely possible events. When modern artists draw on chance —from *le corps exquis* drawings to aleatory music—they are exploring only part of what the possibilizing function of imagination brings within reach. But what *does* it bring into reach?

The possibilizing activity of imagination in art opens up an experiential domain that would not otherwise have been available either to the artist or to the spectator. This domain is one in which *everything appears as purely possible*. Within the medium-bound, spatio-temporal limits of a given work of art, the domain of the purely possible emerges whenever imagining is functioning autonomously. Thus, as we follow Picasso through the numerous stages in which *Guernica* was composed, we become aware that at each decisive step (and taking into account what had already been achieved) Picasso's creating might have taken any number of different directions. Although certain of these directions can with hindsight be said to have been much more probable than others, for Picasso himself in the throes of creation there was no sense of precise probability, of determinate degree of likelihood, with regard to his options. Inasmuch as Picasso's imagination was active—that is, to the degree that he was not merely following some preestablished pattern—each successive step presented itself as only one of numerous possible solutions that might have been adopted. Picasso's imagining possibilized the progress of his painting.[6]

Similarly, and equally effectively, the spectator's imaginative capacities are deployed in their possibilizing power in experiencing works of art. When I watch a movie or read a novel, the development of the plot at any point short of termination is felt to be radically open insofar as my imagination is actively projecting possibilities pertaining to the plot's subsequent course. No matter what my specific expectations may

6. On the specific issue of the composition of *Guernica*, see Rudolf Arnheim, *Picasso's Guernica* (Berkeley: University of California Press, 1962), esp. part III. Arnheim writes that "finality . . . is a state disliked and perhaps feared by Picasso. Variations on a theme already established in the mural let the artist's imagination keep on inventing new shapes for a subject that, like all subjects, is inexhaustible and assure him that his creation continues to live beyond its burial on the canvas" (p. 94).

be, and no matter how well-grounded they are, my imagining still makes room for the possibility of practically *anything happening* in the next moment of viewing or reading—anything, that is, within the limits of conceivability demarcated by the plot itself. Even in contemplating a painting or a piece of sculpture, I can adopt an attitude that is sensitive to aspects or nuances which I have not yet apprehended and which are, for the moment, purely possible in status. It is imagining that makes such possibilizing possible.

Or to be more exact: it is imagining *as autonomous* which introduces the factor of pure possibility into aesthetic experience. Only an autonomous imagination can project, explore, and populate the domain of the purely possible in art. This domain is intrinsic to the very being of works of art, and yet is left unaccounted for in representationalist and expressivist theories, both of which fail to appreciate the autonomous activity of imagination in artistic creation and enjoyment. To recognize the significance of such activity is to achieve a more adequate assessment of the nature of art itself, which cannot be confined to functions of expressing or representing. For in art—whether in making or contemplating it—we not only perceive or feel; we also imagine, thereby entering a realm that would otherwise have remained closed to us. Hence, the acknowledgment of the role of autonomous imagining in art makes a difference, a quite considerable difference, in the way in which we are to understand the transporting and transforming character of aesthetic experience.

II

In this section we shall consider various ways in which autonomous imagining forms part of three prominent psychotherapeutic procedures: Freudian, Jungian, and that of the lesser-known guided imagery school. Manifest in each is the profound affinity between the psychical and the imaginal elements in human existence.

FREUDIAN PSYCHOANALYSIS

Despite my earlier animadversions against certain aspects of Freudian and neo-Freudian psychoanalytic theory—specifically, its failure to distinguish clearly between imagination, fantasy, and hallucination and the inadequacy of secondary autonomy as a model for imaginative autonomy—there are other dimensions of psychoanalysis that are es-

pecially meaningful at this point. These dimensions belong to psychoanalytic *method,* for within the method originally recommended by
Freud and pursued by the majority of his followers we find that imagination plays a quite central role. This is so in spite of the fact that psychoanalysis in its original form placed special stress on emotions and
memory, and on their combination in "abreaction" or catharsis.

It was in fact an *over*emphasis on memory that led Freud, after
several years of therapeutic frustration, to recognize the importance of
imagination in the psychoanalytic process. He came to realize that the
very basis of his seduction theory of neurosis was in jeopardy. What his
patients had tendered as straightforward memories of childhood seduction by their parents suddenly lost all credibility, and Freud confessed
to Fliess that "I no longer believe in my *neurotica.*"[7] The grounds of
his disbelief were not only empirical—how could that many incestuous
acts occur in staid Vienna?—but also, and more crucially, theoretical.
Freud announced triumphantly that he had made

> the certain discovery that there are no indications of reality in the uncon-
> cious, so that one cannot distinguish [there] between the [historical]
> truth and *fiction that is cathected with affect.*[8]

Hence the pathogenic nucleus of a neurosis need not be an actual event
in the patient's childhood—an event which could be unearthed intact,
recalled as such, in the course of analysis—but might equally well be a
fabrication of his imagination. All memories of childhood, in short, are
potentially "screen memories."[9]

As a consequence of this new insight, Freud could no longer hold
dogmatically that "hysterics suffer mainly from reminiscences."[10] He
was also forced to alter psychoanalytic technique itself. Where formerly the primary object of this technique had been the retrieval of repressed memories, now it had to take into account *whatever* came into
the patient's mind during treatment. With this step, free association
became the main methodological basis of psychoanalysis. For free
association is "free" precisely insofar as by its means anything and
everything present to the mind of the patient counts as valid material
for analytical examination and interpretation. What thereby comes
into consideration includes not only ostensible memories but dreams,

7. *Standard Edition,* I, 259 (letter of September 21, 1897).
8. Ibid., p. 260. My italics.
9. See the 1899 essay of this title in *Standard Edition,* III, 301-22, esp. the con-
cluding statement on p. 322: "It may indeed be questioned whether we have any
memories at all *from* our childhood: memories *relating to* our childhood may be all
that we possess."
10. *Studies in Hysteria* (*Standard Edition,* II, 7; in italics in original).

daydreams, imaginings, and fantasies. Common to all of these otherwise disparate items is the form in which they appear in free-associating: an imagistic form. Thus, when Freud first introduces the notion of free association in *The Interpretation of Dreams*, he writes that "as the involuntary ideas emerge they change into *visual and acoustic images.*"[11]

Here we must be cautious, however. Freud's point is not that free association *is* imagination; imagining (i.e., "imaging") is only one form of free association. But the *products* of every type of free association, including real and apparent memories, come clothed in imagery of various sorts. As Freud remarks in one of his earliest reported case histories, "It was as though she were reading a lengthy book of picture-images, whose pages were being turned over before her eyes."[12] In free association, therefore, the patient produces a steady stream of images, and from this we may conclude that imagining is operative at the critical moment of conversion from "involuntary ideas" (i.e., repressed fantasies, thoughts, and memories) into "visual and acoustic images." Imagination is the *metteur en scène* of all that the patient has kept from conscious awareness; it is the dramaturge of depth psychology.

The focus of Freud's research in the years immediately following the abandonment of the seduction theory was, above all, the *dream*. He became increasingly convinced that "the key to hysteria really lies in dreams."[13] For dreams provide an easily available paradigm for a whole series of psychopathological phenomena, including symptoms, parapraxes, and jokes. As Freud investigated the way in which dreams are formed, he uncovered a close alliance between dreaming and imagining. This alliance is found at both of the basic levels of dream formation: latent and manifest. At the latent level, the level of dream-thoughts proper, imagination enters in two ways. First, when the dream-thoughts make use of an already created daydream or fantasy, they are building on the prior work of imagining.[14] Second, the dream-thoughts themselves are often results of imaginative activity: "the unconscious activity of the imagination has a large share in the construction of the dream-thoughts."[15] Since dream-thoughts (especially in the form of dream-wishes) are the ultimate motive forces underlying dreams, Freud accords to imagination a crucial place in dream forma-

11. *Standard Edition*, IV, 102. My italics.
12. Ibid., II, 153. The case is that of Elisabeth von R.
13. Ibid., I, 276 (letter of January 4, 1899, to Fliess).
14. See *Standard Edition*, V, 491-93. Freud warns, however, that such ready-made fantasies typically form only a "portion" of the dream (ibid., p. 493). We must also question whether fantasy activity can be equated with imaginative activity.
15. Ibid., 592. Note the reference to Scherner's notion of "dream-imagination" on the preceding page. Earlier this same notion had been the object of skeptical remarks on Freud's part (see ibid., IV, 83 ff.).

tion, and therein reaches an unexpected agreement with the Romantic view of dreams as products of unconscious imaginative activity.

At the manifest level, imagination plays an even more indispensable role. This level, which is that of the dream proper, is almost wholly composed of sensory imagery arranged in various sequences and scenes:

> Dreams, then, think predominantly in visual images—but not exclusively. They make use of auditory images as well, and, to a lesser extent, of impressions belonging to the other senses. Many things, too, occur in dreams (just as they normally do in waking life) simply as thoughts or ideas . . . *Nevertheless, what are truly characteristic of dreams are only those elements of their [manifest] content which behave like images.*[16]

Freud attributes the imagistic character of the manifest dream to the "dream-work" and particularly to the dream-work's passion for pictorial representation.[17] How does such representation come about? Here Freud's view cannot be considered satisfactory. In chapter seven of *The Interpretation of Dreams*, he proposes that representation in image-form, instead of arising from imagination, arises from a regression to a *memory* of former wish-satisfaction; this memory is then revived to the point of such sensory intensity that its content seems to be actually present to the dreamer. In other words, the manifest dream is a form of hallucination which, as a reactivated memory, is "perceptually identical" with an original experience of satisfaction.[18] Yet why should memory, whose authenticity has already been questioned in psychotherapy, be made so essential to the manifest dream? Freud himself avers that the visual and acoustic images of the manifest dream "are more like perceptions than they are like mnemonic presentations."[19] He also remarks that "in dreams fresh composite forms are being perpetually constructed in an inexhaustible variety" and that such composite forms "could never have been objects of actual perception."[20]

16. Ibid., IV, 49-50. My italics.

17. Thus what Freud calls "considerations of representability" are a crucial factor in the transformation of dream-thoughts into the manifest dream: "of the various subsidiary thoughts attached to the essential dream-thoughts, those will be preferred which admit of visual representation" (*Standard Edition*, V, 344). Such pictorial representability is the only mechanism of the dream-work which is unique to dreams (cf. ibid., p. 671).

18. On regression and perceptual identity, see ibid., V, ch. seven, sec. B, esp. p. 566.

19. Ibid., IV, 50.

20. Ibid., V, 651; IV, 324. Note, however, that Freud remains skeptical about the complete novelty of imagined objects: "The 'creative' imagination is quite incapable of *inventing* anything; it can only combine components that are strangers to one another" (*Standard Edition*, XV, 172; his italics).

If they have never in fact been perceived, then they cannot be *remembered* as having been perceived, and it becomes highly questionable to derive the imagistic component of manifest dreams from the revival of memories. It would be more economical and more plausible to credit the formation of the "dream-façade" to the activity of imagination, which is not restricted to a mnemonic reproduction of prior perceptions. What Freud calls "the wish-fulfilling world of imagination"[21] is perfectly capable of constructing dream scenes in which basic wishes are represented as fulfilled, and this can be done without reactivating memories and without having to attain a hallucinatory state.

Dreaming, in sum, may be seen as a form of imaginative activity—both at the latent level (where Freud explicitly acknowledges its role) and at the manifest level (where, *contra* Freud, imagination proves to be a more likely creator of dream imagery than is memory). Furthermore, imagination provides a link between dreaming and free-associating. For the position of the patient in free association is remarkably similar to that of the dreamer at night: in both cases the subject confronts the imagery that his own imagination has brought before him. Freud himself observes that free-associating "bears some analogy to the state before falling asleep."[22] But he might have gone further and pointed to the fact that in each instance the mind encounters a stream of self-generated visual and acoustic images, only some of which can be classified as strictly mnemonic. By the same token, in dreaming, as in free-associating, there is a proliferation of types and modes of content—often to the point of surfeit and even of absurdity. In each case the imagery is of many different sorts, and what is conveyed to the mind seems kaleidoscopic in its diversity: we are as surprised at the multitude of things that show up in free-associating as we are at what appears in our nocturnal dreams.

A parallel between Freud and Husserl suggests itself. No less than Husserl's method of free variation in imagination, Freud's technique of free association brings us into contact with the many possible variants of particular forms or themes. And just as free variation in phenomenology allows us to penetrate to an eidetic structure or "noematic nucleus," so free association in psychoanalysis gives us access to the pathogenic nucleus of dreams and psychoneurotic symptoms.[23] In both cases the longest way around proves to be the shortest way home: we must investigate all of the available variants before being able to seize

21. Ibid., XIII, 188.
22. Ibid., IV, 102.
23. The noematic "nuclear layer" is discussed in Husserl, *Ideas*, sec. 90. The term "pathogenic nucleus" occurs in Freud, *Standard Edition*, II, 288-92.

the thematic core. Thus Husserl counsels patience in view of the "need for infinite variation," and Freud advises that "it is quite hopeless to try to penetrate directly to the nucleus of the pathogenic organization."[24] Finally, and closely related to what has just been said, *insight* is the aim in both enterprises: eidetic insight (*Wesensschau*) in the one case and psychological insight into the self in the other. Such insight, attained by examining imaginatively projected variations, involves immersion in a form of experience in which possibility is a basic dimension. If the realm of eidetic insight is a realm in which "actualities must be treated as possibilities among possibilities,"[25] the successful outcome of psychoanalytic therapy is a mode of existence in which the patient is free from his own neurosis—in which his ego has gained "freedom to decide one way or the other"[26] and thus to live affirmatively in a world of open possibilities.

JUNGIAN ANALYTICAL PSYCHOLOGY

It is a striking fact that both Freud and Jung invoke Schiller in their earliest considerations of imagination.[27] In *Psychological Types* (first published in 1921), Jung admiringly discusses Schiller's conception of imagination as an essential *tertium quid* lying between sensation and intellect and resolving their inherent opposition. Jung finds Schiller's endorsement of imagination a basis for distinguishing his own position from that of Freud and Adler, both of whom "reject the principle of imagination since they reduce fantasies to something else and treat them merely as a semiotic [i.e., indexical] expression; in reality fantasies mean much more than that."[28] What more they mean is indicated in Jung's contention that "every good idea and all creative work are the offspring of the imagination."[29] Thus, from the very beginning Jung

24. Husserl, *Experience and Judgment*, p. 350; Freud, *Standard Edition*, II, 292 (in italics in original).

25. *Experience and Judgment*, p. 350.

26. Freud, *Standard Edition*, XIX, 50n. (Freud underlines "freedom.")

27. Freud quotes Schiller's letter of December 1, 1788, in which Schiller speaks to his friend of "the constraint imposed by your reason upon your imagination" (cited, *Standard Edition*, IV, p. 103). It is just such constraint that must be given up in free association. Jung discusses Schiller at length in *Psychological Types*, ch. II. (See *The Collected Works of C. G. Jung* [Princeton: Princeton University Press, 1971], vol. 6, pp. 67-146. Subsequent references to Jung's writings will be to *Collected Works*.)

28. *Collected Works*, 6, p. 63.

29. Ibid.

recognizes imagination to be an independent operation of the mind—one which refuses reduction to sensory processes or to intellection. Moreover, he explicitly acknowledges its autonomous status and its intrinsic connection with pure possibilities:

> This autonomous activity of the psyche, which can be explained neither as a reflex action to sensory stimuli nor as the executive organ of eternal ideas, is, like every vital process, a continually creative act . . . it is the mother of all possibilities.[30]

Jung also distinguishes in *Psychological Types* between three forms of fantasy or imagination (the two terms are not differentiated at this point): voluntary, passive, and active.[31] Voluntary fantasy is characterized by superficiality and triviality, thus resembling Coleridge's notion of "fancy." Passive fantasy occurs when one is overwhelmed by the upsurge of one's own fantasies, as is typified in the dream ego's supine acceptance of a sequence of disturbing dream images. In active fantasy, in contrast, there is "a positive participation of consciousness" as the conscious self enters into its own imaginative activity: "the passive process becomes an action."[32] Active fantasy as thus described is the progenitor of what Jung comes to call "active imagination." Distinguishing between fantasy and imagination as a result of his study of medieval and Renaissance alchemy, he limits fantasy (*Phantasie*) to being "a subjective figment of the mind" and promotes imagination (*Einbildungskraft*) into "an image-making, form-giving creative activity."[33] Active imagination represents a special employment of this creative power. Such imagining was first encountered in Jung's self-analysis and then became part of his psychotherapeutic work with patients. In contrast with Freudian method, Jung's use of active imagination does not give particular prominence to dreams.[34] Any imagistic content, whether dreamed or not, will do as a starting point. Nor is it a matter of free-associating upon this fragmentary *point de départ*. Instead of following out a series of different associative pathways, the active imaginer restricts his attention to the initially given material and allows it to exfoliate in imaginative form.

30. Ibid., p. 52.
31. For Jung's nondifferentiation between fantasy and imagination, see *Collected Works*, 6, pp. 427ff. For a more complete discussion, see my article "Toward an Archetypal Imagination," *Spring* (1974), esp. secs. I-II.
32. *Collected Works*, 6, p. 428; and ibid., 14, p. 496.
33. Ibid., 13, p. 167n. and p. 168n.
34. Jung even writes that active imagination "to some extent takes the place of dreams" (ibid., 8, p. 204).

In practice, the technique of active imagination is a form of "vision-ary meditation," and it consists of two phases. (1) At first there is a *focusing* on a particular dream fragment or fantasy-image—a concen-tration on it alone: "you choose a dream, or some other fantasy-image, and concentrate on it by simply catching hold of it and looking at it . . . [you] fix this image in the mind."[35] (2) Then a process of *elabora-tion* ensues as the fixed image alters and is transformed before the active imaginer's own observing mind: "a chain of fantasy ideas develops and gradually takes on a dramatic character . . . you dream with open eyes."[36] But Jung warns that this critical second phase is not merely a matter of "interior entertainment." As in active fantasy, the actively imagining subject must learn to participate in his own psychical pro-ductions with himself as one of the primary *dramatis personae*:

> Although, to a certain extent, he looks on from outside, impartially, he is also an acting and suffering figure in the drama of the psyche.[37]

Through such self-dramatization, the active imaginer is coming to terms with his unconscious being; he is "having it out with the uncon-scious," and thereby achieving a momentary *rapprochement* with what is quite alien to his conscious ego.

It is at this terminal point of active imagining that insight occurs: "this is where insight, the *unio mentalis*, begins to become real."[38] Such insight is not only into oneself, but at the same time into the archetypal constants that subtend the self. For the aim of active imagination is at once personal and extrapersonal; or more exactly, by taking us more deeply into ourselves it brings us into contact with what is more than ourselves. This "more" refers to archetypes, which lend lasting shape and structure to what would otherwise be a sheer "chaotic assortment of images."[39] Archetypes themselves may be defined as "certain collec-tive unconscious conditions which act as regulators and stimulators of creative fantasy-activity."[40] In this light, active imagining becomes a means of drawing out and fastening onto "primordial images"—images

35. Ibid., 14, p. 495. Cf. the similar description at ibid., p. 526.
36. Ibid., p. 496. It is especially in this phase that we see that active imagination "is not a question of 'free association' . . . but of elaborating the [fragment of] fantasy by observing the further fantasy material that adds itself to the fragment in a natural manner" (ibid., 9 [i], p. 49).
37. Ibid., 14, p. 529. The phrase "interior entertainment" occurs at ibid., p. 496.
38. Ibid., p. 529.
39. Ibid., 8, p. 203.
40. Ibid., p. 204. On the same page Jung even suggests that he based the original thesis of archetypes on experiences of active imagining.

that embody and specify archetypal dominants. Such imagining is therefore describable as "a kind of spontaneous amplification of archetypes."[41]

Here we might find ourselves wondering to what extent active imagination as conceived by Jung corresponds to everyday imagining as it has been depicted in this book. It might even seem as if the thetic character of the real has been substituted for the purely possible insofar as active imagining puts us in touch with archetypal material. What could be more ultimate, and thus more real, than such material? Yet, as James Hillman observes, archetypal structures "provide the *a priori* structures within the caverns and dens of [an] *immeasurable* imagination."[42] Precisely as immeasurable, an archetypally attuned imagination deals with what is purely possible—with what cannot be constricted to the empirically real. No less (and often much more) than ordinary imagining, such imagining is an organ of pure possibility.

Although active imagination brings us into the sphere of archetypal dominants—i.e., those structuring elements that unify an otherwise merely dispersed experiential manifold—it does so *only by means of what is intrinsically multiple*. There is never a *single* adequate image of a given archetype; instead, there is a multiplicity of possible images by which the archetype may manifest itself.[43] Jung himself underscores this multiplicity in one of his earliest descriptions of active imagination: "the result of this technique was a vast number of complicated designs whose diversity puzzled me for years."[44] Speaking of the actual products of active imagining, he said that "their variety defies description."[45] Indeed, it is just this variety which marks them as genuine imaginative creations and allows us to view active imagining as continuous with autonomous imagining as depicted in the last chapter. Active imagining involves the free elaboration of primordial images, each of which is an alternative and equally possible expression of underlying archetypal material. These images are not posited as real in any

41. Ibid., 8, pp. 204-205. On primordial images, see ibid., 6, p. 443.

42. *The Myth of Analysis* (Evanston: Northwestern University Press, 1972), p. 179; his italics. For Hillman's own view of an archetypally sensitive imagination, see ibid., pp. 85-87, 168-81, 202, 279; and *Re-Visioning Psychology* (New York: Harper, 1975), pp. 38ff., 85-86, 92ff., 178-79, 198ff.

43. Hillman's recent work has eloquently stressed the essential multivalency of "an archetypal psychology that would give proper due to many dominants, that would recognize . . . a multiplicity of centers and affirm a psychological polytheism" (*Myth of Analysis*, p. 265). See also *Re-Visioning Psychology*, pp. 26, 127, 167ff., 193, 226.

44. *Collected Works*, 8, p. 202.

45. Ibid., p. 203.

empirical sense—or even as quasi-real (i.e., in the sense of hallucinatory dream images). They have the status of pure possibility.[46]

Nevertheless, the products of active imagining are also said to be experienced as "psychically real." In order to understand how this is so, we need to make a basic distinction. The content of what we actively imagine is indeed felt to be psychically real insofar as it may affect and change the psyche of the imaginer himself.[47] But the same content is experienced as purely possible insofar as it is regarded as a particular and variable expression of a fundamental archetypal motif. Despite his emphasis on the subsistent and unifying character of archetypes and on their psychical efficacity, Jung also stresses that every archetype reveals itself in a plurality of possible manifestations:

> The psychoid form underlying any archetypal [i.e., primordial] image retains its character at all stages of development, though empirically it is *capable of endless variations*.[48]

The mention of "endless variations" brings us to a final point. Even more than Freudian free association, Jungian active imagination is a process parallel to Husserl's technique of free variation. For each successive image projected in active imagining is a variation of an archetypal dominant, and the corresponding *in*variability of the dominant itself may be compared to the invariancy of an essence as conceived by Husserl. Jung's very terminology of "alteration," "elaboration," and "transformation" suggests a protophenomenological procedure in which "the material is continually varied and increased until a kind of condensation of motifs into more or less stereotyped symbols takes place."[49] Archetypes, in their inherent constancy, resemble Husserlian *eidē*, which keep appearing in the most variegated expressions and experiences. As preformed patterns, archetypes are analogized by Jung himself to Platonic forms and to Kantian categories, that is, to eidetic or *a priori* factors which shape experience in advance.[50] Like all such factors, they are accessible only through a multitude of possible appearances, and Jung concludes that

46. Cf. ibid., 6, p. 442: "the image has the psychological character of a fantasy idea [i.e., of pure possibility] and never the quasi-real character of an hallucination."

47. This is in accordance with Jung's general principle that "the real is what works" (ibid., 7, p. 217). It is in terms of this principle that we are to understand his claim that active imagining "invests the bare fantasy with an element of reality" (ibid., 16, p. 49). It is in this sense too that archetypes are to be considered real; they too are "psychical realities, real because they work" (ibid., 7, p. 95).

48. Ibid., 13, p. 272. My italics.

49. Ibid., 8, p. 84.

50. For this analogy, see ibid., 3, p. 243.

the archetypal representations (images and ideas) mediated to us by the unconscious should not be confused with the archetype as such. They are *very varied structures* which all point back to one essentially 'irrepresentable' basic form.[51]

In their variety these structures can only be the objects of an autonomous imaginative activity that thrives upon its diverse dealings with the multiple and the possible in human experience.

GUIDED IMAGERY TECHNIQUES

European psychotherapists have for many decades paid special attention to the vicissitudes of imagery and fantasy. Even before the turn of the century, Pierre Janet had been struck by the pathogenic significance of *"rêveries automatiques,"* and he sought to replace the "fundamental image" that lay at the origin of a neurosis with a more benign image.[52] Shortly afterward, Alfred Binet proposed a method of *"introspection provoquée,"* which influenced the Würzburg School and led to Carl Happich's notion of a "meditative zone" of experience in which mental imagery could be easily induced.[53] Another early line of development was opened up by J. H. Schultz, who outlined a series of self-hypnotic exercises in which subjects attempt to imagine various feelings and sensations in different parts of their bodies (e.g., heaviness and warmth in the extremities). This "autogenic training" was designed to relieve a multitude of psychological and even physiological ailments.[54] There were also psychoanalysts who encouraged sustained visualizations as a way of helping patients to reexperience childhood events more vividly.[55]

51. Ibid., 8, p. 213. My italics. Compare Husserl's statement that "to every concept belongs *an infinite extension of purely possible particulars"* (*Experience and Judgment*, p. 329; his italics).

52. See Pierre Janet, *Névroses et idées fixes* (Paris: Alcan, 1898), I, 393-422.

53. Cf. Alfred Binet, *L'Etude expérimentale de l'intelligence* (Paris: Costes, 1922), esp. chs. 6, 7, and 9; and Carl Happich, "Das Bildbewusstsein als Ansatzstelle psychischer Behandlung," *Zentralblatt für Psychotherapie* (1932), no. 5.

54. On Schultz's approach, see J. H. Schultz and W. Luthe, *Autogenic Training: A Physiologic Approach in Psychotherapy* (New York: Grune & Stratton, 1959); and J. H. Schultz, *Autogenic Therapy*, ed. W. Luthe (New York: Grune & Stratton, 1969-70), 5 vols. Although published in English only relatively recently, these books sum up a lifetime's work in the area of guided imagery.

55. See, for example, Pierce Clark, "The Phantasy Method of Analyzing Narcissistic Neuroses," *Psychoanalytic Review*, XIII (1925); and M. Nachmansonn, "Concerning Experimentally Produced Dreams" in David Rapaport, ed., *Organization and Pathology of Thought* (New York: Columbia University Press, 1951).

With the exceptions of Schultz and, more recently, of Hanscarl Leuner,[56] the most thorough research in guided imagery has been done in France, where Eugène Caslant is the pioneering figure. Using a darkened consulting room, he encouraged his subjects to imagine themselves traveling along various directional vectors. Images of ladders, staircases, and flying chariots were evoked so as to encourage imagined movements from one projected level to another. Associated with each level were specific affects and emotions, and Caslant believed that the developmental stage of a patient's "supranormal" powers was indicated by the level he could attain in imagination.[57] Caslant's most enterprising pupil was Robert Desoille, perhaps the single most important person in the history of guided imagery techniques. Desoille called his own procedure *"le rêve éveillé dirigé,"* or the directed daydream. In the experience of directed daydreaming the patient achieves "an intermediate and subtle state between waking and sleeping."[58] Desoille compared this state to that induced by Freud's early use of the "pressure" technique.[59] Closer to Jungian active imagination (especially its focusing phase) was Desoille's stress on "concentration" during the course of the directed daydream. For the latter is conceived as

an internal representation of thought, most often in the form of a visual image—an image which should be very well formed and on which the [patient] must concentrate his attention *without any distraction*, all the while experiencing (if possible) a certain affective state.[60]

Distractions are minimized by the environment Desoille established for the directed daydream: in a semi-dark room the prone patient (with his eyes shut) is invited to engage in reveries whose formal content is suggested by the "guide." To begin with, stationary objects, typically a sword for a man and vase for a woman, are imagined. Soon

56. On Leuner's method of guided imagery, see the excellent account in Jerome Singer, *Imagery and Daydream Methods in Psychotherapy and Behavior Modification* (New York: Academic Press, 1974), pp. 82-91. Singer's book provides a comprehensive survey of the entire field. For a briefer overview, see Mary Watkins, "The Waking Dream in European Psychotherapy," *Spring* (1974), pp. 33-57.

57. See Eugène Caslant, *Méthode de développement des facultés supra-normales* (Paris: Rhea, 1921), passim.

58. Robert Desoille, *Théorie et pratique du rêve eveillé dirigé* (Geneva: Mont-Blanc, 1961), p. 10. See also p. 45: in the directed daydream "the subject finds himself in a state close to sleep"—reminding us of what Freud had said of the patient's similar situation when free-associating.

59. See ibid., pp. 21 and 28 for Desoille's discussion of Freud. For Freud's own account of the pressure technique, see *Standard Edition*, II, 109-11, 270-79.

60. Desoille, *Exploration de l'affectivité subconsciente par la méthode du rêve eveillé* (Paris: Artrey, 1938), p. 189; his italics.

after, the guide proposes a series of basic situations, each of which is correlated with a different area of human experience (e.g., a cave with one's suppressed emotions, a wizard or witch with one's parents). Further, each of these imagined situations involves a characteristic form of movement that is for Desoille "the very sign of life and freedom."[61] The primary axis of all such movement is *vertical*; hence ascending and descending become the most important motions. In an imagined descent—e.g., to the bottom of the sea—the images that emerge are frequently somber or frightening, eliciting affects of sadness or anxiety. If the movement is ascensional, however, one's images are increasingly ethereal and luminous and are accompanied by a peculiar euphoria and joy. It is the ascensional movement that is most crucial in Desoille's view, for its frequency and quality manifest the degree to which the imagining subject has been freed from the problems that brought him to psychotherapy in the first place. At the same time, images of ascension promote the patient's independence of the psychotherapist as guide; as such images become more spontaneously generated, the need for their inducement by another person is correspondingly diminished. In this way Desoille practiced by means of guided imagery what Bachelard has called an "ascensional psychology."[62]

What is significant in the work of Desoille and of others who have continued and systematized his original efforts is not merely the use of ingenious techniques of guided imagery in psychotherapy;[63] of particular interest for our purposes is the stress placed on the dynamic imagery of upward movement. Such movement, by its very nature, exemplifies and symbolizes the themes of multiplicity and possibility we have found to be integral to autonomous imagining. To imagine oneself ascending freely is to represent oneself as rising above the concerns that clutter one's everyday existence—and thus as moving from the plane of care-bound reality to a region of playfulness and pure possibility. In the rising movements of directed daydreams, we enter an imaginary space where, as Desoille himself described it, "everything is possible."[64]

61. Desoille, *Théorie et pratique du rêve eveillé dirigé*, p. 31.
62. This phrase is found in Gaston Bachelard, *L'air et les songes*, p. 129, where Bachelard comments that "through reveries of ascent [Desoille's method] aims to liberate blocked psychical structures and to furnish a fortunate destiny to confused and ineffective feelings."
63. See, for example, the lucid and rigorous book by Roger Frétigny and André Virel, *L'Imagerie Mentale* (Geneva: Mont-Blanc, 1968), passim. The work of Roberto Assagioli should also be mentioned as a further offshoot of Desoille's original work: cf. his *Psychosynthesis* (New York: Viking Press, 1965), esp. pp. 143ff.
64. *Marie-Clotilde* (Paris: Payot, 1971), p. 32.

By the same token, when we imagine ourselves gliding up into a limit-less free space, a multiplicity of optional motions, of unhindered move-ments, suddenly suggest themselves. No longer constrained by gravity —by earthbound duties—we feel free to take on any number of possible projects. In this buoyant and exhilarating state we experience "the power of imagination, the omnipotence of a sublimation that is achieved, wished for, and multiplied in all of its 'correspondences'."[65] By activating the ascensional potentiality of our imagination, we not only lose our symptoms but become psychically free; we attain a form of imaginative liberation that is the ultimate aim of all the varied tech-niques of guided imagery discussed in the foregoing pages. For Desoille as for Caslant, for Janet as for Schultz, guided imagining is the *via regia* of psychotherapy. It is the most effective means for helping the patient to realize that he is a being of possibility, with multiple routes into an open-ended future.

The same therapeutic aim informs the work of Freud and Jung, each of whom views his own brand of psychoanalysis as a privileged path toward an eventual psychological freedom. This commonness of purpose is supported by an overlap in method. In all three kinds of psychotherapy we have examined, imagination has been seen to play a major, if not always explicitly acknowledged, role. This is so despite significant differences in emphasis and in technique—including the choice of what is to count as the paradigmatic imaginative phenom-enon. If Freud takes as his paradigm the night dream, Jung a fragment of a dream or a fantasy (i.e., as a starting point for active imagination), and guided imagery practitioners the directed daydream, in every in-stance imagining is of central importance. And this is so whether imag-ination is conceived as the origin of dream-thoughts and the manifest dream (and as the source of free associations to the latter), as the active amplification of an image from a dream or a fantasy (and thus as a means of access to archetypes), or as the moving force and experi-ential basis of the directed daydream. Such differences in focus and in procedure notwithstanding, autonomous imagining proves to be a fundamental factor in each psychotherapeutic enterprise. It shows it-self to be crucial to the redirection and eventual 'cure' of the psyche in distress—and to its liberation from the locked-in domain of the reality-bound ego. As Eros animated Psyche with his arrows of love and ascended with her to Olympus, so the imagination reanimates an ex-hausted ego by teaching it how to rise into the etheral realm of the purely possible.

65. Bachelard, *L'air et les songes*, p. 143.

III

In contrast with what we find in art and psychology, the role of imagination in philosophy is of largely unsuspected significance. With but few exceptions. Western philosophers have made a profession—a markedly logocentric and ratiocinative profession—out of discounting the importance of imagination in philosophizing.[66] In a climate of derogation and dispraise, any residual esteem for imagination has tended to restrict itself to admissions that imagining is of value in certain enterprises *other than* philosophy, e.g., in artistic creation or in scientific discovery. Only rarely has it been suggested that imagination might have a central part to play within philosophy itself. In what follows we shall consider three quite different areas of philosophical activity in which the role of imagining is of considerable significance.

METHODOLOGY

It is a revealing fact that some of the very same philosophers who publicly denounce imagination make abundant use of imagining in their actual practice, i.e., in their working methods. This use is more extensive than is generally admitted. It occurs above all in the preliminary procedures philosophers employ in the pursuit of their cherished logocentric aims. The result is a paradoxical pattern of denial-*cum*-acknowledgement in which an express denigration is accompanied by a covert recognition of the special utility of imagination in the very process of philosophizing. This pattern may be observed in the ambivalence with which a number of Western philosophers, including Aristotle, Hume, and Kant, view imagination. These thinkers accord a privileged position to imagining in philosophical method and yet hesitate to recognize the importance of imaginative activity in their official philosophies of mind. Let us look at each briefly:

In Aristotle's model of the mind, sensing and thinking are elevated to positions of supreme epistemological value. Imagination, caught in the middle, is said to be "for the most part false" (*De Anima*, 428a 11). Yet in practically the same breath Aristotle suddenly adds that imagining is necessary to thinking, which "will not exist without images" (ibid., 432a 14). This rapid promotion of imagination to a position where it is necessary to thinking in general (and hence to philosophical

66. "Logocentric" is taken from Jacques Derrida, *De la grammatologie* (Paris: Minuit, 1967), pp. 21ff.

thinking as well) occurs unexpectedly and yet with firm insistence.

Similarly, Hume begins by asserting confidently that "nothing is more dangerous to reason than the flights of the imagination," and calls for "a resolution to reject all the trivial suggestions of the fancy, and adhere to the understanding" (A *Treatise of Human Nature*, p. 267). Yet it turns out that the understanding itself is conceived by Hume as "the general and more establish'd properties of the imagination."[67] Thus Hume comes to acknowledge the essential ingrediency of imagining in the very activity of understanding, which is in turn crucial to philosophical thought.

Following the same pattern, Kant denounces the merely "visionary" imagination, which is said to produce "empty figments of the brain," yet contrasts it with an "inventive" imagination, which has the merit of operating "under the strict surveillance of reason" (*Critique of Pure Reason*, A770, B798). In the end, imagination is elevated to a position of central prominence within Kant's epistemology: "a blind but indispensable function of the soul, without which we should have no knowledge whatsoever" (ibid., A78, B103). It is indispensable because it is the source of all intellectual synthesis in the understanding, and such synthesis is what "first gives rise to knowledge" (ibid., A77, B103). Consequently, imagination is again made basic to understanding—i.e., to the faculty of knowledge—and thus to philosophical activity itself.

Descartes is the first modern philosopher to fall into the paradox of denial-*cum*-acknowledgment. In his *Meditations* Descartes describes his method as one in which he has "put aside every belief in which I could *imagine* the least doubt."[68] Further, he sets out to "pretend" or "suppose"—thetic activities that are closely allied with imagining itself—that all of his former beliefs are "entirely imaginary and false" and that he is being deceived by an omnipotent evil genius.[69] To perform such sweeping acts of doubt requires not so much a cancellation of ordinary beliefs as a forceful use of imagination. For a truly systematic doubt employs imagining in its possibilizing power inasmuch as *every possible* object of experience is to be considered dubitable. This

---

67. A *Treatise of Human Nature*, p. 267. See also p. 265: "the memory, senses, and understanding are, therefore, all of them founded on the imagination."

68. *Meditations on First Philosophy*, trans. L. J. Lafleur (New York and Indianapolis: Bobbs-Merrill, 1961), p. 23. My italics.

69. Ibid., p. 21.

means that the philosopher must view as subject to doubt not only everything he has already experienced and held for certain but also anything he *might* experience. And it takes a special effort of imagination to conceive of all of those things which *could* be doubted even though they do not form part of one's present or past experience. The fact that such doubt is solely methodological in character only underlines the essentiality of imagination's role. For it is not through the discovery of new evidence or by adducing logical reasons for doubt, but by an act of imagination that Descartes effects the methodological suspension of belief: he tries to imagine that the world is the kind of place in which the normally unquestioned validity of everyday beliefs does not obtain. Yet, paradoxically, there is scarcely any basis for such a crucial recourse to imagination in Descartes' theory of mind, in which imagination is regarded as adventitious and eliminable. Thus, later in the *Meditations* he condemns imagining as "in no way necessary to my nature or essence, that is to say, to the essence of my mind."[70] What had earlier been indispensable for carrying out the project of the *Meditations* is now declared inessential. In this rapid *volte-face* we observe a striking instance of at once acknowledging and denying human powers of imagining: what is granted with one hand is taken back by the other.

Husserl, a professed admirer of Descartes, presents us with an even more extreme instance of the paradox of denial-*cum*-acknowledgment. His work exhibits to an acute degree a deep-seated ambivalence toward imagination—an ambivalence that involves both a recognition of its critical importance in philosophical method and a disparagement of its epistemological value. The disparagement is expressed, first of all, by a conspicuous neglect: only rarely do we find a detailed description of imagining in Husserl's published writings. Even the ingenious Dresden gallery example in *Ideas* involves a mixture of imagining, remembering, and signifying.[71] When imagination *is* singled out, as in *The Phenomenology of Internal Time-Consciousness*, it is given a decidedly subordinate role. Its basic operation is conceived as a form of "presentification" (*Vergegenwärtigung*), that is, as a modification of a directly giving, presentative consciousness such as is found in perception.[72] In fact, insofar as perception is considered the "basic" or "simple" act (in the language of the *Logical Investigations*), Husserl endorses the primacy

---

70. Ibid., p. 69.

71. Sec. 100. For an ingenious interpretation of this example, see Jacques Derrida, *Speech and Phenomena*, trans. D. Allison (Evanston, Ill.: Northwestern University Press, 1973), p. 104.

72. Cf. appendices I and III of *The Phenomenology of Internal Time-Consciousness*.

of perception: a primacy in terms of which imagination is necessarily secondary.[73]

Furthermore, Husserl's ultimate aims in philosophy are such that imagination appears to be excluded *ab initio* from the pursuit of objective knowledge. To the extent that phenomenology is a "rigorous science," it aims at articulating "a universal conformity to laws of structure on the part of conscious life, a regularity by virtue of which alone truth and actuality have, and are able to have, sense for us."[74] Such conformity and regularity leave little room for imagination's capricious adventures. If conceptually objective truth is found in the non-varying content of experience, imagination cannot by its own action alone embody such truth. For imagination signifies the variable *par excellence*. Its divagations, when unchecked, distract and divert us from what is "absolutely invariable."[75] To use Husserl's own metaphor, the imprint or seal of conceptual truth must be placed *upon* all lower cognitive strata, including the strata of expression and imagination.[76] In this manner the logically necessary is ranked above the actual and the possible, the conceptually certain above the empirically contingent. Logos, god of reason, triumphs—at least in theory—over Eros, god of imaginative desire.

I say "at least in theory," for a closer look at Husserl's writings reveals a very different aspect of his attitude toward imagination. Despite his doctrinal commitment to a resolute rationalism, Husserl takes a surprisingly open stance toward imagining when he considers how best to practice phenomenology. This practice is based on one procedure (i.e., phenomenological reduction) that is significantly parallel to the spontaneous operation of imagination and on another (i.e., free variation) that involves the actual exercise of imagining and "lets it have free rein."[77] In both respects, and also as a fecund source of examples, the role of imagination is considerably enhanced and enlarged, compared with its strictly secondary status in Husserl's theory of mental activity. Indeed, perhaps more than any other post-Romantic philosopher, Husserl accords to imagination a place of prominence in philosophical methodology: "freedom in the investigation of essences ne-

73. Cf. *Logical Investigations*, II, pp. 606-610, 642-47, 682-88, 760-63, and especially 773-95. On the primacy of perception, see Merleau-Ponty's essay of this title in *The Primacy of Perception*, pp. 12-42.

74. *Cartesian Meditations*, p. 59.

75. *Phänomenologische Psychologie* (The Hague: Nijhoff, 1962), p. 73.

76. Cf. *Ideas*, sec. 124.

77. *Phänomenologische Psychologie*, p. 71. This free rein is required for the full performance of free variation, that is, for projecting all of the possible variants of a given *eidos*.

cessarily requires that one operate on the plane of imagination."[78]

It is therefore perplexing that Husserl, while allowing imagination full play within phenomenological method, is not willing to recognize it as an independent act in its own right. What is essential to the gaining of eidetic insight becomes, in the context of epistemology, a mere mode of presentification. There could be no starker contrast than that between the role of imagination in Husserl's conception of methodology and its subordinate rank in his model of the mind, for in this model imagining is considered to be the mere neutralizing of content belonging to memory. It makes little difference that this is "memory in the largest sense" or that imagination is said to be indefinitely reiterable.[79] These concessions to the scope of imagination are minor when compared to the power that the same mental operation is accorded in the pursuit of eidetic insight, where it is responsible for giving us access to "all essential necessities and essential laws—all genuine intuitive *a priori*."[80] The paradox remains, reminding us that for all his obstinate originality Husserl does not overcome the basically ambivalent attitude with which other Western philosophers have also viewed imagination.

Nonetheless, unlike these other philosophers, Husserl does intimate a way of breaking out of the paradoxical pattern of denial-*cum*-acknowledgment. Closer scrutiny suggests a possible exit from the stalemate in which Husserl's predecessors—typified by Aristotle and Descartes, Hume and Kant—were caught. All of these other figures remained trapped in the initial paradox of asserting and denying, at one and the same time, the importance of imagining. Though he does not himself escape this paradox, Husserl at least indicates a means by which it might be avoided: *phenomenological method itself*. It is precisely by making use of imagination that phenomenological method allows us to view imagining unambivalently and in its full significance.

This last insight involves a further paradox: we must *use* imagination in order to give an adequate descriptive account *of* imagination. In

78. *Ideas*, sec. 70. I draw here on the more detailed presentation in my article "Imagination and Phenomenological Method" in *Husserl: Expositions and Appraisals*, eds. P. McCormick and F. Elliston (Terre Haute: Notre Dame University Press, 1976).

79. Cf. *Ideas*, secs. 111-12. To be more exact: imagination is a strictly *non-positing* mode of presentification in contrast with memory, which is conceived as positing (i.e., existence-establishing) presentification. Whereas imagination is a neutralizing of memory-content, memory is a positing of perceptual content as having occurred in the past. In the end, then, all presentification, whether imaginative or mnemonic in character, is a form of re-presentation (*Re-präsentation*) of content originally given in sensory experience. (*Re-präsentation* is interchangeable with *Vergegenwärtigung* for Husserl. Cf. *The Phenomenology of Internal Time-Consciousness*, sec. 17.)

80. *Phänomenologische Psychologie*, p. 72.

contradistinction to the previous paradox, however, this second paradox is positive and productive in character. Where the first paradox
derives from a denial of the importance of imagining, the second reveals an interest in the act for its own sake. And where many former
philosophers take only an indirect and surreptitious interest in this act,
those inspired by Husserl's example will take imagination itself as an
explicit theme of philosophical interest. Yet it will receive this attention not only because of its special role in phenomenological method.
As Husserl implies but never expressly asserts, imagining has its own
importance and deserves to be considered in its own right and not just
as an auxiliary in the realization of more austere philosophical concerns. And if this is true, it is because, using imagining's extraordinary
powers of variability (and above all in free variation), we gain entry
into a "world of *absolutely pure possibilities*, each of which can serve
as a central structure for possible pure variations in the mode of the
arbitrary; and from each [such structure] results an absolutely pure
eidos."[81]

MODAL LOGIC

Modal logic, a comparatively young discipline, has analyzed the
logical properties and peculiarities of necessity and possibility. In the
case of possibility, particular attention has been given to the idea of
"possible worlds," i.e., those discrete *cosmoi* which are quite conceiv-
able yet in themselves are neither actual nor necessary. Ingenious and
intricate systems of logical symbols have been devised to deal with
relationships between propositions in which the factor of possibility
is ingredient. It cannot be my purpose here to enter into any of the
technicalities of modal logic or into the detailed debates over specific
issues that have raged in the last two decades.[82] Rather, I wish only to
point to the role of imagining as an unacknowledged presupposition of
the *practice* of modal logic. In this practice, reference is frequently
made to situations that obtain in one or more possible words—to "states
of affairs across the range of possible words." This is a recurrent phrase
in the discussions of modal logicians, one of whom makes the following
claim:

When we say that David could have been essentially a harpist rather

81. *Phänomenologische Psychologie*, p. 74; my italics.
82. For a survey of these matters, see G. E. Hughes and M. J. Cresswell, *An Introduction to Modal Logic* (London: Methuen, 1968), esp. part III.

than essentially a philosopher-king, we are doing more than contrasting a state of affairs in the actual world (call it "terra") with a state of affairs in a possible world (call it "Canaan"), demarcating a world in which David is essentially a harpist rather than essentially a philosopher.[83]

Even if more than a contrast is meant, however, we can still raise preliminary questions concerning the contrast itself. How do we project "Canaan" (or, more finitely, David-as-harpist) as possible? What mental agency is responsible for entertaining such a nonactual state of affairs?

Following Leibniz, modal logicians often speak as if some form of pure intellection were the only relevant mental operation at work in the construction and consideration of possible worlds. It cannot be denied that such an operation is intrinsic to the practice of modal logic in two crucial ways. First, it is by intellection that we posit the *idea* of possible worlds—that we *conceive* of them in a strictly nonimaginative form. Second, only by intellection can we go on to treat the properly logical problems that constitute the subject matter of modal logic as a distinct discipline. But what about the projection of possible worlds themselves (and not just the idea of such worlds)? How are we to do this in the first place except by a specifically imaginative activity?

To admit the relevance of such an activity is not to confuse conceivability with imaginability. Or to be more precise, it is not to confuse (1) *sheer* conceivability with (2) a form of conceivability that involves imagining in an essential way. In the case of sheer conceivability we have to do with the employment of intellection proper, that is, with the pure *conception* of possible worlds—the idea *per se* of such worlds. In the case of conceivability of the second type, however, it is a matter of conceiving what a *particular* possible world—or a cluster of such worlds —would be like. To do this requires imaginative activity, even though the imagining in question need not be imagistic or sensory. As we know from chapter two, in addition to sensory imagining in various forms there are also nonsensory modes of imagining-that and imagining-how. But the important point is that, whether it is specifically sensory or not, imaginative activity is intimately involved with conceivability in sense (2)—i.e., in what Hughes and Cresswell call the "stronger" sense of conceivability:

> In a stronger sense of 'conceive', one would not conceive (or at least fully conceive) of a world of a certain kind unless one had a complete

83. Amelie Oksenberg Rorty, "Essential Possibilities in the Actual World," *Review of Metaphysics*, XXV (1972), p. 608.

insight into what it would be like to live in such a world.[84]

Although the authors do not refer expressly to imagination in their discussion of the "intuitive" interpretation of models and validity, it is nonetheless implicit in their notion of a stronger sense of conceivability. For how else are we to obtain "a complete insight into *what it would be like* to live in such a [purely possible] world" if not by acts of imagining, and especially by acts of imagining-that and imagining-how? And yet, here as elsewhere, the very existence of such acts is passed over in silence or, if mentioned, is treated in an offhand and unclarified sense.[85] Hence modal logicians presuppose and build upon an imaginative activity which they are disinclined to acknowledge or to clarify.

METAPHYSICS

A final way in which imagining proves itself to be integral to philosophy is found in metaphysical speculation. As in the previous two instances, the significance of imaginative activity is based on its ability to project pure possibilities. But in the present case we must begin by noting that there is a lengthy tradition in the West of refusing to separate the logical and metaphysical aspects of possibility from each other. Thus, for Leibniz possible worlds are at once logically possible (i.e., non-self-contradictory) and metaphysically real (i.e., qua ideas in the mind of God prior to the actualizing of the best of them in accordance with the principle of perfection).[86] In the twentieth century the ascension of the analytical spirit in philosophy has meant that the logical and metaphysical dimensions of possibility have been thrust apart, with the consignment of the former dimension to modal logicians and of the latter to cosmologically inclined metaphysicians. In view of this sharp division of philosophical labor, it is all the more remarkable that the philosopher who has had the most to say on the metaphysical meaning of possibility was also a great logician: Alfred North Whitehead.

For Whitehead, whom we shall take as paradigmatic in his metaphysical interpretation of possibility, the realm of the metaphysically possible is considerably more vast than the region of finite fact. At any

84. *An Introduction to Modal Logic*, p. 78.
85. Thus Rorty writes that "since there is no dearth of possible worlds, [we can] carry out our assignment formally, *by imagining* not one but a cluster of possible worlds" (art. cit., p. 613; my italics). But the nature of such "imagining" is not further specified.
86. Cf. Leibniz, *Monadology*, secs. 41-55.

given moment in the life of the universe there are unrealized possibilities which no finite group of actual entities, however diverse or multitudinous, can fully embody. Hence metaphysical possibility "transcends realized temporal matters of fact."[87] The total sum of such matters of fact is always eclipsed by the totality of purely possible states of affairs. In other words, many things which qua possible might happen have not yet happened or may never happen; and whatever *has* happened might have happened differently.

Here we must become more specific. Three great orders of being are recognized in Whitehead's metaphysical system as set forth in *Process and Reality*: the possible, the potential, and the actual. Regarded by itself alone, what is possible is without effective limits of any kind—and for this reason may never be realized—while what is potential is conditioned by the requirements for becoming an actual entity. Possibilities, which are abstract in character and thus essentially related to what Whitehead calls generically "eternal objects," intervene or "ingress" in actual entities when they are realized. Summing up this line of thought, Whitehead writes:

> The satisfaction of each actual entity is an element in the givenness of the universe: it limits boundless, abstract possibility into the particular real potentiality from which each novel concrescence originates. The 'boundless, abstract possibility' means the creativity considered solely in reference to the possibilities of the intervention of eternal objects. . . .[88]

Although this statement succeeds in relating possibility to radical novelty and thus to what can be envisaged only by imagining, many of Whitehead's discussions in *Process and Reality* tend to obscure the intrinsic link between imagination and metaphysical possibility: affirmation of the link is left largely implicit. Even the "creativity" with which such possibility is identified in the above passage has little, if anything, to do with the creativity of imagination since it refers to the ultimate cosmogonic "stuff" of the universe.[89] When Whitehead singles out the act of imagining itself, he tends to treat it only in terms of its difference from bare sensory perception. In this context it is conceived as a form of "negative perception" wherein we apprehend what is *not* the case with regard to what actually confronts us in perception at a given mo-

---

87. Whitehead, *Process and Reality* (New York: Harper, 1960), p. 46. Note also the following anecdote: "Suddenly he stood and spoke with passionate intensity, 'Here we are with our finite being and physical senses in the presence of a universe whose possibilities are infinite' " (cited in Lucien Price, ed., *Dialogues of Alfred North Whitehead* [Boston: Little, Brown, 1954], pp. 133-34).

88. *Process and Reality*, pp. 336-37.

89. Cf. ibid., p. 33.

ment: e.g., a certain wall as not-grey. Even though imagining in this capacity is said to reflect "the triumph of consciousness,"[90] it is not clear in what the triumph consists beyond the mere transcendence of perceptual givens. In fact, Whitehead's own strictly epistemological considerations lead him to the quite cautious claim that "imagination is never very free."[91]

But when he is thinking metaphysically, Whitehead proclaims that "imagination finds its easiest freedom among the higher categories of eternal objects" and, even more significantly, that "such freedom as it has in fact seems to establish *the principle of the possibility* of diverse actual entities."[92] In such passages Whitehead overcomes the skeptical stance that derives from his reflections on Hume's and Locke's theory of knowledge. No longer restricted to negating activity at the level of sensory perception, imagining becomes the crucial point of connection between the finitude of actual entities and the infinitude of possibilities inherent in eternal objects. Thus it is at the metaphysical level that the full sweep of imaginative powers becomes evident. What had been the mere negation of perception "finally rises to the peak of free imagination, in which the conceptual novelties search through a universe in which they are datively exemplified."[93]

In this way Whitehead promotes imagination into a position of genuine metaphysical significance—which is to say, of genuine *philosophical* significance, since metaphysical speculation and philosophizing are inextricably intertwined in Whitehead's view. Hence the opening chapter of *Process and Reality*, a chapter entitled "Speculative Philosophy," concludes with the following assertion:

> Philosophy is the welding of imagination and common sense into a restraint upon specialists, and also into an enlargement of their imaginations. By providing the generic notions, philosophy should make it easier to conceive the infinite variety of specific instances which rest unrealized in the womb of nature.[94]

These sentences are remarkable for their express acknowledgment of the importance of imagination in philosophy. Only rarely has imagining been so enthusiastically endorsed as an indispensable source of

90. Ibid., p. 245. For further discussion, see ibid., pp. 245-47 and 397-403.
91. Ibid., p. 201.
92. The first quotation is from ibid., p. 175; the second is on p. 202 (my italics).
93. Ibid., p. 245.
94. Ibid., p. 26. On pp. 7ff. Whitehead discusses the methodological significance of "the play of imagination" under the heading of "imaginative generalization" or "imaginative rationalization."

philosophical insight. Still rarer is the realization that the significance of imagining rests upon its possibilizing role, a role that consists precisely in giving to "infinite variety" its proper due in human experience.

We have now witnessed the possibilizing power of imagining at work in philosophical methodology, in modal logic, and in metaphysics. In each instance imagination is responsible for entertaining an open-ended array of freely developed possibilities. As "pure," these possibilities resist reduction to the actual or the necessary—and even to the hypothetical or the potential. If pure metaphysical possibilities "rest unrealized in the womb of nature," the pure possibilities whose formal properties are investigated by modal logicians and whose methodological value is exploited by phenomenologists and (covertly) by other philosophers are themselves no closer to a realized state. In all three cases we have to do with an imaginative activity that directs itself to what *might be* rather than to what must be, or to what is, has been, or will be. Such an activity represents an exercise of what Whitehead calls "imaginative freedom,"[95] that is, what we have termed "freedom of mind." This freedom concerns itself exclusively with the purely possible, and to recognize the pervasive importance of pure possibility is to affirm the truth of William James's prescient claim: "The mind is at every stage a theater of simultaneous possibilities."[96]

The foregoing discussions have shown that the projection and contemplation of pure possibilities by imagination is not only a matter of instrumental significance—i.e., of constituting means to predesignated ends within art, psychology, or philosophy. *Such possibilities are themselves ends* and are experienced as such. This is perhaps most evident in art, where possibilities figure not just as alternative forms of composition or creation but also as part of the finished product itself. As John Dewey wrote, "Possibilities are embodied in works of art that are not elsewhere actualized; this embodiment is the best evidence that can be found of the true nature of imagination."[97] Such embodied possibilities open up the work of art to the viewer in turn, inducing an aesthetic aura or expressive world which is unique to each work and which by its

95. Ibid., p. 202. Note also Whitehead's statement that "self-determination is always imaginative in origin" (ibid., p. 374).
96. *The Principles of Psychology* (New York: Dover, 1950), I, 290.
97. *Art as Experience* (New York: Capricorn, 1958), p. 268. Dewey underlines "embodiment."

very indefiniteness and openness permits a multiplicity of interpretations. A poem, for example, does not present itself merely as actual —as a perceived typographical entity—but more importantly as a vehicle of possibilities: its very "spots of indeterminacy" (Ingarden's phrase) support a multitude of possible insights and values. Similarly, though perhaps less obviously, possibilities are embodied in the contents of psychotherapeutic insight—and in the effects of such insight. The liberated self that emerges from successful psychotherapy is a more fully autonomous being that has made possibility one of its primary categories; its new-found sense of freedom is a freedom to act in any of several openly possible ways instead of being determined by neurotic needs. In philosophy, especially in certain conceptions of methodology and in metaphysics, one comes to realize that there is no more a single possible point of view on a given topic than there is a single possible object or world: to posit one such point of view, object, or world is at the same time to posit the possibility of many. In metaphysical thinking, moreover, the philosopher characteristically seeks to encounter not Being itself but various modes or types of being.[98] In every instance, an alert and alive imagination guides us into *le pays du possible*.

An acknowledgment of the autonomy of imagining in its possibilizing power leads, therefore, to a more adequate assessment of its role in the diverse domains of art, psychology, and philosophy. This role is quite different from what it is often taken to be, being both more significant and more subtle than many previous appraisals have held. Rather than being merely marginal, imagining lies at the heart of making and appreciating art, it is intrinsic to psychological insight and well-being, and it is crucial in certain forms of philosophizing. Thus we are able to answer affirmatively the basic questions raised in the opening paragraph of this chapter. The importance of imaginative autonomy, its actual place in human experience, is considerable. And to recognize this significance is to alter our understanding and evaluation of fundamental human endeavors—endeavors which show themselves to be permeated with the purely possible, thanks in each case to an ongoing imaginative activity.

We may conclude that the significance of such activity is itself manifold, and thereby reflects imagination's own multiple modes of enactment and expression. The theme of the multiple has imposed

98. It is significant that most major treatments of the nature of being—from Plato to Whitehead, and from Aristotle to Weiss—have recognized the essentially plural character of ultimate substance. Plotinus and Spinoza appear to be exceptions in this regard, but even they posit "emanations," or "attributes" and "modes," which diversify a sheer monism into a pluralism of aspects and phases.

itself on us at a number of critical points in this book: first in the guise of the multiplicity of the mental and then in terms of the inherent multiplicity of the purely possible. The connection between the multiple and the possible is further reinforced by the fact that a pure possibility rarely, if ever, occurs in complete isolation; the existence of *one* possibility of a given type implies that there are infinitely many *other* possibilities belonging to the same type—e.g., other possible creative solutions, other possible interpretations, other possible worlds, other possible modes of being. Multiplicity and possibility are indissolubly linked in art, in psychology, in philosophy, in mind, in life.

Pure possibility also implies freedom and specifically the freedom of mind that is manifested in autonomous imagining. To entertain pure possibilities requires a freedom of mental maneuver which such imagining most fully displays. Hume, in many respects a precursor of phenomenology, said of imagination: "Nothing is more free than that faculty."[99] Nothing is more free because no other mental act is as capable of envisaging possibility in its purity and multiplicity. The autonomy of imagining is an autonomy of freely projecting and of freely contemplating a proliferation of pure possibilities. It is an autonomy that is "thin" precisely insofar as it concerns itself with the purity of the possible and not with the resistance of the real. Yet it remains, as Whitehead intimated, "the triumph of consciousness." For it is by autonomous imagining that consciousness comes to know itself in its multifariousness—in the diversity of its digressions and the variety of its vicissitudes. In imagining, the mind moves in many ways. Imagination multiplies mentation and is its freest form of movement. It is mind in its polymorphic profusion. It is also mind in the process of self-completion, and as such includes an element of self-enchantment:

> Heart-mysteries there, and yet when all is said
> It was the dream itself enchanted me . . .
> Players and painted stage took all my love,
> And not those things that they were emblems of.
>
> Those masterful images because complete
> Grew in pure mind. . . .[100]

---

99. *A Treatise of Human Nature*, p. 10. For Husserl's view of Hume as a proto-phenomenologist, see E. Husserl, *Erste Philosophie* (The Hague: Nijhoff, 1956), I, pp. 157-82.
100. W. B. Yeats, "The Circus Animals' Desertion."

Index